Revolution and Reaction:
Bolivia, 1964-1985

James M. Malloy

and

Eduardo Gamarra

Transaction Books

New Brunswick (U.S.A.) and Oxford (U.K.)

Library of Congress Catalog Number: 87-19145
ISBN 0-88738-159-6
Printed in the United States of America

Library of Congress Cataloging in Publication Data

Malloy, James M.
   Revolution and reaction.

1. Bolivia—Politics and government—1952-1982.
2. Bolivia—Politics and government—1982-
3. Bolivia—Armed Forces—Political activity.
4. Movimiento Nacionalista Revolucionario (Bolivia).
5. Bolivia—Economic conditions—1952-1982. 6. Bolivia—
Economic conditions—1982-   . 7. Populism—Bolivia—
History—20th century. I. Gamarra, Eduardo.
II. Title.
F3326.M26   1987   984'.052   87-19145
ISBN 0-88738-159-6

Preface

This book focuses on the two decades of political life in Bolivia from the overthrow of civilian president Victor Paz Estenssoro in November of 1964 until his return to office in August of 1985. It was a period in which the military dominated national politics and acted as the major base of support for various governments. During these years military authoritarianism was not unique to Bolivia but part of a wider shift to authoritarian modes of governance that occurred throughout South America in the 1960s and 1970s. Then in the late 1970s Bolivia again swung with the regional trend and began a tortuous process of return to civil democratic rule.

Bolivian political life during the past two decades was shaped largely by the dynamics set in motion by the great revolution of 1952 and the reactions by national and international actors to the dilemmas posed by the revolution. Of particular importance have been succeeding attempts to reorganize Bolivia's society in terms of competing strategies of state-led economic development and modernization.

The body of the book provides an account of the main contours of political economy in Bolivia from 1964 until 1985. At the same time the authors present an interpretive analysis of the problem of regime formation in Bolivia by focusing on the alternations among various authoritarian and democratic modes of governance. In a concluding chapter the authors provide an analytical focus to tie Bolivia into more regionwide trends around the question of regime formation and transition. The book is written to appeal to general audiences as well as specialists in the field.

Contents

Introduction

On November 4, 1964, the Bolivian military ousted the civilian president, Victor Paz Estenssoro, and pushed aside the ruling national revolutionary movement (Movimiento Nacionalista Revolucionario-MNR). The MNR had dominated Bolivian political life since 1952, when it spearheaded a mass uprising that unleashed a revolutionary process the likes of which had not been seen in Latin America since the great Mexican revolution of 1910. President Paz was one of the major leaders of the MNR and on the eve of his ouster had just begun his third presidential term, after having served completed terms from 1952 to 1956 and 1960 to August 1964. It is both ironic and significant that the same Victor Paz Estenssoro, heading the same MNR, was reelected president in July of 1985 and at this writing (October 1986) holds that office.

The military action of November 1964 was a major development in the political history of Bolivia. It ushered in an era of some twenty-plus years when the military dominated national political life and was the key base of support for a number of governments. During those years military authoritarianism was not a phenomenon unique to Bolivia but part of a wider shift to authoritarian modes of governance that occurred throughout South America in the 1960s and 1970s. Then in the late 1970s, Bolivia again swung with the regional trend and began moving toward more open modes of rule organized within the framework of representational democracy; a process that as we shall see was particularly tortuous in Bolivia.[1]

The book recounts the main contours of national political life in Bolivia from the coup of 1964 to the return to power of President Paz and the MNR in 1985. At the same time we present an interpretive analysis of the problem of regime formation in Bolivia by focusing on the alternations among various authoritarian and democratic modes of governance. Then in a concluding chapter we provide an analytical focus to tie Bolivia into more regionwide trends around the question of regime formation and transition.

To understand the period 1964 to 1985 properly, we must first return briefly to the revolutionary process initiated in 1952. If we cast a historical eye over the past thirty-some years in Bolivia, the military action of 1964 appears not as a counterrevolutionary event that marks a point of discontinuity with the revolution of 1952 but, rather, as a moment of transition within an ongoing process of reorganizing the basic structures of the political economy. We will argue that the military action of 1964 was in many ways a product of the specific political and economic dynamics set in motion by the revolution and in particular by the decisions made and not made by its major actors. We will also interpret the new military-based regime as an attempt to implement by force one of the major ideological tendencies to emerge within the revolution regarding strategies of state-led economic development and modernization, a tendency that reflected the way both national and international factors impinged on the process in Bolivia. Indeed, in our perspective, the entire period from 1964 till the present has been shaped by succeeding attempts to grapple with the central question of the political economy set in motion by the great revolution of 1952.[2]

There is a tendency to forget that the Bolivian National Revolution of 1952 was once perceived as the second (after Mexico's) great progressive social uprising of twentieth-century Latin America. Spurred by worker and peasant militias, the MNR implemented a number of critical structural changes aimed at unseating the old oligarchy of tin magnates and landowners (called in Bolivia La Rosca, the screw) and promised a new era of economic progress and social justice. In rapid succession the largest tin mines were nationalized and reorganized into a new state mining corporation (Corporación Minera de Bolivia, COMIBOL); the old system of landed estates was destroyed and the lands doled out to Indian peasants; the mass of the population was enfranchised for the first time; and the national military was purged, reduced in size, and reorganized. Not without reason, at the time these were considered to be momentous changes.

Once the old regime had been dismantled, the major task of the MNR was to build a new order capable of giving shape to the social energies unleashed by the revolution and at the same time push forward the promised process of economic development and social justice. It was a task that escaped the grasp of the leadership of the MNR in the late 1950s and early 1960s which led to the coup d'état of 1964.

In trying to construct a new order, the elites of the MNR faced three central problems. The first was to define and implement a model of the political economy to promote development as well as to articulate specific strategies of economic growth. The second was to create a set of institutional structures capable of incorporating into a new system key social sectors like organized labor, peasants, and the middle class. The third was to form coalitions among critical social sectors to produce sufficient political power to sustain governments capable of solving the first two problems.

As we will argue in the conclusion, these were problems that have confronted all the national elites of the region since the collapse of economic and political structures brought on by the Great Depression of the 1930s. The major difference in Bolivia was that the failure of the old elites (the oligarchy) to solve these problems provoked the revolution of 1952. Hence, the MNR elite, which at its core was more reformist than revolutionary, confronted these common problems in the politically intense context of hypermobilization and radical reform produced by the mass rising of 1952 and its aftermath. This leads to a theme that is implicit throughout this book; namely, that Bolivia constitutes an extreme case of a common set of problems and trends that pervaded the region during this same period.

When the MNR took power by force in 1952, it was a broad coalition of social groups with various ideological tendencies. The main party leaders—Victor Paz Estenssoro, Hernán Siles Zuazo, and Walter Guevara Arce—were old-line Latin American populists who looked to Mexico, not Moscow, for their ideological inspiration. In Bolivia, as elsewhere in Latin America, ideological issues were and are manifested mostly around issues of economic models of development and derived growth strategies. In broad terms the main-line party leaders, following Mexico, aimed to impose a model of state capitalism. The left of the party, which was increasingly identified with the labor leader Juan Lechín Oquendo, pushed for a more radical approach that would be embodied in a state socialist model. In regionwide terms the old-line party elite looked to Mexico while the leftist party elite anticipated what would come to pass in Cuba after 1959. An interesting aspect of Bolivia, as the text will show, is that all of these early leaders played crucial political roles over the next three decades and into the present. They are still the titans of Bolivian politics.

Aside from purely ideological issues, the question of models spoke to concrete lines of conflict that were ultimately to pull the MNR apart and that still bedevil Bolivian political elites. In all modern societies there is an ongoing tension between the economic imperative to accumulate capital for investment and the political drive to build support by meeting the demands of social groups, which usually means increasing consumption. This tension is heightened in the context of underdevelopment. It is pushed even further in a context of a mass-based revolution, in which the social forces supporting the revolution do so in hopes of bettering their life situation. As Bolivia was to learn, at some point emphasis must shift to capital accumulation at the expense of general levels of consumption. This fact generates costs (restricted consumption) that especially in a capitalist context fall unevenly on the populace. This raises the crucial political questions, which groups are going to pay the costs of capital accumulation and development, and who is going to allocate the costs and make them stick?

These questions were particularly intense in the context of the Bolivian revolution because the MNR was a multiclass organization that assumed a commonality of interests among diverse social groups like the urban middle class, organized labor, and the traditional Indian peasantry. This assumption was to prove fallacious. The fact is that in Bolivia, even after the revolutionary reforms stripped the old elite of its wealth, there was still not enough capital to meet the demands of the MNR's support groups and to accumulate for investment. Hence, a decision as to which groups within the original coalition would bear the costs of development was inevitable.

In the first four years of the revolution, under President Paz the MNR sought to contain the ideological struggle, meet the pent-up demands of its support groups and push ambitious development plans. The result was explosive inflation: the value of the peso fell from 60 to 12,000 to the dollar. The inflation lodged the costs with the urban middle class, which began to turn against the MNR and to support the major opposition party, the Falange Socialista Boliviana (FSB).

By 1956 the central issue had become similar to that which confronts Bolivia today: stabilization of an economy reeling under hyperinflation. At that point the core MNR led by then-president Hernán Siles Zuazo looked to the outside world and especially the United States for aid in solving Bolivia's economic problems. To get that aid, Bolivia had to accept a stabilization program designed by the International Monetary Fund (IMF). Much as today, the IMF austerity program was based on a logic that shifted the costs onto the popular sectors and in particular organized labor. Not unexpectedly, this generated intense conflict between the Siles government and organized labor led by Lechín as head of the mine workers' federation (FSTMB) and the national labor center, the Central Obrera Boliviana (COB).

The stabilization program of 1956 marked the emergence to ideological dominance of the main-line MNR leadership and the state capitalist model. It also showed not only that the assumed commonality of interests in the coalition was illusionary but also that even within the state capitalist model the old belief that the revolutionary elite could push development and distributive social justice at the same time was fallacious. This fact was to set up a line of conflict within the MNR elite itself among those more oriented toward pushing development and those inclined toward populist redistribution. Ironically, that implicit battle would later pit Paz Estenssoro, more a developmentalist, against Siles Zuazo, who later identified with the more populist line.

The conflict between the core MNR elite and the COB was intense, and owing to the existence of armed worker militias, it called into question the authority and capacity of the government to implement its policies. In a move to reassert the authority of the state and to offset the worker militias, the Siles government made the fateful decision to use renewed military aid to rebuild and modernize the armed forces. The revitalized armed forces became a key player in the growing struggle over the definition of models of development and the imposition of the costs of any such centrally defined model. By the early 1960s the armed forces were again a principal political actor.

Models of development and cost allocations emerged as the central points of contention within the revolution, driving the entire process forward. In our view, these remained the crucial issues after the fall of the MNR, and they provide the main analytical focal point around which we have organized this book. Throughout, we view the competition over these issues as the major factor shaping the content of political struggle into the present.

The decision of the Siles government to accept the IMF plan and renewed military aid from the United States highlighted the fact that the revolution did not alter Bolivia's fundamentally dependent position within the Western capitalist system. Indeed, the context pushed the MNR elite into greater reliance on the United States and the international agencies it backed and thereby actually increased and reinforced Bolivia's dependence. The reality of Bolivia's dependence has been a constant external factor shaping (but not determining) the unfolding process of Bolivia's political economy. Dependence has served to limit the options open to national decision makers and to add to the salience of extranational decision-making centers like the IMF and the U.S. government in the internal political drama. Again, dependence is a core theme that runs both implicitly and explicitly throughout this book.

The MNR elite also looked to Mexico for inspiration on how to organize the relationship between the state and society, particularly in terms of intermediary structures to incorporate key social groups. Following the example of the Mexican Partido Revolucionario Institucional (PRI), the MNR sought to establish itself as a dominant inclusionary political organization that would control the state but within a formal democratic framework that allowed opposition so long as it did not pose a serious threat to MNR hegemony. Like the PRI, the MNR adopted a corporatist form of organization that sought to tie functionally defined sectors into the party and the state. In short, the MNR sought to make itself the primary intermediary organization linking state and society, incorporating social sectors, and politically underpinning specific governments.[3]

However, organizational aspiration and reality are two different things. One might argue that a major political achievement of the PRI was its ability to render the Left politically marginal in Mexico and to bring the labor movement into the centrally controlled structure of the party. This was not to be the case in Bolivia. The Left quickly focused around the Lechín-led COB. Owing to the weakness of the MNR elite vis-a-vis the COB, the MNR in the early days of the revolution was forced to accept the COB's demand for the legally autonomous status (*Fuero sindical*) that granted the organization semisovereign control over the workers of Bolivia. From that position the COB successfully demanded co-government status with the MNR, which reinforced its position as a quasi-governmental entity in alliance with the MNR but not an integral part of the party's authority and control structure. As a result the COB's relations with the MNR and the national state were more like interstate than intrastate negotiations. The COB refused to accept the mediation of the MNR as a political party in its relations with the state and any specific government. This development prevented the MNR from assuming the role of structuring the relationship between social groups with the state and specific governments. It also established a precedent of unmediated relations with the state that was to be followed in later years by other class, sectorial, and regional entities.

In addition to the problem of controlling key sectorial organizations like the COB, other problems undermined party unity and called into question the ability of the MNR to make itself into an intermediate political structure capable of underpinning the revolutionary state and generating support for specific governments. The most significant development in this regard was the rampant growth of personalistic factionalism within the party.

Historically one of the realities of Bolivia's dependent mono product (tin export) economy was lack of a broad base of employment. Hence, the state became a principle source of employment, especially for the urban middle class. A major motor of political life for some time had been the struggle to circulate state patronage among dominant political parties and factions; the MNR continued and reinforced this pattern. Within the new revolutionary model public employment was a predominant mechanism to incorporate social sectors into the new regime as well as to link leadership groups to the party structure. Job politics became an important dynamic within the MNR and reinforced a tendency set in motion by the revolution toward a rapid and steady expansion of the size of the state. Not surprisingly, job and patronage seekers lined up in droves to swear the oath of party loyalty.

As party membership swelled relative to jobs in the expanding public sector, the party began to divide into clientelistic cliques formed around various party leaders. The cliques fostered personalistic leadership along with factionalism. The party began to degenerate into a congeries of strongmen heading up personal factions driven more by the dynamics of jobs and patronage than issues of ideology or representing the interests of sectors of civil society. By the late 1950s intraparty strife was as intense as that among parties, classes, and groups.

Internal party conflict showed up dramatically in the legislative assembly. Ostensibly dominated by the MNR, the assembly was in fact an arena for increasingly intense rivalry among party leaders and their cliques. The assembly became a body less interested in enacting laws and representing the interests of civil society than in circulating patronage and enabling factional assaults on executive power. The MNR, in turn, lost its interest-aggregating and incorporating functions and became an instrument through which factions could exploit the state. Neither the party nor the legislature assumed a mediating role between the state and society at large. The state became associated almost exclusively with executive power. MNR executives increasingly governed not through the party but through their personalistic factions, factions that were as intensely opposed by other MNR factions as by opposition parties.

The conflicts and contradictions came to a head in the early 1960s. Newly reelected to the presidency, Paz Estenssoro, backed by the Kennedy administration and its Alliance for Progress, moved definitively to push the state capitalist model and the strategy of emphasizing capital accumulation over consumption. The focal point of this thrust was the multilateral Triangular Plan, in which the United States was prominent, to restructure the tin industry and especially the state mining corporation, COMIBOL. The "rationalization" envisaged layoffs, wage adjustments, reductions in benefits, and a general "disciplining" of labor. It provoked open confrontation with the COB and the Left, led by Lechín, who at the time was also vice-president. The battle escalated, and by 1963 President Paz was deploying troops around the mines in a show of strength that increased the salience of the armed forces chiefs in shaping policy and controlling power. The two most prominent figures were General René Barrientos Ortuño of the air force and General Alfredo Ovando Candia of the army.

In 1964, under prodding by the U.S. embassy, President Paz took advantage of a constitutional revision in 1961 that allowed a president to succeed himself and forced his nomination through a controlled party convention. However, Paz was not able to control the military, which forced him to accept General Barrientos as his running mate. No sooner had the two been elected than Barrientos began to move into all but open opposition to the president.

As he began his new term, Paz was assailed from all sides. The Left and the COB continued to resist his overall economic strategy, especially the cost allocations inherent in the state capitalist model. Party factions arrayed behind other MNR caudillos were frustrated by the Paz faction's grip on patronage and the fact that Paz's reelection meant their exclusion from patronage sources for at least another four years. Both the external opposition and internal party opposition began to conspire to oust Paz and looked to the military as an ally.

When the military moved against Paz in 1964 it had support both within and outside the MNR. This collusion was indicative of two important components of the political system that had developed in Bolivia. First, military intervention sprang as much from the inducement of civilian political leaders as from motives internal to the military. Second, it was clear that any commitment to democratic procedures for rotating political power among the civil elites was, to say the least, tenuous. When push came to shove, all of Bolivia's civilian political leaders from right to left, MNR or not, were as inclined to seize power by a coup as to gain it by electoral means. As we shall see, a large portion of the groups that backed the forced ouster of Paz were in for a rude awakening in the new scheme of things.

The military-based regime quickly consolidated around the charismatic figure of General Barrientos, who became president, and the somewhat less dramatic figure of General Ovando, who became commander of the armed forces. General Barrientos dominated the tone and substance of the new regime. Almost from the outset it was made clear that the Barrientos government would not reverse the policy lines defined by Siles and Paz, in particular the imposition of the state capitalist model. Barrientos declared that his government represented the restoration of the true line of the MNR revolution, which had been distorted by Paz and other MNR caudillos. In practice, this was to mean that the military would push the state capitalist model but without the baggage of Paz and the bulk of the MNR.

Notes

1. For an overview of relevant Bolivian history see Herbert S. Klein, *Bolivia: The Evolution of a Multi-Ethnic Society* (New York: Oxford University Press, 1982).
2. A more extended analysis of the revolution and its aftermath is contained in James M. Malloy, *Bolivia: The Uncompleted Revolution* (Pittsburgh: University of Pittsburgh Press, 1970).
3. For a detailed analysis of the MNR organization, see Christopher Mitchell, *The Legacy of Populism in Bolivia: From the MNR to Military Rule* (New York: Praeger, 1977).

1

Barrientos and the Rise of the Generals

Nothing set the tone of the Barrientos period—and all subsequent periods as well—more than the relationship between the state and organized labor, particularly the miners. The relationship was fraught with intense and violent confrontation as the new government sought to assert its control over labor and to impose by force the costs of the state capitalist development model previously pushed by the main-line MNR and its international backers. Indeed, it was the political failure of the MNR to resolve this issue that led to its downfall and brought the military to the fore.

Given the logic of the situation in 1964, a bloody clash between the new government and labor was all but inevitable, even though labor had helped to bring down the MNR. In retrospect, the events surrounding the coup and its aftermath point up some significant aspects of labor's political situation in postrevolutionary Bolivia. Specifically, they showed that although labor had been part of a blocking veto coalition, it did not have the capacity to seize power in its own right or to play a major role in helping to define and undergird a new regime. In that context, labor was an essentially isolated political force that would have to use all its strength simply to defend itself.

The nature of the relationship that was to unfold between the new regime and labor was signaled when Barrientos, speaking as president of a junta of military commanders, declared that theirs was to be a "revolution within the revolution" aimed at restoring the tradition betrayed by Paz and the factions of the MNR. The new regime was dubbed Revolución Restauradora (restoring revolution); a theme that Barrientos was to hit over and over during his ascendancy over Bolivian public life. In a speech on May 1, Juan Lechín Oquendo showed that he grasped the full implications of the government's self-definition when he declared that it was determined to follow the same antilabor policies as Paz Estenssoro.

The regime's drift into confrontation with labor was given a significant

9

goad in February of 1965. After a review of the situation in the mines, the commission of the Triangular Plan described the results of the first two phases of the plan as disappointing and called into question the wisdom of financing a third phase. Fatefully, the commission concluded that "labor union anarchy" continued to be the major obstacle to the rehabilitation of COMIBOL. The government was told, in effect, to bring labor to heel and to assert its authority in the mines or forgo further financial assistance under the plan. This development gave eloquent demonstration of how the internal logic of an approach to the political economy and significant outside pressure could combine to push the entire flow of politics in Bolivia in a particular, in this case tragic, direction.[1]

The gathering struggle began to take shape in the early months of 1965. The newly appointed president of COMIBOL, Colonel Juan Lechín Suarez (half-brother of Juan Lechín Oquendo), made it clear that the regime intended to implement the third phase of the Triangular Plan and agreed with the commission that labor productivity and "indiscipline" was a key problem. Lechín Oquendo and the FSTMB fired back, accusing the regime of bending to foreign imperialist interests. As they had since the early 1960s, the leaders of the FSTMB argued that COMIBOL's major problems were mismanagement and a bloated bureaucracy of political appointees. They pointed out that some 115 new staff people had been added by the new government since 1964. In that context debates over the specific causes of COMIBOL's financial distress were largely beside the point; deeper issues were at stake. The battle that was looming would not be over technical problems or short-term economic policy but over authority and control; the relative power of the state and state managers, and groups like organized labor. At the deepest level, it would be over the position of the labor Left vis-á-vis the state and the model of the political economy that was being constructed.

The crisis came to a head somewhat symbolically in May, the month of labor. During the traditional celebrations on May 1, 1965, Lechín Oquendo and other leaders denounced Barrientos and the junta for the line they had taken, and exhorted the unions and workers to gird for a long struggle. The Barrientos government in turn, with a tactic it was to use often, sought to discredit Lechín Oquendo personally. The minister of interior attacked Lechín as antinationalist because, he asserted, Lechín surreptitiously had become a Chilean citizen; because of the history of Bolivia's relations with Chile, there were few more politically serious charges that one could make against a national leader. This was followed by accusations that Lechín Oquendo was involved in cocaine trafficking.

The campaign against Lechín culminated on May 15, when after further charges that he was at the head of a subversive international communist plot, the military police whisked him into exile in Paraguay. In the days previous the major leaders of organized labor formed, under the leadership of the COB, a broad defense front made up of the miners, teachers, and factory and construction workers. In response to the exiling of Lechín, the front called for a general strike. The strike failed, for reasons that are many and complex, but the failure demonstrated that at base labor was deeply divided over many issues and that classwide actions were very difficult to achieve. Significantly, the regime was able to drive a wedge into the front by entering into bilateral wage negotiations with specific groups. The teachers, responding to an offer of a wage rise, cut their own deal with the government and broke ranks. By late May the only groups holding together were the miners (FSTMB) and the factory workers (*fabriles*). The government bent them into submission.

On May 17 the regime issued decree #07171, which declared that the mandates of the leaders of all unions were suspended until further notice; it was the first of a host of decrees that would completely reorganize labor relations in Bolivia. The mine unions responded by declaring the mines "free territory," and workers in the Kami mine seized twelve members of a military patrol as hostages. Lechín Suarez declared COMIBOL to be in a "state of emergency" on May 23, and under the terms of the decree empowered management to take all necessary steps unilaterally to "rationalize" the corporation's operations.

The army invaded the mining camps and declared them to be military zones. Bloody battles broke out in a number of mines. The fighting quickly spread to La Paz, where factory workers tried to stop troops from moving into the Milluni mine near the city. There, as in the camps, the government called in the air force, which bombed and strafed in support of the ground troops. Within forty-eight hours it was over—the workers were cowed and, by all accounts, casualties were heavy. Under the vigilance of military commanders, the miners and fabriles went back to work.

On June 1 the regime issued a set of decrees defining labor's status. The COB was abolished, and all current leaders were continued in suspension. The government declared it would supervise a reorganization of the unions by which all leaders with proven connections to parties or other political groups would be excluded from participation. A general wage freeze was initiated for an indefinite period.

In the mines the measures were even more draconian. All decision-making authority was lodged in the COMIBOL management, which promptly moved to "rationalize" the work force. Under a new formula, wages were cut from 40 to 50 percent, and subsidies on a variety of foodstuffs in the camp stores were removed, thereby raising prices dramatically. The company then moved to reduce the work force; in June alone over 1,300 miners were laid off; most losing any accrued benefits.

The most significant change was that the whole system of co-government and workers' control, one of labor's greatest achievements in the revolution of 1952, was abolished. The move undercut the basis of labor's political influence and precluded any further possibility in the short term for pressure to move the revolution in a socialist direction. In the mines, other state enterprises, and the private sector, all legal bases for worker participation were eliminated, and an "authoritarian" model of decision making based on technical and managerial expertise was initiated. As far as the relative distribution of power and influence among groups was concerned, this new package of decrees did in fact add up to a "revolution in the revolution."[2]

The new military-backed government had shown its will and, in the short term at least, its capacity to assert its authority over labor. Perhaps in recognition of that fact the Triangular Plan commission conducted a new review of COMIBOL in August and concluded that the situation had changed for the better. Its report stipulated that the government was now in conformity with the preconditions of the plan and that the third phase could be implemented. After some further negotiations in October 1965, new contracts were signed in March of 1966.

But, the drama of Barrientos, the military, and the miners was not over. To keep its control over labor and particularly the miners, the regime had to maintain a heavy hand over them. There were two more bloody invasions of the mines. The first occurred after the miners sought to regroup and assert their power during late August 1965. Troops entered the camp of the Llallagua mine on September 21, and again many lives were lost. The miners were temporarily submissive. The most notorious clash took place in June of 1967. At that time the eyes of the world were on Bolivia as the Barrientos government was stalking a guerrilla movement launched by the legendary Ché Guevara in Nancahuazú. The Bolivian Left split deeply over what position to take in regard to the movement, and the recriminations engendered by the movement and Ché's death were to last for some time. Some labor groups, including the miners, saw an opportunity to reassert themselves and moved to seize it.

The FSTMB in clandestine meetings drew up a set of demands that included a restoration of pre-May 1965 wage levels, reinstatement of fired workers, and a return of the old labor organizations and leaders. A series of demonstrations in support of the demands were to culminate in a general assembly of the FSTMB to be held in the Catavi-Siglo XX mining complex on June 24, 1967. The assembly was to press the workers demands formally as well as mobilize worker financial support for the guerrillas. The challenge to the embattled Barrientos government was stark and clear.

The day prior to the meeting, June 23, was the traditional festival of San Juan, a winter festival with deep roots in the Andean culture. The Night of

San Juan (*Noche de San Juan*) coincides with the coldest period in the bleak Andean highlands. The celebration's theme is the forces of cold and darkness versus those of light and warmth. Throughout the highlands in both spontaneous and organized fiestas people dance around fires in front of houses, in squares, and other central places and as the night wears on the boldest begin to leap through the fires. The revelry is fueled by copious amounts of alcohol imbibed in powerful hot drinks. In the dawn hours of June 24 each year cities are covered by a blanket of smoke from the fires and a large part of the populace slips into the stupor of a heavy hangover.

The Noche de San Juan is a particularly important festival in the high, cold mining camps. And the fact is that in a hard drinking culture, there are few who consume alcohol like the miners, who seek respite from their grim work and the barren landscape. On nights like San Juan both men and women dance with abandon and drink, as they put it, *hasta el suelo* till one is on the ground. It does not take much imagination, then, to picture what the camps are like the morning after.

On such an early morning on June 24, 1967, the military surrounded and then invaded the camps in what most witnesses described as a brutally murderous way. Whatever the nature of the invasion, the fact is that the miners were again blasted into a hate-filled submission. And whatever arguments the government advanced to justify its actions (there were many), the fact is that on that morning a new symbol of the long violent oppression of the Bolivian miner was created. To the litany of earlier bloody encounters recounted in the camps was added "La Noche Triste de San Juan"—the sad night of San Juan.[3]

The invasion of San Juan took on such significance because it conjured the image of a cowardly sneak attack against drunk and defenseless miners. In any event, that action more than anything else came to symbolize the ongoing struggle between Bolivian labor and Barrientos, the man and leader. It was another bloody page in the history of the relationship of the miners and the military, and helped lock in the image of the military as an institution more adept at beating on Bolivians than defending them from any foreign foes. The sad fact is that the Bolivian military has lost every war it has fought and prior to defeating Ché Guevara in October 1967, its only victories were over Bolivians.

Although there were no further major battles between the regime and the miners, it is clear the government's control over labor was tenuous throughout Barrientos's tenure. Costs were imposed on labor, unions were dismantled, and labor's demands were suppressed, but the movement was not destroyed nor was its combative spirit definitively crushed. At best the government was able to hold a lid on the sociopolitical pot. To keep it there, the Barrientos regime paid dearly in time, energy, and resources.

Even more, it paid in a besmirched image that in the eyes of many diminished the legitimacy of the president himself, and in the long run the armed forces and its claim to be the tutelary institution of the nation.

Economic Policy

The Barrientos regime was not an ideological one in the sense of defining new coherent visions of Bolivia's future. In most instances policy emerged in specific contexts and reflected short-term solutions designed to buy the regime breathing space. Given Barrientos's general orientation, however, policy in most areas flowed along the lines defined by MNR governments since 1956; this was particularly true of economic policy. The tendency to follow the MNR path was reinforced by the constraints imposed by external actors. In addition to the obvious influence of the triangular commis sion, Bolivian economic policy was also influenced by the U.S. AID mission and by the IMF, which continued to conduct annual standby loan reviews.

Economic policy in this period, then, was not characterized by any bold departures or new directions. Rather, it was a policy of consolidating and enforcing the state capitalist model implicit in the approach of the previous eight years. In some senses the major contribution of the Barrientos regime in the area of economic policy was to provide the muscle to impose the policies on recalcitrant groups, such as organized labor. The major change was political, involving a shift from the populist, more or less accommodationist approach of the MNR to a new politics of de facto authoritarian force.

Looking back, one can see that the Bolivian economy went through three fairly clear phases between 1952 and 1969. The first confused years of the revolution were characterized by negative growth and hyperinflation as the country groped for a new definition of its future. The period 1956-60 was one of stabilization and a shift toward the state capitalist model in which negative growth continued but inflation was dramatically reduced. The 1960s saw a pattern of relatively stable growth within the framework of the state capitalist model. The continuity of the Barrientos regime with that of the Paz regime is quite striking. It is plain that the major change between the two was in the political, not the economic, realm.[4]

In the economic sphere the policy differences in the Barrientos period were ones of emphasis and nuance. In sectorial terms the Barrientos regime focused on consolidating the public sector while it emphasized a revitalization of the private sector. This tilt toward the private sector was signaled by a new law for the promotion of investment decreed in 1965. The incentives provided by the law plus the new "climate of labor relations" created a favorable environment for private investors, who responded by increasing their investments from about U.S. $3 million in 1963-64 to approximately $47 million in 1966, a trend that continued until 1970.

The overall tilt toward the private sector stood out in the critical sectors of mining and hydrocarbons. In mining the keystone was the consolidation of authority in COMIBOL under the Triangular Plan, as a result of which the corporation began to post a formal pattern of profit between 1966 and 1969. The government also opened the possibility of some denationalization of mining with a new scheme of joint ventures. Under this the rich Matilde zinc mine was granted to a United States-based consortium of Philips Brothers and the U.S. Steel Corporation; U.S. Steel also received a contract to work the tailings of some of the major mines. The major development in mining, however was the growth of the so-called medium mine sector.

By 1968 there was a fairly rough balance between the state and the private sector in mining, with production split 55 percent and 45 percent. The private sector, in turn, was divided into what were termed small mines and medium-sized mines. The small mines were labor-intensive operations that split among themselves a minor portion of the sector's overall production. The small mines multiplied after 1965 as their owner contractors (many former mine policemen) hired laid-off miners. In the main these were primitive enterprises that paid low wages and provided no social benefits. Because most of them sold their production to COMIBOL, they amounted to a system in which the state corporation extracted surplus from its former employees at a fraction of the previous cost.

The more important companies were those of medium size, medium only in relationship to COMIBOL. In fact, most were large, modern, and capital intensive. In the late 1960s there were twenty-six medium sized companies with a total capital of U.S. $9.5 million and a work force of some 4,728 workers; roughly a third were nationally owned, a third foreign owned, and the remaining third in mixed corporations. Aside from the incentives of the 1965 investment law, the Barrientos government stimulated the medium-sized mines with a favorable tax policy. In general such mines outperformed COMIBOL and increased their production at a faster rate throughout the 1960s. By 1969 the medium sized miners (organized in their own trade association, Associación Nacional de Mineros Medianos, ANMM) constituted one of the most powerful economic forces in the country.

A critical growth area in the 1960s and 1970s was petroleum. Here the Barrientos government followed the policy of opening the sector to foreign private investment begun by the MNR in 1955. By the mid-1960s the Gulf

Oil Corporation monopolized private petroleum production. Gulf controlled some 80 percent of total production; the state petroleum company, YPFB, 20 percent. In the period 1963-68 Gulf dramatically increased its production from 18,500 cubic meters to 1,886,200; that of YPFB declined from from 501,600 cubic meters to 497,400. Gulf was obviously an important economic force in Bolivia.

Aside from these two crucial areas, private economic activity also grew in manufacturing, construction, commerce, finance, and commercial agriculture. Thus, by 1968 a new and vigorous private sector produced by the revolution began to assume a prominent position. It controlled some 75 percent of GNP and engaged some 85 percent of the workforce (these percentages includes traditional Indian peasant smallholders). Although the private sector clearly profited from the Barrientos government's approach to political economy, the public sector was hardly diminished as an economic force. Overall, government, particularly in employment, was a growth sector in this period, and the state's share of total investment grew to a substantial 52 percent in 1968 from a not negligible 40 percent in 1959. The thrust in this period was toward recalibrating the relationship between the public and private sectors within the state capitalist model.

Within both the public and private sector, the Barrientos regime, following the MNR's lead, obviously favored large, modern, relatively capital-intensive corporate operations over small-scale traditional activity. This was particularly true in agriculture. Although private agriculture employs the bulk of the labor force, mainly in small traditional peasant farms, its share of GNP declined during this as well as previous periods. The diminution reflected the clear antitraditional bias of the regime shown in the small share of total investment that went into the agriculture sector. Moreover, the bulk of investment in the sector went to the emergent agro-industrial groups of eastern Bolivia.[5]

In retrospect, the Barrientos period stands out as a time of transition in the structure of the economy, again along lines laid down in the previous years. The major component of the transition was a relative drop in the share of the GDP of the productive sectors of the economy and a concomitant rise in the share of social infrastructure and services. The shift was characterized by declines in the share of agriculture and mining, relatively stable shares for manufacturing, energy, and transportation, and increased participation by hydrocarbons, construction, commerce, finance, general government, and housing and other services. The full significance of the shift would not become evident until the 1970s.[6]

The Barrientos years saw some diversification in exports, with a rise in the export of hydrocarbons, manufacturing, and agro-industrial products. Still, the Bolivian economy remained one of the most dependent in Latin

America. The economy remained dependent on foreign trade in terms of its participation in the GDP, and the central government relied heavily on foreign trade to produce revenue. An important feature of the economy's openness and dependence was the fact that Bolivia had almost no leverage in the markets where its products were sold.[7]

In spite of the regime's openness and favorable policies, there was little direct foreign investment coming into Bolivia between 1964 and 1969. The Barrientos regime remained dependent on foreign aid to underwrite its budget and investments. Although the United States favored the regime and provided substantial aid, especially in its first two years, there was a steady restructuring of the pattern of aid in the late 1960s. Direct grants to the budget declined sharply and other modes of indirect assistance increased. Most significantly, the regime had to increase its rate of foreign borrowing to cover its budget deficits. Foreign indebtedness began to increase sharply in the late 1960s; a trend whose full significance would become apparent in the 1970s.

Political Dimensions

Politically, the period 1964-69 was an inchoate one as Barrientos tried to bring to the fore and capitalize on some internal trends that began to appear in the later years of the MNR. The MNR was a populist coalition led by the middle class that tried to mobilize support within the middle class, workers, and the peasantry. The realities of the situation of scarcity, however, began to rip the movement apart. In the period 1952-56 the costs fell on the middle class by means of inflation, alienating that crucial sector. After 1956 the Siles government, under pressure from the IMF, sought to stabilize the economy and take pressure off the middle class, but the IMF-designed plan shifted the costs to labor, thereby creating tension between the MNR leadership and the working class, particularly the miners.

In his struggle with labor Siles made a number of moves that in effect pointed the way to a potential new power coalition. Foremost, Siles, backed by renewed U.S. military assistance, began to rebuild the military that had been all but destroyed in 1952 as a counterweight to the workers' militias. Second, Siles sought to mobilize the peasantry, and particularly called

% GDP Growth 1960-69

1960	1961	1962	1963	1964
4.30	2.09	5.58	6.42	4.81

1965	1966	1967	1968	1969
6.90	7.01	6.32	7.18	4.76

upon the more organized peasant groups that had their own militias to back him. Implicitly, Siles began to fashion a coalition around the military, peasants, the urban middle class, and external actors such as the United States and U.S.-backed multilateral institutions like the IMF. During his second tenure (1960-64) Paz sought to base himself on the same coalition, which became quite evident in his clash with the miners in August 1963.

Barrientos basically tried to mobilize and solidify the same coalition. In addition, he looked to private-sector entrepreneurial groups that were emerging as a result of the state capitalist development strategy and various regional interests, especially his own Department of Cochabamba and new eastern power centers like Santa Cruz. Although Barrientos was in the main successful in welding these groups into a base of support, the coalition was rather tenuous and problematic throughout the period.

In immediate power terms, the two pillars of the Barrientos regime were the peasants and the military. These were the groups he rode to power and when push came to shove, as it often did during the late 1960s, Barrientos turned to one or the other or both to guarantee his continued tenure. The two were welded into a formal alliance in support of Barrientos, known as the *pacto militar-campesino* (the military-peasant pact). The formal pact has a rather cloudy history, and when it was actually made is difficult to establish. What is sure is that it had its roots in the late 1950s and early 1960s when the Bolivian armed forces became very active in the grass-roots development projects known as *acción cívica* (civic action). These projects brought the military into direct and sustained contact with the peasants of some regions, and officers like Barrientos were thereby able to build personal ties to key peasant leaders.

In part because of his background as the son of an Indian woman from a provincial Cochabamba town, Quechua-speaking Barrientos was particularly successful in forging links to ambitious peasant leaders in the Cochabamba Valley which was perhaps the single most important center of organized power among the peasants. He then used these links to all but force himself onto the ticket as Paz Estenssoro's running mate in 1964. During the coup of November 1964 Cochabamba was Barrientos's power base, and in the hasty negotiations that followed the fall of Paz, the air force general used his peasant support and the spectre of a peasant uprising to persuade, if not coerce, the army and General Ovando to install him as president.

Once in power, Barrientos looked for occasions to "ratify" formally the pact symbolically linking these two power groups. The rhetoric around the pact defined the military and the peasants as the key groups in Bolivia's future, stressed the military's commitment to agrarian reform and rural development, and pledged the two groups to support each other in the struggle against communism and other threats to the nation. The reality was that in the context of the mid-1960s the pact amounted to an anti-Left and anti-labor alliance; it demonstrated then that an alliance of peasants and the middle class was a more practical reality than an alliance of peasants and the working class that had long been heralded by the Left.

Because of the agrarian reform of 1953, the mass of Indian peasants were among the major beneficiaries of the revolution. After the reform the traditional agricultural areas saw the demise of large landed estates and the rise of a class of small peasant freeholders. During the early 1950s, unions (*sindicatos*) proliferated throughout the countryside, and in many areas armed peasant militias also appeared. However, the degree of organization, level of political consciousness, and simple orientation toward the national arena (long dominated by *mestizos* and whites) varied considerably. The picture was complicated further as thousands of peasants went into unfamiliar lowland areas as part of government-sponsored or spontaneous colonization projects.

Given their sheer numbers (60 percent of the population) and their weight in the economy, the Indian peasants obviously were a potential source of great political power. The MNR as a movement sought to tap into that power base, and by and large did manage to establish a formal political monopoly in the countryside. But, as factionalization developed in the MNR, ambitious individuals and factions, often from the position of minister of peasant affairs, attempted to build their own specific links with peasant groups. Again, the situation was complex and variable, but as the revolution progressed, relations between national political groups and the peasants were increasingly mediated by an emergent stratum of peasant leaders (*dirigentes campesinos*) who controlled unions and militias. By the late 1950s and 1960s, these dirigentes often battled with each other for control over specific regions and groups of unions; sometimes forming ties with one national faction or another. In this way a mutual dependency often developed, and in most cases an individual's or a group's power in the countryside was less a function of their ties to the peasant mass than ability to develop clientelistic ties with established dirigentes.

This was the context in which Barrientos created his much-vaunted popular base in the countryside. His ties were particularly strong among leaders of the Quechua speaking peoples in the Cochabamba Valley, and later he built links to powerful dirigentes of Aymara-speaking groups around the Lake Titicaca region of the Department of La Paz. These two areas were the most organized and armed and therefore constituted the major foci of power in the countryside.

Once in power, Barrientos worked hard on his image as the maximum leader of the campesinos. He traveled widely by helicopter, donning a poncho here, drinking and dancing there, and everywhere distributing personal largess ranging from schools, to potable-water systems to soccer balls and uniforms for schoolchildren. Essentially, he built an image of patrimonial authority in which he was the patron in a personalized relationship of dominance and dependence. He was the one from whom good things would flow in return for supportive dependence.

Given the complexity of the Bolivian countryside and our relative ignorance of that diverse reality, it is extremely difficult to determine how popular Barrientos actually was among the mass of campesinos. What does seem to be the case is that behind the facade the real key to Barrientos's power in the countryside was his clientelistic ties to certain dirigentes. Basically, he used patronage to co-opt some peasant leaders, force to eliminate others (often the rivals of his clients), and some remote groups he simply ignored. There was very little in the way of true resources that went into the traditional agricultural sector; what did go was highly visible but low-cost "gifts" that were doled out on a personalized and particularistic basis. The operative logic seemed to be that where the peasants were politically sophisticated and their leaders loyal, they gained; where they were politically marginal or the support of their leaders in question, they were either ignored or punished. Indeed, in some politically weak areas the former landowners and/or townspeople were able to reassert their hegemony over the land and local peasant groups.

The picture in the countryside, then, was hardly of one piece. Barrientos's power was based on pockets of support that turned on his links to peasant dirigentes. By all accounts his real power base was the Cochabamba Valley; but here as well as elsewhere that power base often fluctuated according to the shifting fortunes of rival local dirigentes and his ability to back, buy off, and support local winners. In sum, it was a complex variable reality that beneath the surface was in a considerable state of flux.[8]

In any event, the campesinos did constitute both a symbolic and a real card that Barrientos could play in the unfolding political game. Barrientos used that card as a positive goad with other groups, such as the military, by seeking to demonstrate the popular support he had mobilized for his military-backed regime. He played it quite often in a negative threatening way, raising the spectre of multitudes of Indians marching against any civil or military factions that might try to unseat him. Throughout the 1963-69 period, whenever Barrientos was on the political defensive (which was often), he or his supporters arranged for dramatic actions by peasant groups, ranging from demonstrations to blockades around cities. On the whole Barrientos played his campesino card with great skill, but on occasion he did stumble badly.

Barrientos's relationship with his other pillar of support—the military—

was equally complex and variable. The military was severely traumatized by the revolution of 1952, in which it came close to being destroyed. As it was, the military was severely reduced in troop size (to about 5,000), officers were purged, and in general the institution was downgraded. The remainder of the officer corps either became dedicated members of the MNR or institutionalists who tried to keep a low profile for themselves and the armed forces.

In the context of the struggles of the late 1950s (IMF stabilization) and the early 1960s (Triangular Plan), the fortunes of the military began to change. Utilizing renewed U.S. military aid (renewed in 1958), the MNR began to rebuild the military as counterweight to the various localized sources of armed power (worker and peasant militias, and in the East, local figures) that had arisen during the revolution. It is not surprising that the MNR sought to assert a coercive capacity of the central state, that is, an organized armed force. As the cohesion of the MNR collapsed and institutionally unmediated conflict increased, the military was pulled into the political arena—a position that with changing fortunes it has held to this day.

Under Barrientos the military became a central political institution in a broader sense than simply being a source of deployable armed force. Military officers assumed important political posts at the local, provincial, and national levels, and important managerial posts in a variety of state enterprises. In addition, the military continued with direct ties to peasant groups and crucial political elites in places like Santa Cruz, the Beni, and other traditionally isolated regions. As many Bolivian politicians are apt to put it, the military increasingly became like an armed political party of sorts.

The military took full advantage of the situation to enlarge its share of national resources. U.S. military assistance increased dramatically in the 1960s: $.1 million in 1958 to $3.5 million in 1968. At the same time government spending on the military grew apace; between 1964 and 1968 alone, more than 100 percent, the largest single increase in the current account during that period. About 12,000 men were under arms in the early 1960s; over 20,000, in 1968. They were equipped with modern weapons, thereby steadily surpassing in firepower the worker and peasant militias that were still using World War II-vintage weapons. Under the pacto militar-campesino powerful dirigentes tried to negotiate an upgrading of the weaponry of their militias, but the military was out to assert its monopoly over the capacity to organize force and no significant upgrading took place. The military clearly treated the campesinos as a junior partner in the pacto, which it saw mainly as a way to manipulate and use peasant groups rather than as a basis for autonomous peasant power.[9]

The more central the military's political role—constantly reinforced by the fact that by the late 1960s the military was the only significant national institution—the more the military was internally politicized and subject to the same strains that had ripped at the unity of the MNR. As the military suppressed the MNR and asserted its titular political role, it began to import into itself the structural conflicts manifested in the larger society. This would have caused serious strain even in a highly institutionalized and professionalized military, as was seen in Brazil, Argentina, and neighboring Peru; but the Bolivian military at that point was still a rather tenuous force from a professional and institutional point of view. It therefore quickly began to divide into personal and ideological factions that undercut the hierarchical authority structure of the institution and diminished its capacity to act as a coherent institutional force.

The reality was that —like the situation with the campesinos—Barrientos increasingly was supported less by the military as an institution than by factions within the military. Because factions and factional coalitions formed and reformed for a variety of complex and often contradictory reasons, the nature of the support flowing from the military was fluid and ever-changing. Aside from the larger political game, then, Barrientos had to become adept at manipulating military politics as well. In sum, the military hardly formed a coherent and stable pillar of support for Barrientos. Throughout his tenure it waxed and waned according to circumstance. By the late 1960s he was looking over his shoulder to fend off rivals in the military who wanted to put themselves in his place.

The shaky nature of Barrientos's relationship with the military evidenced itself during the coup of 1964, and he assumed the presidency only after intense negotiations with General Alfredo Ovando, who controlled the army and harbored his own presidential ambitions. Barrientos served as the singular president for only a few months. Perhaps as a form of payment for crushing the miners and factory workers in May of 1965, the army forced Barrientos to accept General Ovando as his co-president as of May 25, 1965. The two served together until January 1966, when Barrientos resigned so as to meet the legal requirements to run for the presidency in elections called for July 1966. It seems rather clear that prior to this turn, the two generals had made a deal whereby Barrientos would be a constitutional president for one four-year term and Ovando would be president for the next term. To guarantee the deal, Ovando was to serve as chief of the armed forces throughout the Barrientos presidency.

The Quest for Legitimacy

Thus, in 1966 the military leaders sought to legalize the new situation and establish a regime based on constitutional legitimacy. The elections of July were to be for both the presidency and a legislative assembly. The elections were held under the terms of the Constitution of 1947 (under which the MNR had acted), but the new legislature (a standard bicameral body) was simultaneously to function as a constituent assembly and draft a new constitution (which went into effect in 1967.)

In preparation for the elections Barrientos set about building a civil political force to mobilize support and provide the base for a new government. Eschewing the MNR (many factions of which would have been glad to support him) and its old right-wing rival, the Falange Socialista Boliviana (FSB), Barrientos started from scratch and ended by sponsoring the formation of a specific pro-Barrientos party, which, in imitation of the Christian Democrat parties popular throughout Latin America at the time, was called the Movimiento Popular Cristiano (MPC), the Popular Christian Movement.

Although the MPC drew heavily from middle-class politicians, including former members of the MNR, it was organized by military officers personally loyal to Barrientos. The prime mover was Major Hugo Bozo Alcozer who, along with other officers, took a leave of absence from the army to devote full time to the effort. As leader of the MPC, Bozo was charged with coordinating the military-peasant pact and generally organizing peasant backing for Barrientos.

The MPC was a classic personalistic party that revolved around the personality and political fortunes of Barrientos. It was actually more a personalistic faction oriented toward the distribution of jobs and patronage than a true political party or movement. As such, it was a product of the dynamics of intraelite factional struggles over jobs and patronage that had long run through, and in a sense undermined, Bolivia's political life. This basic theme of personnel circulation was and is rooted in the structural nature of the Bolivian middle class.

Like much else in Bolivia, the middle class was a product of the unbalanced economic structure generated by Bolivia's outward-oriented export model of dependent capitalist development. As a result of the fact that sources of hard wealth have been few and subject to monopoly control, the middle class has been a specific kind of dependent class that relies on salaries and fees to underwrite its social status. Occupationally, it is a class of liberal professionals, and in recent years also of technical specialists and white-collar employees. The reality is that a substantial portion of this class has been and is dependent on the state for employment. Because access to state jobs has always been politically determined, the middle class early on spawned a "political class" that has always been driven as much by the pursuit of jobs as ideology or other factors. The number of state jobs has never been enough to absorb the whole "political class," so it has always split into antagonistic job-hungry factions.

The middle class is mainly an urban stratum heavily concentrated in the capital city of La Paz. Although it is relatively small, perhaps 5 percent of the economically active population, it has great weight politically because it has staffed the state apparatus and produced most of the nation's political leadership since the 1920s.[10] Most of the major political parties, movements, and ideologies in modern Bolivia, including the MNR, originated in the urban middle class and then reached out to other groups. Whatever contradictory ideologies have been produced by the middle class, it is evident that the bulk of its numbers have been "statist" in the sense of looking to government as a primary employer. This bureaucratized social stratum is a pivotal class politically, in our view, and its dynamics help account for the expansion in size and role of the state in post-1952 Bolivia. Moreover, the political logic of this stratum and its numbers relative to available jobs has guaranteed that at a deep level job-faction politics (which Bolivians call *empleomania)*, is a driving force of the political game whatever other kinds of ideological, class, and regional conflicts are at stake. Intraelite job-faction politics is so rooted in the socioeconomic structure that it forms a kind of deep political structure in its own right; and constitutes a basic theme that runs under and through the drama of public life. This dynamic was one of the key factors that fragmented the MNR and led to Paz's downfall.

The MPC was a product of this underlying structure. It was almost exclusively a collection of middle-class *políticos* drawn from a variety of parties and groups, including many factions of the MNR. An artificial creation, it had no institutional links to other social groups or classes. As a cabal, or what Bolivians call a *camarilla*, revolving around Barrientos, it was in a sense epiphenomenal to the larger political struggle. The job-hungry cadres of the MPC were unable alone to mobilize any mass support for a Barrientos presidency or provide an institutional base for a new regime.

Recognizing this basic fact of political life, Barrientos attempted to broaden his formal political base by creating a front of political parties and groups called the Frente de la Revolución Boliviana (FRB), the Bolivian Revolutionary Front. The FRB embraced first three classic party/faction groups: the Partido Social Demócrata (PSD), a pre-1952 party drawn from reformist sectors of the prerevolutionary elite; the Partido de la Izquierada Revolucionaria (PIR), a pre-1952 quasi-Marxist party that had been compromised by its propensity to serve in any government that offered posts; and the Partido Revolucionario Auténtico (PRA), a formal offshoot of the MNR formed in the 1960s by the long-standing MNR leader Walter Guevara Arce. These parties added little to Barrientos's coalition other than some well-worn political names and more job-hungry factions ready to cash in on his presidency. Like the MPC, none had any real structural links to major classes or sectors in the society. In addition to the parties, the FRB enrolled the organization of veterans of the disastrous Chaco War of the 1930s with Paraguay, the *excombatientes*, they were little more than a specialized middle-class interest group.

The most significant nonparty group to enter the FRB was the peasant bloc, the *bloque campesino*. It was formed by pro-Barrientos dirigentes, especially those from the Cochabamba Valley, and maintained its independence within the FRB. However, the bloc was integrated into the MPC and under the direct tutelage of Barrientos, as coordinated by Hugo Bozo. Together the two officers controlled the nomination of peasant candidates for Congress and after the elections pulled the strings of the ostensibly independent peasant brigade of deputies, the *brigada campesina parliamentaria*.

Barrientos led the FRB into the elections of 1966 amidst much fanfare. His running mate was the well-known civilian politician of the PSD Luis Adolfo Siles Salinas, the half brother of Hernán Siles Zuazo. The FRB campaigned around the theme of the restoring revolution. Barrientos linked himself to the spirit of the revolution and to two famous reformist military presidents of the 1930s and 1940s; Germán Busch and Gualberto Villarroel. In so doing, he focused the campaign on his personality and implied that the true revolutionary tradition of Bolivia sprang from the armed forces in the form of strong individual leaders rather than from civil political movements. As expected, Barrientos and the FRB swept the elections polling some 680,532 votes against the combined 331,568 gathered by the five major opposition groups. By tradition, Barrientos and his new government were sworn in on August 6 (Independence Day), 1966.

René Barrientos served as constitutional president of Bolivia until his death in May of 1969—less than three years. It was a period rife with violence, rumors of coups, scandals, and old-fashioned political combat. Given his personality and style, Barrientos projected himself to center stage and all but encouraged an intense political dance around his person. Although there was a sitting legislature, he manipulated it by means of his majority when he saw fit or simply ignored it when to do so served his purpose. For example, he did not submit any budgets for congressional approval but issued them by decree. For all practical purposes, Barrientos exercised de facto dictatorial power. His authority was checked less by the legislature than by the direct pressure of key support groups and/or pressure from the military high command. Behind the constitutional facade, Bolivia lived under an authoritarian regime of a rather personalist and patrimonial type. But it was an authoritarian game in which the leader had to juggle contending pressures constantly to hang onto power.[11]

One of the more dramatic episodes of the Barrientos reign was the struggle between the regime and the guerrilla movement led by Ernesto "Ché" Guevara. Although important in the regional history of guerrilla movements, especially the transition from a rural to an urban focus, Ché's movement was in many respects epiphenomenal to the political dynamics of the Bolivian situation. In structural terms the movement had little effect other than to inspire a number of other brief guerrilla episodes and perhaps to provide some inspiration for a new left-wing political group that emerged among young middle-class Bolivians in the 1970s—the Movimiento de la Izquierda Revolucionaria (MIR), Movement of the Revolutionary Left.

Ironically, Ché's movement gave the Bolivian military a chance to gain some much-needed prestige nationally and internationally. If the military has a corporate personality or institutional mentality it is no doubt shaped a great deal by the fact that the armed forces have lost every foreign war they have fought in. Bolivia has no days of national victory to celebrate and the armed forces have no great triumphs over foreign foes to legitimate their claims to be the protectors of the nation. Indeed, the memory of the particularly ignominious defeat at the hands of Paraguay in the 1930s was still fresh in both the public and military consciousness.

Hence, it was a bit of a triumph when the army tracked down, bested in combat and killed the legendary Ché Guevara. There was a brief swelling of national pride that spilled over into prestige for the military, but the achievement was soon tarnished. As more and more information came out, it became apparent that the United States had played a large role in the episode, a fact that demonstrated the dependence of the armed forces and the regime on the United States; which in turn demonstrated Bolivia's fundamental dependence on and vulnerability to the international structure of power.

Further, rumors that a wounded and exhausted Ché was actually shot on order of the high command after he had surrendered also chipped away at the image of the officer corps. Finally, any remaining positive effects were lost in 1968 during the infamous Arguedas affair.

Barrientos Under Pressure

In August 1968 Barrientos's close friend and interior minister, Captain Antonio Arguedas, fled the country when it was revealed that he was responsible for a copy of Ché's diary getting into the hands of the Cubans, who promptly published it. Arguedas wandered about Latin America and Europe for a number of weeks while he was denounced and vilified as a traitor in the Bolivian press. The matter took an unsavory turn when it became apparent to all that the intensity of the personal attacks on Arguedas by Barrientos, Ovando, and other officers was motivated in part by the fact that they themselves had been negotiating privately to sell the publication rights to the diary to the highest bidder among Western magazines. Arguedas, it seems, had done them out of a substantial bonanza. Then Arguedas made a dramatic return to Bolivia to face charges. In an airport interview he revealed that he had been on the payroll of the U.S. Central Intelligence Agency for years, even when he was a minister of state. In a confused and emotional outburst, Arguedas declared that he was in fact a Marxist, and that he sent the diary to Cuba because of personal revulsion at his own behavior and to protest the extent of CIA penetration of the Bolivian military and the Barrientos regime. He named names and detailed contacts in such a manner as to paint the regime as little more than a puppet of the CIA and the United States.

The whole matter was never really resolved prior to Barrientos's death, and many questions remain unanswered, but it left a bad smell and clearly did not help either Barrientos or the military. Their evident greed was at best deplorable, and questions about corruption in high places and the patent use of public position for private gain began to be raised in public. The legitimacy of the regime and more basically of the armed forces was being undermined.

Corruption and abuse of public position are not new to Bolivia—or most other nations for that matter. Moreover, the issue of corruption draws one into a world of rumor or innuendo where the issues are not always clear and specific charges are hard to prove. Still, the issue is a troublingly real one and among things at stake is the "legitimacy" of a regime. And, extensive rumors and innuendo create public images that themselves become important political facts.

Such was the case in Bolivia in the late 1960s. The Barrientos regime acquired a corrupt image; one that was to plague it and subsequent regimes. Just as important—in some senses more so—the officer corps also acquired a corrupt image, which likewise has stuck to it since. Aside from the Arguedas affair, rumors flew regarding bribes by Gulf Oil (later proved in U.S. courts) and other corporations, other kinds of bribes and kickbacks, embezzlement, and more. Military officers holding government posts were often drawing two salaries, and the public view was that Barrientos gave them specific license to find creative ways to augment their salaries. Some posts, such as chief of customs, were considered to be particularly juicy plums, and at a minimum military officers and politicians were perceived to escape the heavy import taxes on luxury goods like posh foreign cars. The standing joke was that on Sundays you could identify the ranks of mufti-clad officers corp by virture of the quality of the cars they drove down the main street—Mercedes Benz or BMW being the favorite of generals. In any event, the claim to a moral right by the military and the government to "discipline" the miners in the name of national austerity began to appear hypocritical.

The corruption issue was linked to, and in a sense was an outcropping of, the mode of governance that began to settle in under Barrientos. Basically, it was one in which the distribution of the jobs and patronage generated by the state became the primary means by which Barrientos was able to cling to power. This kind of clientelism was nothing new in itself, but what was new was (a) the scale of patronage, (b) that it was becoming *the* primary mode of governing, and (c) that increasingly it flowed directly from the president and was not mediated by political parties or other institutions. Barrientos more and more came to relate to critical sectors, classes, and institutions through his direct clientelistic ties to specific factions and individuals within them; such beneficiaries were able to use the patronage to assert their dominance over rivals. Public authority in Bolivia began to degenerate from an abstract frame of rules and procedures to a personalistic and particularistic interchange; the president was treating public resources as private resources to be distributed to further his own purposes. This development not only undercut the credibility of public life in Bolivia but guaranteed that in every sector, class, and institution those not tied into the patronage net would become part of the general opposition seeking to undo the government. Such motivations began to override more general kinds of class, sectorial, and institutional interests as an engine driving the political process forward.

The image question raised by the Arguedas affair took a fascinating and almost comedic turn in 1968. Two self-styled independent legislators, Marcelo Quiroga Santa Cruz and José Ortíz Mercado, let loose a political storm when they formally called for a congressional investigation of Barrientos's behavior in the Arguedas affair; behavior that they charged was part of a pattern of unconstitutional, illegal, and antinational actions. These were charges in the Bolivian context at the level of the Watergate affair in the United States. Barrientos lashed out at his accusers, calling them every name in the book from traitors to one of those hyphenates whom Bolivian politicians are marvelous at creating, namely, *rosca-comunistas*, or oligarchs who are communists. The exchange quickly degenerated into ever-greater calumnies; at one point Barrientos, who himself had carefully cultivated a macho image, cast heavy aspersions on Marcelo Quiroga's sexual orientation.

More revealing was that in this essentially constitutional struggle Barrientos simply ran roughshod over Congress and his two adversaries. He used his control of the assembly to have his accusers' congressional immunity lifted. Thereupon he brought countersuits against them and at different times had both thrown into jail. The whole matter of charges, countercharges, suits, and countersuits dragged on for months and dominated the headlines. In one particularly bizarre incident, police broke into the Supreme Court building where Quiroga was giving testimony and hauled him off to jail; the executive branch was less than attentive to the constitutional prerogatives of other governmental branches.

The Arguedas affair and its aftermath with the two legislators was only one gust in a political storm that swirled around Barrientos and his government in 1968 and 1969. Although the government had effectively quelled the miners and most of the rest of labor in 1967, Barrientos found himself in a deadly political duel with the politically important teachers' union throughout most of 1968. The biggest union in Bolivia and strategically placed in the scheme of social influence, the largely lower-middle-class teachers have for some time been one of the key groups in Bolivia. Their power is attested by the fact that in this and subsequent periods spending for education rivaled, and at times surpassed, that for defense. The major portion of the budgets by far was for salaries. In the main the teachers have often furthered their own goals to the detriment of larger "working-class" goals. In May of 1965, for example, they responded to government blandishments and broke with the general strike, thereby tremendously weakening the COB's position. When they moved into a confrontational mode with Barrientos, then, it was a critical matter.

As he dealt with the teachers, Barrientos found himself otherwise assailed from all sides by opposition parties, including the MNR, the FSB, and a host of others. It was readily apparent that even as they maneuvered for position in any future elections, the parties and the "outs" of the "political class," which they in the main represented, were plotting and scheming to bring down Barrientos by any means. Barrientos fought back, accusing them of sundry political sins and using force against them. Throughout 1968 and 1969 the government announced time and again the discovery of coups plots, guerrilla organizations, and potential uprisings. The announcements were often followed by the declaration of states of emergency and the subsequent arrest, imprisonment, and exiling of prominent opposition leaders. The comings and goings of politicians, parties, and factions, and the plots and subplots that kept appearing were so numerous that it became difficult to follow the game and the players without a political score card.

As he reeled under opposition pressure, Barrientos turned to his key bases of support among the peasants and in the military. He countered popular actions against himself with public demonstrations and roadblocks by the campesinos. And on more than one occasion, he threatened under the terms of the pacto militar-campesino to unleash the peasants on his adversaries. Then serious cracks also began to appear in these two pillars of support.

Under some pressure from U.S. and international technical advisers, Barrientos made the political mistake of announcing in December 1968 his government's intention to levy a tax—*impuesto único*—on the agrarian sector. A protest came roaring in from the countryside and buffeted the beleaguered Barrientos, who feebly tried to justify the tax. On one occasion he was literally driven from the altiplano town of Belén, where he had gone to attempt to explain the move. Obviously shaken by that experience, Barrientos backed away from the tax, but not before significant political damage had been done.

The episode of the impuesto único also put into relief many features of the political reality. For one thing, it revealed the illusionary nature of Barrientos's control over the entire peasant sector; a fact that was quickly ratified by the formation of the new independent peasant bloc—Bloque de Campesinos Independientes—that countered the dirigentes pledged to Barrientos. Significantly, the bloc and student groups formed an alliance aimed at fighting the tax and defending university autonomy. Tensions mounted as rival groups of dirigentes struggled to control key regions and subregions. It was clear that the peasants were as divided and fragmented as every other sector, that they could respond easier to what they were against rather than what they were for, and that any one person's ability to rally the peasantry as a unitary political force was problematic to say the least. The support of the peasantry was both an intricate and contingent matter.

So, too, was the relationship between Barrientos and the military. The more the military became the tutelary political institution of Bolivia, the more it mirrored the complex personal and ideological forces working against national cohesion. Like everything else in Bolivia, the military was split into factions, in its case factions formed around particular officers, many of whom made little attempt to disguise their presidential aspirations. As in the 1964 coup, the cohorts negotiated with and forged links to civil groups both in and out of the government. This definitive politicization was fostered as much by civil political groups as any dynamic inherent in the military, for the reality was that all civil factions and parties had come to see an alliance with factions of the military as the one sure and quick way to power. Ambitious officers at all levels found themselves courted by civilian políticos eager to convince them that with the politicos' aid each could be the next great leader of Bolivia.

Increasingly, then, Barrientos had to enter the game of playing individuals and factions within the military against one another, as well as against the gaggle of civil political groups that flocked around the military. Support was again a negotiated item that was always contingent and subject to change as the context changed; not to mention that it was a marketable item the price of which rose steadily throughout the period and fed into the corruption undermining public institutions.

The complexity of Barrientos's relationship with the military was epitomized in the role played by Ovando. As chief of the armed forces, Ovando ostensibly supported Barrientos, yet he was openly negotiating with opposition groups like the FSB to form a civil coalition to underwrite his upcoming bid for the presidency in 1970. Other officers more or less openly opposed and plotted against Barrientos; the most prominent among them was Chief General Vasquez Sempértegui of the army.

Adding to Barrientos's problems was the steady decomposition of his civil political bloc, the FRB, during 1968. The leaders of the constituent parties battled with one another for standing with the president, and for ministerial and other posts for their followers. They either claimed to be the president's most ardent supporters or threatened to leave the government to serve the larger national good. By midyear the political picture was one of a swirl of activity around the figure of Barrientos as parties, sectors, and factions formed and reformed into supporting or opposition coalitions. Barrientos had to dance as fast as he could to cling to the symbols of power and the presidential chair.

The Regime Collapses

Things came to a head of sorts in July and August of 1968 when Barrientos provoked a constitutional crisis with the legislature. As the result of earlier actions, Bolivia was at that point under a declared state of emergency (*estado de sitio*) that gave the president extraordinary powers to deal with his opponents. Nonetheless, the drumfire of the opposition was strong; the Arguedas affair was still a hot issue, the confrontation with Quiroga Santa Cruz and Ortíz Mercado had begun, and a series of clashes with university students had erupted. Concerned that the opposition was using Congress as a forum, Barrientos, under a quirky interpretation of the assembly's constitutional authority under the Charter of 1967, announced that the legislature would not be reconvened as scheduled on August 6.

In the full-scale constitutional battle that ensued, Barrientos, who as vice-president had opposed his chief, Paz Estenssoro, suffered the irony of his vice-president, Siles Salinas, challenging his authority. Reeling under the blows of both his civil opponents and ostensible civil supporters, Barrientos formed an all-military cabinet. Constitutional niceties gave way and the essentially military and authoritarian nature of the regime came to the fore.

Faced with the possibility of a military dictatorship, the politicians in

Congress signaled their willingness to deal. At the eleventh hour, a complex arrangement was put in place. The pro-Barrientos parties essentially agreed to get their act together and dominate the legislature, to avert the move by Quiroga and Ortiz for a congressional investigation, and generally to bring about a docile and friendly assembly. To give substance to the deal, the assembly leaders agreed to a continuation of the state of emergency, to accept the military cabinet, and to cede to the executive extensive decree powers. Although Congress was reconvened, it was an emasculated body, and for all intents and purposes Bolivia was under a military-based, personalistic, authoritarian regime.

Barrientos's shift to the military brought him a modicum of relief, but not for long. The formation of a military cabinet was aimed not only at bolstering the leader's hand with his civil foes but also consolidating some base of power in the military itself. In fact, the move actually provoked Barrientos's military opponents to move against him. On August 22, the president's most visible opponent in the military, Army Chief Vasquez Sempértegui, declared his intention to deliver a blow of state (*golpe de estado* or coup d'état). After several tense days of maneuvering within the military, Barrientos was able to contain the golpe and ease out Vasquez Sempértegui. However, he by no means eliminated the opposition in the military and thenceforth had constantly to cast an eye over his shoulder as he dealt with his civilian foes.

The political situation did not stabilize. In many respects it worsened, and as it did, Barrientos's reactions became more flamboyant and erratic. Throughout late 1968 and early 1969 Barrientos all but publicly gave up on his civilian front of parties, which he found himself denouncing almost as often as his formal opposition. Perhaps in an attempt to overcome the mediating influence of the old line *políticos* who controlled the parties in the front, he sponsored an attempt by some of his supporters to form a single pro-Barrientos party, the Partido Revolucionario Barrientista (PRB).

The formation of a single pro-government party in that context made a great deal of sense. The political reality was such, however, that the various cadres that dominated sectorial groups like the peasants and the various microparties of the Frente would not give up their little power bases to enter into one organization controlled by Barrientos and his political lieutenants. Hence, the PRB ended up being little more than another cabal of job-hungry middle-class *políticos* drawn from the "political class" with no ongoing links to any groups, sectors, or classes other than themselves. Barrientos had come to recognize the futility of attempting to build a legitimating civil base out of the existing pool of professional *políticos* and began to denounce all parties and politicians. The fact is that he was bereft of any stable and manipulable links to the populace at large. At best, he could act as a man kneading political dough from which he would pull forth now this organizational shape and later some other. There was no shortage of politicians who in return for a position were willing to put together almost any kind of civil party, movement, or front. But any combination Barrientos came up with was of precious little help in generating stable support, even as it made heavy claims on patronage resources and immediately provoked all of the out factions, parties and groups to plot and scheme among themselves.

Frustrated with trying to build a civil political base, Barrientos was not above seeking to intimidate or force civil society into aquiescence. All along, he had encouraged his campesino supporters to menace the rest of the society through mass demonstrations, boycotts, roadblocks, and the like. Then in the constitutional crisis of July and August of 1968 he began to talk ominously of arming the peasants to back his regime. In fact, he had already distributed arms to loyal groups in Cochabamba, as was demonstrated during a peasant congress in late August 1968 when leaders brandished new automatic weapons. One can assume that Barrientos's threats and actions did not sit well with the military. Hence, once the all-military cabinet was formed, he toned down his rhetoric, although his backers among the peasant dirigentes continued to call for the arming of a peasant support base.

By January 1969 the president was again publicly threatening the populace at large. In his New Year's speech he threw down the gauntlet and declared that if the opposition would not let him govern with laws, he would not hestitate to govern by force. On January 20 he again said he would forcefully crush his opposition, and to give the threat teeth, he announced formation of a special armed group to enforce "order and discipline," FURMOD. The implication was that FURMOD was to be a paramilitary police force of the president himself, organized by his closest trusted lieutenants. Such a unit, it was plain, imperiled the military and its monopoly on the capacity to use force. That this was no mean issue to the regular army had been demonstrated in 1964 when it disarmed the national police (Carabineros), which in the 1960s was perceived to be directly loyal to Paz Estenssoro.

The announcement of FURMOD probably was meant as a challenge by Barrientos to his foes in the military as well as to the civil opposition. At a minimum it signaled his lack of confidence in the solidity of the military's support and in all likelihood his awareness that military factions were regularly plotting with civilian groups. In any event, the possibility of a personal praetorian guard evoked a response from the regular military. In April General Hugo Suárez resigned from the cabinet in protest and another prominent general, Rogelio Miranda, voiced opposition. In the following months the public definition of the FURMOD kept changing from that of a personal paramilitary unit to some more regularized expression of the official military. In early April 1969 the government announced that FURMOD would be constituted as a regular army unit subject to the usual chain of command. The military had made it clear, first, that the military more than any other group or individual would be the arbiter of the political situation, and, second, that it would maintain its monopoly over the capacity to exercise force.

As April wore on, the political pot continued to boil. On an almost daily basis the government denounced the subversive intent of the opposition and reported the discovery of some plot or other. The regime was preparing the ground to declare a new state of emergency and assert a more authoritarian mode of rule. As the new crisis loomed, however, it was becoming evident that Barrientos and his government were increasingly on one side and the generals on the other.

It seems in retrospect, that by late April 1969 there was a growing differentiation between Barrientos the individual and his retainers and the general notion of a post-MNR regime rooted in the military and oriented to imposing a specific model of development in Bolivia. Again in retrospect, it seems that the officer corps and numerous other groups were willing to contemplate the possibility of sacrificing the former to save the latter. The signs and portents were there. Barrientos's ability to keep all the political balls in the air was fading rapidly. Unless he did revitalize his government, his days were numbered. In Bolivia then, as now, nothing in politics was, or is, certain, and Barrientos might well have been able to hang on indefinitely. But he was running scared and showed it in a flurry of airborne visits to the countryside to drum up peasant support yet once again. On one such visit to the town of Arque, the presidential helicopter piloted by Barrientos collided with a high-tension wire. In a burst of flames he was dead and the political game was wide open.

Summary

The Barrientos government was in a real sense a product of the political failure of the MNR to resolve the fundamental contradictions of the revolutionary process it launched in 1952. The MNR's greatest failure was political. It had not built an institutional framework that could mediate and contain the demands of different groups and simultaneously mobilize support for a state-centered development process. The central contradiction was that between a state capitalist development strategy and a populist political strategy. In confronting the dilemmas of a populist-based state capitalist political economy, the MNR (and subsequent regimes) found its options severely limited by the extreme scarcity of surplus capital and by dependency on the international economic system and the leverage this gave international actors in Bolivian affairs.

The Barrientos government emerged in response to the central contradiction of the late stage of MNR rule; namely, to enforce the state capitalist strategy by reversing the populist thrust of the revolution. Thus, the Barrientos period marked a political break with the previous phase of the revolution and also represented an ongoing global economic strategy. The Barrientos years were marked by political discontinuities and substantial political volatility against a backdrop of substantial stability in the economic sphere. The overall "good" performance of the economy in these years was, a part of a recovery begun in the early 1960s. Between 1960 and 1969 the average group rate was 6.43 percent per year.

The key to the regime's approach to the political economy was its commitment, backed by the United States and other international actors, to use force to impose the costs of accumulation inherent in the model on the previously powerful working class and, by, extension on the traditional Indian peasantry. This fact led to violent clashes with labor, especially the miners, who were a focal point of conflict not only because of the issue of costs inherent in the model but also because of the specific eastward-oriented policy begun by the MNR and continued by Barrientos.

The government had, in that context, to move with force to break the political back of the labor Left. This it did in a series of bloody clashes and a policy of steady repression of labor leaders and organizations. Although the government was able to contain labor's demands and to suppress its modes of political expression, it was unable to eliminate the labor Left from the political picture entirely, leaving the labor Left looking for an opening to return.

The period from 1964 to 1969 was marked by economic growth and monetary stability. There was a growing opening of the economy to the international system, and therefore a consequent increase in Bolivia's dependency on processes over which its decision makers had virtually no leverage. Also, the economy was undergoing a structural shift: a decline in the relative role of the productive sectors, especially mining and traditional agriculture, and a rise in the relative role of social infrastructure and services. This period saw a shift, too, in the government's reliance on foreign capital from direct grants (large) and direct foreign investment (negligible) to foreign borrowing.

Although it was carried out in the name of anti-imperialism, the revolution of 1952 and the subsequent adoption of a state capitalist development strategy actually increased Bolivia's economic dependence and vulnerability. Moreover, the revolution led to an increase in the direct involvement of foreign governments and international agencies in the nation's internal affairs. The United States developed what it considered to be a great stake in Bolivia's future, which it sought to encourage along lines acceptable to it. In the late 1950s and early 1960s direct aid helped keep the central government afloat and increasing military aid helped create the capacity to exercise force at the center.[12] This allowed a coercive imposition of the costs of the U.S.-favored development strategy and simultaneously engendered the wherewithal for a revived military to project itself into the core of political life. There were moments of tension between Barrientos and the U.S. embassy in La Paz, but the United States generally backed Barrientos and his policies to the fullest.

Aside from the U.S. government, international agencies, often influenced by the United States, played a substantial direct role in shaping events. Most notable was the IMF and its ongoing monitoring of Bolivia's monetary stability, and the Triangular Plan, which defined and demanded a specific approach to the state mining sector. Foreign private capital did not play that great a role, with the notable exception of the Gulf Oil Corporation, which all but controlled the key oil sector and became rather enmeshed in the Barrientos government.

This is not to argue some simple determinism in which external dependence causes governments to become nothing but the expression of the interests of external powers. Rather, it points up a situation in which powerful domestic forces and interests converged with key external sources of power to define and back a specific approach to development in Bolivia. Furthermore, scarcity and dependence meant that at certain critical junctures foreign actors were able to limit the options of the Bolivian policymakers whose overall approach they supported.

The costs of the development approach enforced by the Barrientos government fell first and most directly on labor, mainly through wage freezes and specifically on the miners through wage cuts and layoffs. Contrary to government rhetoric, the traditional peasantry was also a big albeit indirect loser. The government's overall approach, its reliance on large corporate enterprises in both the public and private sectors and a policy of supplying the cities with cheap food discriminated against the traditional agrarian sector.[13] Because the costs were more indirect, the government could avoid direct confrontations with the peasantry and even play at mobilizing peasant support. The one occasion when the government tried directly to extract surplus from the peasantry (the impuesto único) brought on an immediate violent response that made the government back off.

There were also winners. Most notable were entrepreneurial groups in the private sector that benefited from a "stable" labor climate, government investment policies, and other direct and indirect incentives. The urban middle classes also benefited, from stable prices, expanded employment opportunities, and a general upsurge in such activities as construction, commerce, and finance, not to mention relatively inexpensive foodstuffs and imported consumer goods. International actors benefited indirectly from the implementation of policies they favored; again, with the exception of Gulf, U.S. Steel, and some small-scale investors, foreign capital as such was not much involved. In regional terms the big gainer was the East, and particularly the Department of Santa Cruz, which was able to tap directly into the wealth produced by the oil industry and was favored in the government's overall investment strategy. The full significance of this pattern would become clear in the 1970s.

One result of this way of distributing costs and benefits was a growing concentration of income at the upper end of the scale. Income data are scanty, especially for this period, but available data highlight the effects of the development model imposed in the 1960s. By 1970, some eighteen years after one of the most significant massed-based revolutions in Latin America, Bolivia still had one of the most negatively skewed patterns of income distribution: the ratio between the per capita income of the richest 5 percent and the poorest 20 percent was 50:1; the figure for the rest of Latin America was 31:1.[14]

Although the economic sphere was characterized by continuity, growth, and stability, this was not the case in the political sphere. Whether one looks at the golpe of 1964 as cause or effect, it did signal that a significant process of political decomposition was under way. The mode of rule practiced in the Barrientos years fed into and accelerated that process. Barrientos tried but was incapable of building a viable set of institutions to link the state and civil society. Among both political and civil associations the unmistakable trend was fragmentation and disintegration. This was more than evident in the disarray in the countryside, divisions in the working class, fragmentation in other groups, and the hyperproliferation of civil parties and factions.

In the absence of any legal or de facto civil structures to mediate the relationship between the state and an increasingly atomized civil society, the military was perforce thrust into the breach; for by the late 1960s it was the only national institution of any consequence left. However, Bolivia highlights the fact that the military can provide a power base to resolve a crisis or break through political immobilism but cannot alone provide a stable base of rule for any great length of time. As the cases of numerous other Latin American countries show, the military cannot generate any long-term base of legitimacy in the populace at large. However common coups may be (in Bolivia they are very common) in Latin America, military regimes are viewed as governments of exception and, therefore, by nature transitory.

Once in power the Bolivian military was in a sense invaded by the virus of factionalism, a condition antithetical to the corporate hierarchical character of the military as an institution. The military began to reproduce within itself the conflicts ripping at civil society, and the result was internal fragmentation, undermining of the chain of command, and the beginning of decomposition. By the time of Barrientos's death, the military was no longer a stable base for the regime and, in fact, had become a contributing element to the general level of instability.

Barrientos had put together a coalition of sorts from among the groups that benefited by the economic model, international actors, and factions of the military and the peasantry, but as time went on he was incapable of keeping these disparate elements together to undergird his governance. In part because of his personal style and in part because of the structural reality of Bolivia, he had to resort to a personalistic mode of authoritarianism based upon the manipulation of clientelistic networks, which networks became the primary mechanisms for mediating between the state and various groups, fragments, and segments of civil society, not to mention the military.

The process of political decomposition had many important consequences in Bolivia, among which three are worth noting at this point. First, it set in motion a regression from more modern abstract modes of rule within a formalized legal framework to more primitive modes of personalistic rule. Second, it created a situation in which the state was disconnected from and set above civil society; and to the extent that the military became identified with the state, it—as an institution—was increasingly set against civil society. Third, the reversion to a personalistic and clientelistic mode of rule reinforced a tendency among all segments of the political process to see the state as an almost predatory entity whose primary purpose was to generate distributable patronage.

One final critical trend during this period was the steady rise in both political and economic significance of the eastern sections of Bolivia, and most particularly the Department of Santa Cruz and its capital city, Santa Cruz de la Sierra. Because the full significance of this trend was to be felt in the 1970s, we will discuss it in subsequent chapters. For now let us simply say that this trend carried within it a significant shift of the geopolitical distribution of power and added another complicating factor to the national political game.

Notes

1. The Triangular Plan is discussed fully in Melvin Burke, "The Corporación Minera de Bolivia (COMIBOL) and the Triangular Plan," Latin American Issues Monograph Series (Meadville, Pa.: Allegheny College, 1986).

2. There are many discussions of labor relations in this period. See, for example, relevant chapters of the following: Guillermo Lora, *A History of the Bolivian Labor Movement* (London: Cambridge University Press, 1977); June Nash, *We Eat the Mines and the Mines Eat Us* (New York: Columbia University Press, 1979); Gregorio Iriarte, *Los Mineros* (La Paz: Ediciones Puerta Del Sol , n.d.).

3. A detailed account of the San Juan episode is presented in Sergio Almaraz, ed., *Guerrillas y generales sobre Bolivia* (Buenos Aires; 1968).

4. A detailed analysis of economic policy that emphasizes continuity between the approach of Barrientos and the MNR is presented in Richard Thorn, "The Economic Transformation," in *Beyond the Revolution: Bolivia Since 1952*, ed. James M. Malloy and Richard S. Thorn, (Pittsburgh: University of Pittsburgh Press, 1971).

5. This interpretation is based on Melvin Burke and James M. Malloy, "From National Populism to National Corporatism: The Case of Bolivia (1952-1970)," *Studies in Comparative International Development* 9 (Spring 1974): 49-73.

6. This structural pattern is documented in L. Enrique García-Rodríquez, "Structural Change and Development in Bolivia" in *Modern-Day Bolivia: Legacy of the Revolution and Prospects for the Future*, ed. Jerry R. Ladman, (Tempe: Arizona State University, Center for Latin American Studies, 1982), pp. 165-92.

7. Juan Antonio Morales "The Bolivian External Sector after 1964," in *Modern-Day Bolivia: Legacy of the Revolution and Prospects for the Future*, ed. Jerry R. Ladman (Tempe: Arizona State University, Center for Latin American Studies, 1982), pp. 193-232.

8. For general overviews of the situation in the countryside after the revolution, see the following: Fernando Calderón and Jorge Dandler, eds., *Bolivia: La fuerza histórica del campesinado* (La Paz: Centro de Estudios de la Realidad Económica y Social, 1984); Silvia Rivera Cusicanqui, *Oprimidos pero no vencidos* (La Paz: Instituto de Historia Social Boliviana, 1984).

9. For discussion of the military and politics, see William H. Brill, *Military Intervention in Bolivia: The Overthrow of Paz Estenssoro and the MNR* (Washington, D.C.: Institute for the Comparative Study of Political Systems, 1967). Gary Prado Salmón, *Poder y Fuerzas Armadas 1949-1982* (La Paz: Los Amigos del Libro, 1984); Charles D. Corbett, *The Latin American Military as a Socio-Political Force: Case Studies of Bolivia and Argentina* (Miami: University of Miami, Center for Advanced International Studies, 1972).

10. Analyses of social structures in Bolivia are not numerous. One is José Medardo Navia Q., "Análisis de la estructura social en Bolivia," *Revista de Cultura,* no. 7 (Cochabamba, 1983): 79-92.

11. Political issues especially involving political parties and the legislature are dealt with at length in Eduardo Gamarra "Political Stability, Democratization and the Bolivian National Congress" (Ph.D. diss, University of Pittsburgh, 1987).

12. For an analysis of U.S. economic and military assistance during this period, see James W. Wilkie, "U.S. Foreign Policy and Economic Assistance in Bolivia, 1948-1976," in *Modern Day Bolivia: Legacy of the Revolution and Prospects for the Future,* ed. Jerry R. Ladman (Tempe: Arizona State University Center for Latin American Studies, 1982), ch. 6.

13. The issue of low investment in agriculture is discussed in Burke and Malloy, "From National Populism to National Corporatism."

14. The major attempt to assess income distribution is *Reformal fiscal en Bolivia: El marco económico general* (La Paz: Ministerio de Economía y Finanzas,

1977). For a discussion of the general issue of revolution and inequality, see Jonathan Kelly and Herbert S. Klein, *Revolution and the Rebirth of Inequality. A Theory Applied to the National Revolution in Bolivia* (Berkeley: University of California Press, 1981)

2

Populism, the Military, and the Left

Upon the death of Barrientos the military became the determiner of who would succeed to the presidency, and how. After some discussion the high command essentially permitted the civilian vice-president, Luis Adolfo Siles Salinas, to assume the office. There was little doubt, however, that the real power brokers looked on Siles Salinas as a purely interim figure on the way toward a new and more powerful government based at least in part on the military. There was also little doubt that General Ovando and the bulk of the officer corps simply assumed that Ovando would be the next strong president. The real question was whether Ovando and his backers would seek a constitutional mandate in the elections scheduled for May of 1970 or whether they would seize power.

Ovando was a commanding figure in Bolivian politics solely because of his position within the military. His role and presence within the military was substantially more significant, however than his place in the hierarchy. He was one of the few ranking officers to have survived the purges and general downgrading of the regular army that followed the revolution of 1952. In those years of difficulty for the military, Ovando demonstrated his skills at behind-the-scenes political infighting and slowly won the confidence of key MNR leaders. He moved up the hierarchy quickly, becoming chief of staff in 1957, army commander in 1960, and armed forces commander in chief in 1963.

As a senior officer, Ovando was a central actor in helping the army through the bitter early 1950s after the force had been reduced to around 5,000 men, its budget had been drastically cut, and its role had been preempted by armed civil militias. Although Ovando effectively feigned loyalty to Hernán Siles, Paz, and the others, he made it clear in later years that he neither forgot nor forgave the indignities that he believed had been visited upon him and the military. His resentments fueled his single-minded drive to recoup and expand the position of the armed forces in national life of Bolivia.[1] Owing to Ovando's skills at dealing with the MNR leadership, he rose to a position of command at the same time that the center Right of the MNR began to look to the military as a counterweight to the worker militias. Under him budgetary support supplemented by renewed U.S. military aid increased significantly, and the force level of the army grew steadily to some 12,000 men on the eve of the golpe of 1964.

Ovando also presided over important changes in the makeup and organization of the officer corps. In the early 1950s, the officer corps, which had previously been the bastion of the old elite, was opened to the sons of the lower middle class. As they responded to the opportunity, the army was infused with newcomers who looked upon a military career as a mode of moving up the social scale. Ovando traded on this drive to rebuild the army and imbue it with an agressive sense of corporate self-interest.

Ovando most skillfully expanded and diversified the army's functions. Through a civic action program it became involved in development projects at the grass-roots level. By performing these relatively benign tasks in the "national interest" the army was able not only to legitimate an increase in personnel but also to establish its presence throughout Bolivia, becoming thereby a critical mechanism in the MNR's avowed goal of national integration.[2]

At the same time Ovando helped to project the military as a kind of national referee charged with resolving disputes among local armed groups. Thus, in the early 1960s the military attempted to restrain a bloody struggle among rival campesino dirigentes in Cochabamba. When arranged truces repeatedly broke down, the region was put under military control. As we saw previously, it was during this pacification program that links were forged between the officer corps and key peasant leaders. Concurrently, the government used the military as a wedge into a complex struggle among rival local MNR bosses (caudillos) in the eastern regions of Beni and Santa Cruz. That area, too, became a military zone and officers began to exercise governmental authority as official "interventors;" it is by no means coincidental that the first military prefect of Santa Cruz in 1960 was General René Barrientos.

Finally, Ovando presided over an important process of modernization and professionalization of the entire military. U.S. military aid was used to increase the firepower and sophistication of the military's arsenal such that the arms of the worker, peasant, and local militias were made relatively obsolete and insignificant. The military became an active and willing component of the U.S. hemispheric security policy, which paid off not only in cash and hardware but also technical assistance and greatly expanded training of Bolivian officers in the United States. By 1963 Bolivia's small officers corps had more graduates from the U.S. Army's Special Warfare School than any other Latin American country.

In the early 1960s Ovando helped weave these strands into a new concept of the role of the military. Basically, the military was projected as the single most "national" institution in the country. Because of its defense, development, and politico-administrative functions, it had become the de facto linchpin of the authority of the central state and also of the ongoing process of defining a model of the political economy to actualize the thrust of the "National Revolution" embarked upon in 1952.

In sum, Ovando had helped to change the image of the military from that of an object of the revolution's wrath to that of an institution that in some important senses embodied the purpose of at least one powerful tendency within the revolution. The new roles for the military were given institutional form in 1960 with the establishment of the School of High Military Studies (Escuela de Altos Estudios Militares). Each year high-ranking officers and civilian leaders drawn from the principal sectors of the society came together as a class to study the full range of issues that shaped the strategic and development prospects of the nation. This melding of strategic and development concerns around a linkage between civil and military elites was elevated to national institutional status in 1961 with the creation of the Supreme Council of National Defense. The council which included key officers and the top constitutional civil leadership, was the major advisory body on matters of national security and defense defined very broadly and inclusively.

It is not surprising, then, that within the military Ovando was perceived as an institutionalist who was in some senses the chief architect of the new armed forces. His internal authority within the military was great, especially among the younger officers. That support allowed him to maintain control of the military throughout the Barrientos years, and in spite of growing internal pressures, to hold the military in line behind the air force general.

It is important to note that both Ovando and the institution itself defined the revived military as an integral and legitimate part of what was called the process of the "National Revolution." Not without reason, Ovando and other generals asserted a revolutionary heritage that was independent from and equal to that of the MNR. Again not without reason, Ovando and others traced the concept of the "National Revolution" to the reformist military regimes in the 1930s and 1940s of Toro, Busch, and Villarroel. Historically, this strain of military populism had at times converged with civil populism, such as the MNR, but the two remained separate and on occasion blame each other for the failure of regimes like Villarroel's.[3] The image of the military as a revolutionary force was always nurtured by Ovando and was much behind the military's view that in 1964 it did not abrogate the revolution of 1952 as a process but rather assumed

its legitimate role as guardian of the revolution in the face of the incompe-
tencies and betrayals of the revolution by the MNR.

In an open letter to the armed forces in 1968, Ovando laid out this
history and revealed his bitterness toward the MNR. Just as important, he
all but claimed the role of titular guardian of the revolution for the armed
forces, and by extension established his claims on the presidency as the
man who had brought the military back to its rightful place. These historical facts carry weight in accounting for the actions Ovando eventually
took, the peculiar twist he was to give his government, and the complex
and contradictory role that the military has played in shaping Bolivian
public life since November 1964.

In the weeks after Barrientos's demise Ovando began openly to run for
the presidency, and everyone was convinced that both he and the military
wanted his presidency to be constitutionally legitimate. The fact was,
however, that although he was a master of palace intrigue, he was a bust at
the parry and thrust of public political maneuver; indeed, it was that very
lack luster public persona that had forced him to give the presidency to
Barrientos in 1964. At the same time that Ovando faltered, Siles Salinas
began to play his own political game in which he sought to assert his own
presidential authority in the short term and to be the kingmaker in 1970.
Siles started to push the candidacy of the popular mayor of La Paz, General
Armando Escobar Uría. During July and August, Ovando's electoral
chances were looking less and less certain. The situation had so deteriorated by September that speculation was not *if* Ovando and his backers
would seize power by force but *when*. The question was answered on September 26 when in a bloodless golpe Ovando, backed by the military,
unceremoniously dumped Siles Salinas and appointed himself president.

Having grabbed power, Ovando set out to make his mark. In a series of
dramatic speeches he declared his intention to mount a truly "revolutionary" government that would revive and put back on track the "National
Revolution" process begun in 1952. His government, although based on
the military, gave prominent place to a number of young civilians with
solid, if yet untested, "revolutionary" credentials. The most prominent
were the two congressmen who had done battle with Barrientos, Marcelo
Quiroga Santa Cruz, minister of mines and energy, and José Ortíz Mercado, minister of planning. Other key civilians were the influential news-
man Alberto Bailey, the new minister of information, the Christian
Democrat leader José Luis Roca as minister of agriculture, and successful
mining entrepreneur Antonio Sanchez de Lozada, the new minister of
finance. It was stressed at the time that whatever their party affiliations, the
civilians entered the government as individuals, independent of any party,
ideology, or program other than that to be elaborated by the regime.

Thus, in his "revolution" Ovando created a government that looked toward a popular mandate but consciously did not make any alliances or links to existing civil parties, nor did he try to create a new personalistic or officialistic party. The institutional base was the military. Civilians were to be influential in the early months but did not constitute a power bloc within the government, either in the sense of a cohesive, focused group or in the sense of representing an important element of power in the society. Politically, this was to be very much a revolution launched from above, if at all.

There is little evidence that Ovando was an ideologically concerned or committed individual. On the other hand, it is clear that he was a nationalist who was deeply tied to the military as an institution and to its tutelary role in national development. Hence, at the least Ovando had a broad if vague set of nationalist and developmental values and was in search of an ideological program to give shape to his general goals and to justify his and the military's assumption of power. To some extent one might say that Ovando looked to the military to provide the capacity to rule and to his cohort of civilian ministers to give form and shape to that rule.

The programmatic thrust of the regime was contained in the concept of what it called El Modelo Nacional Revolucionario de Desarrollo (National Revolutionary Model of Development). This central concept and its then-stylish use of the language of "models" obviously showed the influence of the civilians and particularly of Ortíz Mercado, who was to build and elaborate on the concept in drafting one of Bolivia's first coherent national plans, *Estrategia Socio-Económica del Desarrollo Nacional, 1971-1991.*[4] The fact that the civilian programmatic stamp appeared so soon attested that men like Ortíz Mercado and Quiroga Santa Cruz had been informally advising Ovando long before the coup. Given this fact, it is probably both unfair and inaccurate to see the Ovando regime as simply adopting an ideological cover upon seizing power or as uncritically imitating the revolutionary-oriented military government established in neighboring Peru in 1968.

The path that the Ovando government embarked on, although clearly influenced by a number of external factors, is also traceable deep in recent Bolivian political history. As we shall see in a moment, the national revolutionary model of development, as practiced by the Ovando government, constituted a revival in modern garb and language of the original state capitalist approach of the national revolution, with a renewed emphasis on the values of nationalism, an activist state, and populist mobilization. In this respect the approach was one of national populism enforced by the military, or, in essence, military populism. As we noted above, this kind of military populism was not new to Bolivia, and Ovando could in truth trace his government's roots to the military experiments of the 1930s and 1940s, strain of national populism that since then had developed alongside and in interaction with that articulated by civil forces like the MNR. In purely Bolivian terms, the Ovando government in a sense turned the clock back to pre-1964 and raised again many of the issues and points of conflict that had set the tone of the political debate at that time.

The Ovando approach also clearly reflected central trends in the broader Latin American context. The language of government documents was internationally very *au courant* and used especially heavily the relatively new and then very fashionable language of *dependencia*, or dependency. In this respect there was a linguistic overlap with the Peruvian *Revolution of the Armed Forces* mounted by General Velasco Alvarado in October of 1968. Indeed, Ovando and his ministers proudly compared their government to that of Peru and talked of the two constituting an ideological confederation.

A careful reading of the government's critical documents reveals, however, that in Bolivia (Peru as well) the language of dependencia was somewhat superficial and did not reflect any attachment to the neo-Marxist roots of that emerging theoretical doctrine. The real underlying theoretical frame was derived from the national popular movements, like the MNR and its Peruvian counterpart, the Alianza Popular Revolucionaria de America (APRA); that came of age in Latin America in the 1930s and 1940s and from the corpus of economic theorizing developed by the UN Economic Commission for Latin America, known in Latin America as CEPAL. The CEPAL doctrine was particularly influential through individuals like Ortíz Mercado as was reflected in the government planning documents. The role of Ortíz and the other civilians was the Bolivian version of what was to be called in other Latin American contexts a ruling pact based on an alliance between the military and civil technocrats. In Bolivia it was a rather tenuous alliance, and the civilians were more político-technocrats.

Central to the thrust of both national populism and CEPAL was the notion of a state-stimulated and state-led process of capitalist growth in which the state would overcome internal structural barriers to development and modernization while it simultaneously mediated with the international system so as to overcome the consequence of a peripheral country's weak (or dependent) position in the stratification of the international political economy. Derived from this was the critical role of the state in controlling nonrenewable national resources, articulating and implementing a national plan, sponsoring economic diversification, and to some extent protecting national industries, especially import-substitution industries. An important derivative of the CEPAL doctrine was the concept of small nations' overcoming the constraints of size by entering into regional and subregional economic associations; multiple-country organizations that would go beyond customs unions or common markets and create zones for protected, state-led capitalist growth.

These underlying notions and concepts appeared immediately in the *Mandate of the Revolution of the Armed Forces* promulgated by the new government on September 27, 1969, which quickly began to be manifested in policies. Following CEPAL logic, the regime sought to restructure its relations with the international system by diversifying its options through actions like renewing relations with the USSR and other socialist bloc countries. One of the more important initiatives in this respect was the active role taken by Bolivia along with Peru pushing the Andean Pact and basing it on the protectionist principles embodied in the controversial "decision 24," which from its signing in 1969 was the ideological basis of the pact until its reformulation in the late 1970s.

Internally the regime also made some dramatic moves. One of the most significant was the lifting of the repressive lid imposed during the Barrientos years and a consequent attempt to rekindle the populist base of the "National Revolution's model" in an attempt at social mobilization of both workers and peasants controlled from above. In effect the Ovando government sought to revive the populist dimension of the revolution even as it sought to maintain a state capitalist thrust. It sought, in other terms, to renew a relationship with the working class without the mediation of the labor-based parties of the Left and their avowed commitment to Marxian-socialist models of development.

By far the most dramatic, almost immediate, act of the new government, was the nationalization of Gulf Oil's Bolivian holdings on October 17, 1969. Although it was the one move most imitative of the Peruvian generals, who had nationalized the holdings of the International Petroleum Company, IPC, the year before, it was also a symbolic initiative that sprang from the Bolivian context and pulled together the government's bid for popular support by beating the nationalist drum even as it significantly boosted the functional role and power of the state.

Oil had long been a symbol of nationalism in Bolivia, as in the rest of Latin America. In fact, in 1937 during one of the early military populist regimes, Bolivia had nationalized the holdings of Standard Oil and created a state oil corporation, YPFB. Then in 1955, partly out of conviction and partly out of the realities involved in pursuing U.S. aid, the revolutionary government of the MNR encouraged the influx of foreign private corporations with the generous terms of a new oil code, the Davenport Code. However, in the early 1960s as ideological divisions became a focal point of conflict, opposition to the MNR on both the left and right began to raise the issue of the code and the emerging power of Gulf Oil, which at that point was beginning to pass YPFB in its share of production.

As the 1960s wore on, the code in general and Gulf Oil in particular increased in salience. The debate gained in intensity when the question of natural gas (in which Bolivia is rich) was posed along with that of oil. The capacity of the issue to touch nationalist nerves was so strong that even Barrientos, who behind the scenes clearly favored Gulf's activity in Bolivia, felt constrained to make some rhetorical gestures and flourishes in that direction. Because oil went to the heart of strategic questions and to critical notions of national security, the question was obviously of some significance to the military, and by the mid-1960s it was clear that nationalistic anti-Gulf sentiment was running strong, especially among younger officers. The whole matter took a critical turn in the power game that emerged after Barrientos's death. In Siles Salinas's complex manuvering to save his lame duck government, he began to try to preempt nationalist sentiments by playing the oil card. Hence, even as he came to power, Ovando was in a sense on the defensive as far as the oil issue was concerned.

In sum, it is obvious that whatever else was at work the nationalization of Gulf Oil flowed rather logically out of Bolivia's political situation. Even so it was a matter of some debate within the new government, where numerous voices counseled caution. The more aggressive national populist wing of the civil group led by Marcelo Quiroga carried the day, and the government orchestrated a highly public and dramatic seizure of Gulf's holdings. As the soldiers were marching, into Gulf's property, the government promulgated the decree and declared October 17 as the Day of National Dignity. That day turned out to be the highest point of the national populist civil influence in the Ovando regime.

Reactions to Military Populism

Ovando also made a direct bid for support from the Bolivian working class. He repealed a law of state security passed under Barrientos and generally loosened the reins on trade union activity, permitting clandestine organizations and leaders to come back into the open. In a highly publicized gesture to the miners he announced that the mines were no longer military zones and had all troops withdrawn. Then he promised to improve the miners' economic conditions and to study the repeal of the measures enforced in COMIBOL back in May of 1965.

Ovando made it clear that he distrusted the old left-wing politicians and parties and that he preferred a direct link to labor organization. Ovando's aversion toward parties of the Left had many causes, but the key was the reality that he and some of his prime advisers, like Ortíz Mercado constantly insisted upon: they were designing a "national revolutionary," not a socialist, model for Bolivia. Ovando was putting state capitalism and populism back on the agenda, but he was by no means open to a resurgence of the forces behind the state socialist alternative associated with the old labor Left bloc of the early MNR days—in essence, a regime of military populism that like its Peruvian counterpart sought popular support, especially from workers, but without the political baggage of the traditional Left parties connected to labor. Perhaps to drive that point home, on the very day that Gulf was nationalized, Lechín Oquendo was yet again hustled into exile. In doing so, the government stressed that it was disciplining Lechín the politician, not a bona fide labor leader.

Ovando also continued the prior Barrientos strategy of looking to the peasantry for support. But, Ovando did not have the public presence of a Barrientos, and in the context of his development strategy there was little in the way of concrete rewards to offer. Circumstances dictated, then, that he continue to try to build clientelistic links with certain dirigentes. Manipulating peasant leaders was never easy even for the agile Barrientos; once Barrientos was gone, it became even more difficult. Tensions between rival leaders, especially in the Cochabamba Valley, broke into violent confrontations in which a number of dirigentes, including one of Barrientos's main backers, Jorge Solíz, were killed. At best, then, Ovando was able only to put together a paper coalition of dirigentes who backed him in the name of the *campesinado* (peasantry) and hope that the rest of the fragmented countryside remained quiescent.

Another social sector returned to the forefront during the first months of the Ovando regime, university students. In Bolivia, as elsewhere in Latin America, the university has been a highly politicized institution that looms large in the nation's political life, and at times students have played a decisive role in political events. In recent years the universities in Bolivia, especially San Andrés in La Paz, had tended to be a base of opposition to whatever government was in power. Students were prominent in the overthrow of Paz. Under Barrientos the university became a base of Left opposition, and students continually tried to form pacts with the labor movement and peasants to undercut the entire thrust of the government. Hence, the university was an object of concern and the Barrientos government subjected it to the kinds of repression and control that it visited on the labor Left.

As with labor, the repressed political energy of the students, although contained by the regime, was waiting to burst forth. In the heady first days of the Ovando government leftist students carried out their own declared "revolution" in the university, reasserting the role of students in university governance, ousting the authorities appointed under Barrientos, and imposing new more left-oriented officials. Other student political tendencies surged forward as well to contest with the Left within the university, and the campus of San Andrés in particular quickly became a microcosm of the renewed ideological struggle that was again surfacing.

The Ovando government pumped a great deal of effervescence back into Bolivian political life. It seems apparent that its aim was to carry out some kind of controlled populist "revolution" from above, but from the outset the government had no structural links to any of the groups it was mobilizing and made no real effort to forge them. The result was that the regime never had real control over the process of social mobilization, and in the end tended to float above and apart from a society that was pulling in a myriad of directions. Ironically, Ovando, who through real and symbolic gestures sought to galvanize broad popular support, ended with little more than the guarded, cautious and conditional support of popular groups even as he generated serious opposition from many of the groups that had benefited under Barrientos.

The emphasis of the regime on popular mobilization and a reassertion of a tutelary state set off alarm bells throughout the private sector. In spite of the regime's exhortations regarding an active and crucial role for the private sector in the future, Bolivia's fledgling national bourgeoisie was uncomfortable with the climate created by the new government.

The displeasure of the private sector was more than matched by that of the United States government and the Gulf Oil Corporation. Here again the situation was similar to the reaction to the Velasco regime in Peru, and particularly its nationalization of IPC. If anything the U.S. government was even more negative toward the Ovando government because, aside from the nationalization issue, it saw the new government as undoing what it deemed to be positive achievements of the Barrientos period, especially regarding the control of labor, the suppression of the Left, and the boosting of the private sector—achievements that the United States had backed with heavy outlays of financial and technical assistance. As a result of the change in the tone of relations, U.S. aid to Bolivia dropped off considerably over the next months.

Gulf Oil itself mounted a counterattack against the regime that had a real sting to it. Gulf was able to tie up the marketing of Bolivian oil and to bring to a halt financing for a gas pipeline to Argentina. When the hoopla surrounding the nationalization died down, it looked for a short while as if Bolivia might end up sitting on large quantities of gas and oil that it could not market. It was reality that soon forced the government to deal with Gulf on the compensation issue. After months of negotiations Bolivia had to offer a fairly generous package to Gulf. Although who won or lost is debatable, the Ovando government had not enhanced its image. The nationalization of Gulf began to seem a maneuver that had been poorly thought out and in the short run was costly. This reaction was especially strong in Santa Cruz, where the opposition of the private sector, other elite groups, and the Gulf workers was open. The nationalization of Gulf had a sharply negative effect on the economy of Santa Cruz, but the opposition of Santa Cruz went deeper and was to have long-term political consequences.

Santa Cruz had long perceived the state, especially when controlled by a populist government, to represent an attempt by sierra, *Kolla*, Bolivia to assault the wealth and resources of lowland, *Camba*, Bolivia. Hence, throughout its recent economic emergence, Santa Cruz had relied heavily on its own private sector and the ability of local government to share in the royalties on oil and gas production. The nationalization of Gulf was a strike at the regional development strategy of Santa Cruz, which reacted with undisguised hostility toward Ovando and the perceived pro-Kolla populism.[5]

Ovando's revival of the populist dimension of the revolution provoked substantial opposition to his government domestically and internationally but did not generate a stable base of countervailing power. Most important, the government was not able to mobilize much more than the very tentative and conditional support of labor. Just as important for the political long term was that failing any government-created alternative, workers' relationship with the state continued to be shaped by the long-established leftist unions, parties, and personalities. For this reason, for example, worker pressure forced the government to permit exiled Lechín Oquendo to return and assume his customary role as *dirigente máximo* (chief leader) of the Bolivian workers.

A certain skepticism on the part of workers toward Ovando and the military was of course to be expected. The memories of May and September 1965, of the massacre of the Noche de San Juan in 1967, and the defeat and execution of Ché Guevara were all too fresh to permit uncritical acceptance of Ovando and the military's apparently newfound national populism. For these reasons alone, the average worker was bound to look askance and be suspicious.

More telling yet was the fact that the leaders of the key Left parties and unions perceived something else to be significantly more fundamental than the sincerity of Ovando's populism. For them, the issue was not the revival of populism within a state capitalist framework but a revitalization of the alternative state socialist model of the revolution that had been behind the original battles of the late 1950s. At its best the Ovando regime was a limited vehicle that had to be superseded.[6]

The organizational and ideological position of the labor Left was re-affirmed and consolidated in the spring (fall in Bolivia) of 1970. In April the FSTMB held its 14th Congress in the Siglo XX mine camp. Yet again Lechín was reelected executive secretary, and yet again a radical political thesis that had been adopted by a commission representing various parties was approved by the congress. Then in May the COB, again under Lechín, adopted a general class position of the labor Left after considerable infighting among various groups. It painted the military regime as essentially a manifestation of the local bourgeoisie that at best could realize capitalism in Bolivia. One part of the document spoke of support for the broad anti-imperialist aspects of the regime's nationalism. In another part, however, the real issue was put sharply: given the inherent limitations of the regime, the working class would have to take advantage of the democratic opening provided by the government to take control of the process and push it in a socialist direction.

Ovando correctly saw that the COB thesis challenged his government ideologically and simultaneously made it obvious that the government would not be able to conduct a top-down mobilization of labor for its own purposes. He therefore publicly denounced the thesis, and the regime and labor entered the summer (Bolivian winter) of 1970 dancing a tense minuet of mutual suspicion and distrust.

The organized Left's intention to radicalize and push the situation forward had a deep impact on the government. Even more than Barrientos, who at least had some illusion of personal popular support and constitutitional legitimacy, Ovando was completely dependent on the military for his continued rule. Six years of direct involvement in politics had, however, undercut whatever corporate unity might have existed in the military and infused it with the same kinds of ideological and factional antagonisms that pulled at civil society—not to mention that a taste of power and its attendant perks had stimulated personal ambitions in any number of officers. Even Ovando was unable to contain these divisions, and probably even less than might have been the case earlier now that his own claims on power more or less ratified if not legitimated the personal ambitions of other senior officers. From the government's first moments it was evident that at least two broad quasi-ideological factions were forming in the military. One faction had a vague national populist tendency in support of the government's efforts and aside from Ovando was increasingly associated with General Juan José Torres, who served in Ovando's former position of overall armed forces commander in chief. The other faction was an even more vague rightist group that had no confidence in the government's policies and in particular feared the consequences of a populist mobilization out of control; it began to coalesce around Army Comandante General Rogelio Miranda.

At first the national populist group in alliance with the more radical civil ministers held the initiative, but as months passed and the government failed to assert control over a popular base, the internal balance of power shifted steadily to the right. As the organized Left consolidated its political position, so too did the Miranda forces in the military. Shortly after the COB's declaration the group brought its full pressure to bear against the radical civilians, forcing the ouster of Quiroga Santa Cruz, the most radical civilian minister, and in effect induced Ovando to tilt rightward. It was evident, however, that in doing so Ovando was confirming his weakness not only vis-à-vis the Left in civil society but the Right within the military as well.

In July the political situation heated up considerably. As the month opened Lechín Oquendo and Ovando engaged in a public mutual denunciation match. Shortly thereafter Quiroga Santa Cruz entered the fray, denouncing the shift to the right in the government and warning of the danger of an "Argentine"-style coup. Then on the ninth the Mirandistas all but neutralized General Torres by arranging for the abolition of his post of overall military commander. Later in the month Quiroga Santa Cruz's close ally, Alberto Bailey, resigned his ministry and denounced Ovando's being surrounded by the Right.

While this jockeying went on in government, the focus of politics shifted to the university and student politics. For some months the government had feared the power of the Left in the universities. In May the police, in violation of university autonomy, entered the San Andrés campus in La Paz and confiscated a substantial number of pamphlets urging guerrilla action. In late June students hit the streets, provoking violent clashes with the military. On July 20 the government's fears materialized. A group of young men, many of them university students, seized hostages at the dredging operation of the U.S.-owned South American Placers Company in a region known as Teoponte. The Teoponte guerrillas' short existence ended in late October with the violent deaths of all but a few of the original eighty-odd participants. This small and essentially poorly planned and executed guerrilla episode, although militarily insignificant, had an impact of considerable importance in the subsequent evolution of Bolivian politics.

The group traced itself to the movement of Ché Guevara and the organization derived from it by the Peredo brothers, who had fought with Ché, called the Ejército de Liberación Nacional (ELN, the National Liberation Army). The Teoponte ELN was made up mainly of students of a diverse range of political and ideological backgrounds, including an important strain of religiously based radicalism forming in the Catholic church and the Christian Democratic party. The group's image was of a misguided but nonetheless pure strain of leftist idealism that sought to transcend the confines of the present political impasse. In this sense the members signaled that a substantial portion of the oncoming generation was alienated not only from the Right's expressions of the revolution but also from the traditional parties and groups of the Left as well. They in effect rejected the existing parties of the Left as morally bankrupt and politically compromised. Their action was to go down in the symbolic world of Bolivian politics as a blood sacrifice that would spur on the radical tendency in the church as well as inspire the formation of what was to be the only true new political expression on the left, the Movimiento de la Izquierda Revolucionaria (MIR), which rose to prominence in the 1970s.

In the immediate context of 1970 the Teoponte guerrillas created a crisis of considerable proportions for the Ovando government. The crisis escalated when right-wing students, supported by the ministry of interior, some said, denounced the guerrillas and seized control of the main building of the university in central La Paz. These dual actions highlighted that middle-class youth was polarized ideologically, just like the larger society. More immediately ominous was the fact that the actions demonstrated that the government of Ovando was rapidly losing control over Bolivian society.

The tensions continued and escalated through August. To an already complex situation was added a rash of rumors and public stories that spoke of chicanery in the military, illegal arms shipments to Israel by Ovando and Barrientos for big bribes, Ovando's involvement in Barrientos' death and more. Into these were woven complex explanations tying Ovando and other officers to a recent rash of murders of prominent political figures and journalists. Whatever the truth of any of the charges and rumors an unmistakable stench of corruption began to settle around Ovando and the military.

By late August, Ovando was struggling mightily simply to cling to office. Indeed many were convinced that had it not been for the tragic death of his only son in an air crash, the increasingly hapless Ovando would have been ousted in early September. As it was he did fall only a month later.

In September another symbolic turning point occured. After almost a year of negotiations and bombast the wheel came full circle. Forced by circumstances Ovando announced a most generous settlement of some $78 million (later it proved to be more) in compensation to Gulf. The Left denounced the move and others simply pointed to the stupidity of the original nationalization. Ovando stood alone bereft of political dignity and visibly sunk into a depression by the loss of his son.

On October 6 General Miranda moved to oust Ovando in what seemed at first a most effective manuever. The ensuing seventy-two hours, however, confirmed that the armed forces were in an advanced state of ideological, factional, and personalistic disarray. At one point Ovando was out, and then he was back in; then both he and Miranda were out and a junta of service commanders apparently in. But then things took an ominous turn. The COB called for a general strike, in effect announced itself in rebellion. As the country slid toward civil war, General Torres reentered the scene, put himself at the head of the Left, seized control of the airport above La Paz, and began to menace the capital with attacks from the air. Perhaps driven by memories of 1952 when there were armed workers in the streets, the officer corps pulled itself together and handed the presidency to Torres. There was little doubt, though, that all the unsettled matters brought back to the fore by Ovando's sally into military populism were still there. The key question was, could Torres straddle the populist tiger unleashed by Ovando and at the same time control the military?

Torres and the Left

J.J. Torres became president of Bolivia on October 7, 1970, but served for less than a year. On August 21, 1971, he was overthrown after a brief civil war. As president, Torres was never effective; he was on top but not in control. The hallmark of the Torres interlude was a lack of central authority. It was a situation driven by forces beyond the management of the state or any specific government.[7]

Two foci of power were behind the coming to power of Torres: the military and the labor Left. The two forces hardly formed a natural alliance. The fact was that even though both were involved in his coming to power, neither was able to provide a base of support for Torres or for the "national revolutionary" regime he said he wanted to form.

The military came down on the side of Torres by default. In the face of its internal fragmentation and the collapse of the chain of command, the military responded to some residual sense of institutional identity and endorsed Torres. He was the only officer who had a broad constituency in the military and even a remote possibility of containing the popular sectors on the left, which the military was reluctant to confront openly—at least then. Still, the support of the military was contingent upon Torres's reigning over the popular sectors and not allowing the situation to go too far in a radical revolutionary direction. The military imposed a set of populist limits that precluded any definitive movement on his part to socialize the process.

The labor Left, on the other hand, backed Torres because he was the only viable progressive alternative to Miranda and a right-wing putsch. From the outset it saw Torres as another petit bourgeois general with no real revolutionary program beyond the vague populism of an Ovando. Continuing support from the Left, then, was contingent on the willingness of Torres to be driven toward a more revolutionary position by the Left. The upshot was that the Torres government came to be little more than a small group of civil and military políticos without stable ties to any social sectors. They were in formal charge but able to do little other than respond momentarily to the pressures of a multiplicity of mutually antagonistic groups.

The Left made the state of affairs clear almost immediately. During the maneuvering October 6-7 the labor Left formed a joint command of parties and unions to back Torres and then bargain with him. This *Comando político* (political command) demanded autonomous control of 50 percent of the cabinet as its price for entering the government. The logic was the same as that underlying the COB and FSTMB positions during the Ovando administration: in a petty bourgeois military government the Left must stake out a true revolutionary position, take substantial power in hand, and then pull the rest of the regime foward. The key to that was to go beyond the co-government of the early MNR years to a situation of co-participation in the process of governance at all levels. When Torres balked at its demands (as it knew he would), the Comando político sought to establish itself not simply as an interest sector oriented to pressuring the government but as an autonomous source of authority that would enter into a species of intergovernmental relations with the Torres government over the future thrust of the Bolivian revolution. To this end, the labor Left moved to organize a parallel set of quasi-governmental institutions that would crystalize and legitimize its autonomous power. The main vehicle for this bifurcation of governmental authority was to be a popular assembly that would constitute the internally generated legislative authority of the popular sectors. Thus, as a price for its contingent support outside the government, the Comando político demanded that the government provide the resources for the labor Left to call and form the Asamblea Popular.

Torres was assailed by a variety of other social sectors as well. One of the more important sources of pressure was the departmental jurisdictions, which lobbied hard for projects and local objectives. Behind that was the fact that the regionalism that had been building since 1952 was becoming stronger and adding a new dimension to the already intense class and sectorial struggles.

Torres obviously saw himself as some kind of nationalist revolutionary and therefore the support of the labor Left was important to him. But, like Ovando before him, Torres wanted to shape that support from the top down. At that stage, however, there was not much short of radical structural change that he could do to back his anti-imperialist rhetoric and meet specific labor Left demands. About the only substantial foreign holding for him to nationalize was the Matilde mine, which he did, but that was negligible, really. In addition, he widened contacts with the socialist bloc and entered into some lucrative aid agreements with the USSR, especially in the areas of mineral processing. The major concession he offered the miners was a return to the salary schedules of May 1965, which, although significant, was somewhat offset by the decline in purchasing power of those salaries in the interim. Most of his other moves were largely symbolic, like the releasing of Regis Debray, who had been held by the military since his involvement in the Ché Guevara episode. The most significant and in the long run fatal gesture he made toward the Left was to create an environment in which various groups, parties, and unions could start to carry out a substantial process of mobilization from below in almost all sectors including workers, the peasantry, and university students.

The universities, which were again firmly under the control of the Left became a particularly intense focal point in the escalation of ideological radicalization. Students spearheaded an assault on the more visible manifestations of a continued U.S. presence in Bolivia, like the Peace Corps and binational education centers; both programs were shut down by the Torres government. In a particularly dramatic action students from San Andrés led an assault on the property of a research institute (IBEAS) run by U.S. Dominican priests, which they "appropriated" and made part of the property of the university. Meanwhile labor unions pressed their demands in strikes and public demonstrations, and in the countryside peasants seized properties, blocked roads, and generally took matters into their own hands. As the months wore on the Torres government came to appear as secondary to the real forces at work.

The climate of agitation and radical effervescence that was developing was hardly to the taste of the military, particularly because of the sense of loss of control over the process. Almost from the beginning factions began to form against Torres, and within two months attempts were made to unseat him. A harbinger of the military's distaste for the government's "permissive" attitude toward spontaneous mobilization on the Left came in late October, 1970, less than a month into the regime. As part of his national revolutionary posture Torres offered the olive branch to the remaining Teoponte guerrillas, safe conduct if they laid down their arms and reintegrated themselves into the society. However, when the guerrillas presented themselves for processing, they were summarily executed by local military commanders who were obviously responding to a different set of orders than those of the president. Of the original fighters who had set forth in July fewer than ten survived.

Meanwhile the various groups on the Left continued to mobilize across a broad spectrum. By the winter months (Bolivian summer) the efforts of the labor Left went toward "preparing the masses" for the popular assembly that was to convene on May 1, 1971. As the months wore on, the anticipated assembly began to dominate the national political consciousness. To some, the Asamblea seemed to offer the possibility of a true popular democracy in Bolivia; to others, it loomed as a body that could degenerate into some kind of Bolivian Soviet with Torres playing the role of Kerensky. All and sundry came to see it as a potential turning point.

The Asamblea Popular

The Asamblea was organized and dominated by the formal organized Left operating mainly through the Comando político. A substantial portion of the Left wanted to make it an alternative popular government and a base for the radical transformation of Bolivian society. Whether or not it would ever come to that, the Asamblea at a minimum was to be a manifestation of the who and what of the formal Left, a demonstration of the Left's ability to articulate a coherent vision of Bolivia's future, and to unite in converting the vision into reality.

In 1971 the Left was a fragmented and contradictory melange of parties and groups. The fragmentation was in part a reflection of the general decomposition of all organized political expression in Bolivia that had not let up throughout the 1960s. In part it was a manifestion of a general tendency throughout Latin America since the 1920s for the Left to split continually along ideological, personal, and sectarian lines. Indeed, the situation in Bolivia was almost prototypical.

One of the most salient features of the Marxist Left in Latin America has been its relative lack of success in achieving power and carrying out social transformations that embody its ideological images. Among the more important reasons for that has been that indigenous national popular movements preempted the role of leaders of the forces of change and captured a substantial part of the Marxist Left's clientele. As a result the Marxist Left since the 1930s and 1940s has had to struggle to define itself not only vis-à-vis the entrenched elites of the status quo but also vis-à-vis the reformist and revolutionary images of the national populists. Battles within the Left regarding positions to take in the face of the national populist challenge fed into its inherent predisposition toward sectarian fragmentation.

In Bolivia the Marxist Left was deeply affected by the political success of the MNR and by the fact that the MNR largely shaped and defined the revolutionary process begun in 1952. Moreover, the MNR was particularly adept in preempting the "nationalistically" focused concept of social and economic transformation. In so doing, the MNR—whatever its weaknesses and ultimate failures—clearly appropriated the capacity to define the terms of the nation's political debate and monopolized the capacity to create the symbolic content of politics in the postrevolutionary era.

Throughout, the Left was forced into a mainly reactive and to some extent defensive position. At one and the same time the Marxist Left had to defend its "nationalist" bona fides, to adopt a position toward the MNR and its revolution, and to detail the alternatives it offered. In some senses the government context created by Torres and particularly the calling of the Asamblea marked the first time since 1952 that the Marxist Left was definitively center stage and able to seize the initiative in defining the political debate in its terms. The fact is that owing to the cacophony that arose from the labor Left, it failed to seize the day.

On the eve of the Asamblea there were three major tendencies among the forces that made up what we have been calling the labor Left. One revolved around Juan Lechín Oquendo and the party he formed after his break with Paz over the Triangular Plan: Partido Revolucionario de la Izquierda Nacional (PRIN, the National Left Revolutionary Party). As might be expected, the PRIN was anchored in the labor movement, especially the miners, but it also drew from left-oriented segments of the dependent middle class. In truth, the PRIN was a left fragment of the MNR, and orientation therefore, while avowedly socialistic, was more fundamentally a syndicalist variant of national populism. But it is important to note that Lechín's position of influence in the upcoming Asamblea would be substantially more than that of the PRIN itself; for as always Lechín entered it not only as a party leader but also as secretary general of the COB and the top leader of the miners. Moreover, historically Lechín was probably the single most important figure preempting support among labor from the Marxist Left.

The Marxist Left was fragmented into a congeries of splinter groups but the central split was between the more historically orthodox descendants of the Soviet-focused communist movement and followers of the great Marxist heretic Leon Trotsky. One of the curiosities of Bolivia is that it has produced one of the most long-lived and influential Trotskyist parties in the world: the Partido Obrero Revolucionario (POR, the Revolutionary Workers Party). Historically, the POR had its main influence among the miners and university students, and owing to the efforts of its leaders, such as Guillermo Lora, the POR has had an ideological influence on the Left far beyond its actual numbers. By the late 1960s, the POR, like the rest of society, had fractured into at least three identifiable groups.

The more orthodox communist Left was divided between the main-line pro-Moscow Partido Comunista de Bolivia (PCB) and a pro-Chinese offshoot. In addition to these were the multiplicity of groups spawned by the influence of the Cuban revolution and the upsurge of guerrilla movements in the 1960s, including Ché and the ELN in Bolivia. There were also a number of others, such as the Espartaco group (which took Rosa Luxemburg as its inspiration), formed mainly by university students and that reflected a growing dissatisfaction with the traditional Left parties among young people.

In the relatively small world of Bolivian politics university students have always played an important role, and in the main their energies have gone toward the Left. By the late 1960s, Left-oriented students were alienated from the existing array of parties and groping for both new ideological inspiration and some new strategies and tactics. Thus, on the eve of the Asamblea university students were an inchoate force subjected to a flux of ideological and organizational strains.

One of the more interesting new strains to emerge in the 1960s and to impinge on the world of the Left was radical Catholicism. The post-Vatican II new church appeared in Bolivia before it did in many other parts of Latin America, probably because of the process of the national revolution. In any event radical Catholicism showed up first among foreign priests and nuns ministering to the miners and other working-class groups, and then was carried over into middle-class young people such as the youth wing of the Christian Democratic party. Because of their basic alienation from existing groups and because of the variety of new strains of leftism circulating among them, university students were not easily controllable by the established leadership of the Left. Consequently, this important group was a bit of a loose cannon on the Left: forceful in projection but unpredictable as to direction. In the main, however, students tended to press both Torres and the Asamblea leaders to move in more radical directions quickly.

The peasantry also loomed as a force in the Asamblea, but again the picture is murky. The notion of a conservative peasantry uncritically backing the military was surely fading fast. New currents and organizations were emerging in the countryside, vague and ill defined as yet, running from classical leftism to strains of indigenist populism. Perhaps because of this great diversity and variability, the main-line Left parties more or less openly gave low priority to the peasantry and focused their main energies on the workers and the middle class.

As far as the Asamblea was concerned, a key question regarded the linkages between the main-line Left parties and the working class. Although data are skimpy, the little we have indicates that the connections are and have been complicated. It seems that the bulk of the workers are not ideologically Marxist. They tend toward union-focused bread-and-butter populism, which is to say that ideologically they come closest to the historical national populism of the MNR. However, in the battles over stabilization, the Triangular Plan, and soon, the traditional Left parties became by default the main speakers for the interests and concerns of most worker groups, especially the miners. To this acquired legitimacy was added the fact that many leaders of specific Left parties had substantial personal prestige among workers because of their individual skill, dedication, and courage as union leaders. Hence, the Left parties were able from time to time to represent labor because of the circumstance and events. Such was the case in 1971, when in effect the Left parties—because of the weight of recent history—were able to act as if they were in fact the vanguard of the working class.

Although the Asamblea was to begin on May 1, 1970, the process of selecting and accrediting delegates proved to be so arduous and complicated that activities that day were purely ceremonial; the first working day did not come until June 24. The fact that the assembly began its actual labors on the anniversary of the massacre of San Juan was more than nostalgic symbolism; it was also a message to Torres and his government of the labor Left's deep distrust and residual hatred of the military. Those emotions had also been expressed on May 1 during the inaugural parade, when the main body of worker groups refused to march directly behind General Torres when he attempted to put himself at the head of the parade.

The delegates to the Asamblea were chosen by a variety of local-level electoral and appointive procedures set up by unions and other organizations recognized by the Comando político. The assembly makeup revealed basic realities about the Left. Most particularly, it showed that the Left was dominated mainly by elements from the middle and working classes, and that in national terms the peasantry was clearly a junior partner. Of the 222 delegates, 60 percent represented trade unions; 24 percent, middle-class organizations; 10 percent, peasants; and, the official left parties the remaining 6 percent.

The minor representation granted the peasantry, the largest single group in the nation, was again reflective of some important realities in Bolivian politics. First, it resulted from the fact that in spite of perfunctory bows to the ideological formulas of multiclass alliances and worker peasant pacts, Left politics has always been dominated by segments of the middle class in a tense but ongoing relationship with organized workers. Second, it also reflected the tendency of both populist and Marxist ideology to denigrate the peasantry as a political force, a perspective that showed up in development models that saw the peasantry as at best "traditional" folk who needed to be pulled into modernity. Third, since the 1960s governments pushing the state capitalist development model were to some degree successful in playing off the peasantry against the workers, and therefore some bitterness lingered between the two.

In terms of political affiliation, other than the parties' formal delegates, the makeup of the assembly was also quite interesting. About 76 percent of the delegates openly claimed some party affiliation, and the rest said they were unaligned or independent. The aligned ran the gamut of political organizations. The so-called labor command of the MNR, now tending to form around former president Hernán Siles, who had by then adopted a left-wing image, was about 24 percent of the assembly; the MNR labor group was also part of the Comando político, which organized the assembly. Lechín's PRIN directly controlled about 13 percent. A socialist group and the PCB (Peking line) constituted about 7 percent each. The new MIR group (made up of a left offshoot of the Christian Democrats, the university Espartaco group, an offshoot of the POR, and some independent Marxist groups) was 6 percent; the main-line POR of Guillermo Lora, 4 percent; and the traditional right-wing Falange Socialista Boliviana, FSB, 3 percent. Although the PRIN did not dominate, Lechín Oquendo was still the nation's top labor leader, and as a result he was elected president of the Asamblea.

In formal legal terms the Asamblea was empowered only to express the views of its members. This being the case, the most practical thing it could do (other than to lead to a revolution) was to formulate a Left program of government to press on Torres. The Asamblea could, in effect, demonstrate what a labor Left government would look like and how it would act. Short of mounting an alternative government (an issue that divided the delegates), the Left's task was to create an image and build its own organizational solidarity. In terms of cohesion the Asamblea was all but condemned to failure. From the beginning the meetings were characterized by acrimonious debates that involved a variety of party groups, ideologies, social sectors and personalities. As was often the case in the Left, delegates spent more time and energy squabbling than in confronting their erstwhile political and class enemies.

In articulating a labor Left alternative model of governance, the Asamblea touched on some key policy issues. Aside from some dealing with questions like wages, unemployment, and social security, it raised three such issues that spoke to crucial matters of power: holding previous governments and the military accountable for corruption and actions against the people; full worker participation in the management of COMIBOL, other state enterprises, and in some cases private companies; and the organization and deployment of armed power, and especially the role of militias vis-à-vis the military. The Asamblea perceived right-wing coup attempts to be imminent and therefore claimed for itself the right and responsibility to organize a popular defense against such an eventuality.

The Asamblea pressed hard on all three issues. It called for the establishment of popular tribunals to investigate, judge, and punish various prominent military officers and government officials. The old arguments for cogovernment were rephrased and the demand escalated to equal participation and, more important, effective control of the management of state enterprises. The more radical Left (like the POR) argued forcefully that such participation would be only a step toward working-class control of the revolutionary process. The more openly radical groups pushed hard for the Asamblea's being taken as a prelude to a full "peoples' government" that at a minimum would have dual power and authority with the Torres government.[8]

No single position emerged as the consensus of the Asamblea. And, as we noted, it had no power to transform any of its views into reality. It did, however, create a climate and set a tone for the political debate in Bolivia, a debate in which momentum seemed to be slipping out of the hands of the state and into those of popular organizations that were increasingly acting independently. Workers, peasants, students, and other groups were pursuing their own local objectives against the wishes of not only the government but also national Left leaders. Students seized buildings and appropriated property, like that of IBEAS; workers called for strikes and demonstrations to back their demands; and peasants blocked roads and in places like Santa Cruz invaded holdings not their own. Throughout Bolivia there was a growing sense of things falling into disarray. National elites had to run harder and harder to keep up with the social forces they had unleashed.

Anti Left Reactions

Not surprisingly, the Torres government, the Asamblea, and the general climate created by the two brought about serious opposition both within the country and elsewhere. Those who had benefited from the state capitalist model defined in the latter years of the MNR and then enforced by the Barrientos government were alienated by the Torres government and the reemergence of the labor Left. The major external opposition came from the United States, which saw first Ovando and then Torres as undoing its carefully crafted policies. Most particularly, it deplored the breakdown of controls on labor, the subversion of the management concepts pushed by the Triangular Plan, and the possibility that the revolution would veer in a socialist direction. Indeed, the Nixon administration was unhappy not only with what was going on in Bolivia but also in Peru and in Chile under Salvador Allende.

U.S. reaction was framed in the context of a broader ideological struggle then occurring in Latin America. While leftist and/or populist regimes seemed to hold the initiative in Peru, Bolivia, and Chile, right-wing military regimes held sway in the more powerful countries of Brazil and Argentina. Brazil appeared to be a new kind of authoritarian model of development; a model that many began to perceive as integral to any mode of capitalist development in the continent at that time. Aside from symbolizing one way of achieving capitalist development, Brazil also began to project itself as a force in the area, making plain that it was concerned with the ideological coloration of its neighbors and that it was displeased with leftist and populist governments like that of Torres. Brazil's interest in Bolivian politics was heightened by the fact that it had begun to look to eastern Bolivia as a source of critical materials like natural gas and to some extent as an outlet for Brazilian investment.

Internal opposition to the Torres government and the Left in general arose principally in the private sector, regional groups, and the military. In the Bolivia of the early 1970s the private sector constituted a relatively new and as yet inchoate political actor. Private-sector entrepreneurial groups were a product of the revolution of 1952 and especially the implementation of the state capitalist model during the 1960s. As in most of the rest of Latin America, the bourgeoisie was a hothouse product of state policies, and certain of its constituent groups were still dependent on state action. The sector as a whole had not as yet been able to coalesce into a self-conscious class able to define and act on its own vision for the nation. The leading components of the private sector at that point were the owners of medium-sized mines; infrastructure groups, especially construction; commerce and banking; and the emergent agro-industrial groups of Santa Cruz and the Beni.

Although private-sector groups were as yet incapable of projecting a positive vision around which to cohere as a class, they were able to rally together in significant degree on the negative basis of responding to the perceived generalized threat from the Left. This stance was organized nationally by an association of private entrepreneurs, Confederación de Empresarios Privados de Bolivia (CEPB), which became the principal interest group of the private sector. The confederation openly challenged the Left and the Asamblea, and called for a return to the policies of the Barrientos period.

There was, then, a relatively clear class division between labor and the Left parties and the inchoate bourgeoisie operating through the CEPB. The Left sought to radicalize the Torres government and ultimately achieve some kind of joint power with it. The bourgeoisie, on the other hand, was flatly opposed to Torres, not so much because of his policies or goals but because he was perceived to be weak and incapable of controlling the Left. The more or less open aim of the bourgeoisie eventually became to topple Torres and reestablish a strong central authority able to impose "discipline" on what from their perspective was an increasingly unruly populace.

The Torres government was also subjected to mounting pressure from Bolivia's diverse regions. Throughout the country, municipal governments and regional civic groups seized the opportunity to press the government for pet projects that would be financed by the central government. In doing so, they were not loath to contribute to the general disorder by declaring strikes, blocking roads, and so on.

The most contentious region was Santa Cruz. There, opposition was spearheaded by the municipal government and the local civic association (*comité cívico*). As in the past, Santa Cruz objected to the Torres government not only because of its specific economic policies, such as control over oil and gas revenues, but also because it represented, to it, a populist articulation of Kolla Bolivia. Local elites were particularly upset by recently arrived migrants who, at the urging of the Left, were invading land-holdings. The elites clearly feared losing control over the migrants, who until then had fed cheap labor into the region's economic boom, and blamed the Torres government for events having come to such a pass. The aim became to displace Torres and to rein in the peasants, labor, and the Left, to return to the pro-Santa Cruz model pushed by the center Right of the MNR and Barrientos. The opposition coming from Santa Cruz over-lapped with the general reaction of the private sector, but it also had a decidedly regionalistic and quasi-racialist dimension that went beyond class struggle per se.

Quite early on, then, the Torres government found itself in the position of confronting antagonistic sectors of the civil society and not having any solid connections to supportive sectors. The Left proffered generalized support for the process and talked of a willingness to resist "counterrevolu-tion" but offered only the most contingent of direct support. Moreover, the Left constantly pushed in a direction that reinforced the Right's opposition to Torres without providing any real countervailing force to that opposi-tion. Unable to mobilize and control sustained support on the left or from the popular sectors, Torres even more than Ovando and Barrientos was dependent on the military to retain his presidency.

In the Bolivia of 1970-71 real power was in the hands of the military. The military's pivotal role was reflected in the fact that all key groups sought to forge links with one part or another of the military and to press it to intervene in their behalf. Hence, the already fragile coherence of the in-stitution began to buckle as it was subjected to the perturbing currents within public life. Even were it not predisposed to act directly in politics, the military would have been pulled willy-nilly into the political fray by forces that wanted to enlist its power against their perceived political en-emies. The private sector and regional groups pressed particularly hard for the military to intervene against the Left.

The military had its own reasons to contemplate direct intervention. By 1970-71 it was obviously divided ideologically. The principal division was over state capitalism, in the context of national populism versus the anti-popular mode of state capitalism implemented by Barrientos; there is no evidence for any major factions pushing for a Marxist or state socialist model. However, even those who might back a military populist-style regime à la Peru were, like the Peruvians, oriented toward a process that flowed from the top down. For both Left and Right factions, the issue of control was central. Furthermore, for everyone the memories of 1952 and the near destruction of the military were fresh and a constant reminder of the dangers for the military in a situation of uncontrolled mobilization. Thus, from the outset there was serious opposition to Torres within the military. In fact, he was not in power a month before a plot was uncovered. This original opposition from the Right expanded to embrace other segments as the Torres government demonstrated its inability to control the process of mobilization by the Left. In January of 1971 a major coup attempt failed, but it signaled that opposition to Torres within the military was broadening rapidly.

In retrospect it is clear that the turning point within the military was the inauguration of the Asamblea. The assembly launched a direct threat to the corporate self-interest of the military in at least two crucial areas. First was the call for popular tribunals that would investigate the military and hold it accountable for past antipopular actions. Even more fundamental however was the call from the assembly to rearm worker and peasant militias and convert them into a base for a popular defense of the revolution. This attempt represented a direct threat to the functional purpose of the military and provoked an institutionalist response that for the moment overrode ideological and personal factional differences. The threat was heightened when it was revealed that elements of the Asamblea were forging links to noncommissioned officers and encouraging them to form a people's military outside the official chain of command.

By July of 1971 the political situation was almost completely polarized, and the Torres government teetered in the middle. The Asamblea, whatever else it did, galvanized the class and regional opposition to Torres without providing his government with a predictable base of support, at least at a political price that Torres was willing to pay. Finally, the radicals in the assembly so threatened the military itself—both as an institution and in its role as the ultimate source of social control—that it provoked the officer corps to put aside factionalism and unite to defend its common corporate interest.

Driven by a threat to its corporate self-interest, the military became the de facto spearhead of all the opposition to the Torres government. By August it was obvious to everyone that a military-based move would be made against the government. The questions became (a) whether Torres would seek to defend himself by heeding the Left's call to arm the workers and students, and (b) whether or not the sectors in the popular assembly could in fact mount a defense against an action led by the armed forces. The fact was that Torres as a military man could not bring himself to distribute arms to irregulars, even in the name of some populist revolution, and so it was evident that there could be no effective popular resistance to a coordinated military action. It is doubtful, of course, whether such resistance would have taken place even if Torres had supplied arms to the Left, for when the blow came, it was from a military fighting for its very life.

The movement to overthrow Torres was set afoot on August 20, 1971. Significantly, it began with civic demonstrations in Santa Cruz that were quickly taken over by military officers. The rebellion, headed by Colonel Hugo Banzer Suárez (who had led the abortive coup in January) and Colonel Andrés Selich, spread from Santa Cruz and, finally, to La Paz. Resistance was light in most of the country, but university students in La Paz were of another order; land and air attacks were necessary to eliminate the last stronghold of support for Torres. On August 23, Torres fell. The new government moved with systematic ferocity to crush the political and union structure of the labor Left and thereby intimidate any possible naysayers.

The movement that overthrew Torres brought a number of significantly new dimensions to the Bolivian political scene, and it brought to a head many tendencies that had been at work during the 1970s. First, it reflected the underlying geopolitical shift that had been under way since the 1960s. This was the first successful rebellion in the twentieth-century Bolivia that had its base outside the capital. Moreover, it was not a simple old-time coup d'état but a military-civil movement that had it met with resistance, would no doubt have prosecuted a drawn-out civil war. Although the military was at the head, the movement was openly backed by major political parties like the MNR and FSB, by civic associations, and by the principal organizations of the private sector. Indeed, it was no secret that private-sector groups had in the previous months assembled a substantial war chest. The rebellion in effect embraced almost the entire center Right of the fundamental class polarization that had come to the fore under Ovando and Torres.

Geographically, the rising confirmed the new salience of Santa Cruz. Aside from the movement's originating there, it is clear that Banzer's emergence as the paramount leader of the new government was more than a little due to the fact that he was a *camba* and therefore trusted by the *cruceño* elite. The nation was put on notice that Santa Cruz had come into its own politically, and that it intended henceforth to play a key role in shaping national political life. Events had put into sharp relief the ongoing problem of regional tensions and the potentially violent split between Kolla and Camba Bolivia.

It is difficult to demonstrate to what degree foreign powers like the United States and Brazil directly supported the rising. It is quite clear, however, that both the United States and Brazil welcomed the overthrow of Torres and the new Banzer government. In the months prior to the rising Banzer had taken refuge in Brazil and had been able to move rather freely between Brazil and Bolivia. In fact, many observers argued at the time that the Brazilians, with U.S. encouragement, were rather active in bringing about the entire operation. It is probably of more than symbolic significance that the unit that spearheaded the rising was a ranger battalion trained and equipped by the United States right down to green berets. In any event, the Banzer government quickly received the open support and encouragement of the United States throughout most of its tenure.

Summary

Although short, the Ovando-Torres period was very significant in the Bolivian context and highlighted some regional political trends as well. It showed that in a real sense Bolivia was still struggling with the issue of bringing some kind of closure to the revolution begun in 1952, specifically, to establish some new model of development. It revealed that there was a struggle among three alternatives. The root division was between a state capitalist alternative versus a state socialist alternative, but this division was complicated by the fact that the state capitalist model had two variants, a populist and antipopulist variant.

Both Ovando and Torres attempted to seize the middle ground by basing their governments on the populist variant of the national revolutionary or state capitalist model. The approach provoked opposition from key private-sector groups and their domestic and international allies because of the issues of capital accumulation (i.e. costs) and fundamental questions of authority and control, but was able to win only tepid and contingent support from the labor Left, mainly because most of the Left parties were by then committed to pushing the state socialist model. Labor itself, under most circumstances, would probably have backed a populist approach had it been able to deliver in bread-and-butter terms. But, given resistance on the right, the weakness of the populists, and the memories of recent repression, labor was inclined to follow the lead of the proven leftist union and political leaders.

The period also showed that in power terms there was a kind of stalemate among the approaches. The Left had demonstrated its ability to survive but it was not capable of defining and sustaining its own alternative regime.

The Right, on the other hand, could establish its antipopular state cap-italist model only by means of a military-backed authoritarian regime willing and able to force the popular sectors into submission. But as the swing from Barrientos to Ovando and Torres showed, this approach was only a short-term solution and could not provide the basis for any long-term legitimate rule.

At that point it was doubtful that any civil-based model of democratic governance could have emerged in Bolivia. The fundamental nature of the struggles invariably brought force and, therefore, the military to the fore. It was evident that implementation of any of the three models would need military backing and produce some kind of authoritarian regime. The Ovando and Torres governments showed that the military was divided ideologically and could well back some kind of leftist regime in the sense of a national populist approach. However, in any such model, the issue of control at the center and the corporate integrity of the armed forces quickly loomed large. This fact almost guaranteed a conflict between the populist military and the Left because the central theme of the Left was based on distrust of the military and a strategy of seizing control of the process from it. Hence, once the Left challenged the military's ability to control the process and by extension the survival of the institution, the military overcame its ideological differences and swung rightward.

This basic struggle over models of development and the cost allocations implicit in them was not unique to Bolivia. As in many other times Bolivia was an extreme case of some fundamental themes running through the politics of a number of Latin American countries. Just as Ovando and Torres were symptomatic of an interlude of experimentation in military populism, such as occurred in Peru and Ecuador, the overthrow of Torres was a signal of a broad antipopulist reaction that would swing through the region during the 1970s; both Peru and Ecuador shifted to the right even as Allende fell in Chile and the military ended the experiment in revived Peronism in Argentina.

Notes

1. For discussions on the role of Ovando, see Charles Corbett, *The Latin American Military as a Socio-Political Force: Case Studies of Bolivia and Argentina,* (Miami: University of Miami, Center for Advanced International Studies, 1972) and Gary Prado *Poder y Fuerzas Armadas 1949-1982,* (La Paz: Los Amigos del Libro, 1984).
2. A lengthy analysis of the process of military diversification of functions after the revolution is contained in William Brill, "Military Civil Action in Bolivia." (Ph.D. dissertation, University of Pennsylvania, 1965).
3. A particularly critical view of the military by a prominent MNR leader is

Guillermo Bedregal, *Los militares en Bolivia: Ensayo de interpretación sociológica* (La Paz: Los Amigos del Libro, 1971).

4. *Estrategia socio-económica del desarrollo nacional, 1971-1991.* (La Paz: Ministerio de Planificación y Coordinación, 1970).

5. The historical roots of regionalist sentiment in Santa Cruz is treated in José Luis Roca, *Fisonomía del regionalismo boliviano* (La Paz: Los Amigos del Libro, 1980).

6. A prominent left wing leader's view point is contained in Guillermo Lora, *A History of the Bolivian Labor Movement* (London: Oxford University Press, 1977).

7. For an account of the trials and tribulations of the Torres government by a prominent insider see Jorge Gallardo Lozada, *De Torres a Banzer: Diez meses de emergencia en Bolivia* (Buenos Aires: Editorial Periferia, 1972).

8. Views of the Asamblea are as conflictual as the meeting itself was. Two different views of the Asamblea with significant information are Jerry Knudson, *Bolivia's Popular Assembly and the Overthrow of General Juan José Torres* (Buffalo: Council on International Studies, State University of New York at Buffalo, 1974), and René Zavaleta Mercado, *El poder dual en America Latina* (Mexico: Siglo XXI, 1971).

3

Banzer and Neopatrimonial State Capitalism

The military uprising of August 1971 brought army Colonel Hugo Banzer Suárez to power as president of Bolivia. Before he was done, the diminutive Banzer ruled with a strong hand for some seven years. His tenure was unprecedented in modern Bolivian history and marked the longest unbroken presidential term in memory. For much of that period Bolivia experienced an upsurge of economic growth and, in aggregate terms, substantial prosperity. Hence, Banzer's term was very significant in the recent history of Bolivia and in many respects had more impact on the political economy than any government since the early days of the revolution. The significance of the period is recognized in Bolivia where today it is referred to simply as the Banzerato.

To many observers at the time, inside Bolivia, and out, the seven years were a period of firm social and economic progress rooted in political stability and continuity. The retrospective picture is somewhat different; the vaunted political stability was extremely superficial. Actually, Banzer was constantly threatened not so much by the declared opposition but by intrafactional struggles in his own ostensible ruling coalition, a coalition that was based more on personalistic factions than on groups or classes and was always in a constant state of flux. Throughout much of his term, especially the later years, Banzer spent most of his energies simply clinging to the formal trappings of power not in active governing. Furthermore, although he ruled as a strongman and when pushed could deliver brutal blows to his opponents, the reality was that when it came to practicalities, his was a government in precarious control.

The superficial stability masked numerous ironies. One of the most significant was that even as Bolivia apparently was experiencing economic development, it was simultaneously experiencing political retrogression. If political development, at the least, involves the articulation and coordina-

71

tion of a variety of modern institutions, then during the 1970s Bolivia actually went through a process of political decay. In this respect the Banzer government continued and in a sense completed the process that began in the early 1960s. By the late 1970s the substance of the institutional infrastructure of Bolivian public life had all but disappeared. This fact is, in our view, crucial to an understanding of the present political situation in Bolivia, and particularly the immense difficulties the nation faces in trying to establish some mode of civil democratic rule.

Another point bears stating. Although this period did evidence substantial growth rates and some outward signs of prosperity in the cities, the reality was that neither constituted meaningful economic development. By the late 1970s the economy had little more to show than exhausted mines, depleted petroleum reserves, declining agricultural outputs, stalled construction projects, and a massive foreign debt. The roots of the present severe economic crisis are firmly set in this period. Moreover, as we will soon see, the superficial boom of the early 1970s was bought at a very high price socially, economically and politically, a price that was paid mainly by the popular sectors, especially workers and peasants. The justification for the price and its allocation was the much-touted trickle-down theory. The problem was and is that when the boom faded there was precious little to trickle down except more costs.

The Banzer regime was not uniquely perverse or wholly responsible for all of Bolivia's present ills. The fact is that the regime flowed out of trends and intimations going as far back as the revolution of 1952. In our view, the regime, although harsh and clearly anti-Left was not in any real sense counterrevolutionary. Rather, it was a part of the ongoing process of trying to impose on the forces unleashed by the revolution a new societal model of political economy. Moreover, the particular variation on the theme of state capitalism followed by the Banzer government was a direct descendant of the strategy pursued by Barrientos as well as the main wing of the MNR before him. The Banzer regime was, in fact, an integral part of the ongoing struggle over new definitions, allocation of costs, and formation of ruling coalitions endemic not only to the Bolivian revolution but to all modern revolutions.

Fragmentation and Polarization

The rising that brought Banzer to power had come precariously close to being a civil war. As such, it reflected a society that had become completely polarized ideologically. To one side stood the group that articulated what we might call the rightward limits of the revolution. Politically, it was made up of the mainline old guard of the MNR, a variety of other civil parties that had come to accept the revolution as irreversible, and of course the bulk of the military. It favored a state capitalist development model but emphasized capital accumulation over popular consumption, i.e., an anti-populist version of state capitalism. On the other side stood the Left, comprising the labor left wing of the original MNR, a myriad of ideologically Marxist groups, and some components of the officer corps. The Left was further divided into two main camps: one espousing the original MNR populist state capitalist vision, and the other seeking to push the revolution out of the original parameters defined by the MNR toward a state socialist alternative. As the Ovando and Torres governments showed, the fundamental division of the Left undercut its ability to mount a coherent government as well as defend itself from an aggressive and relatively coherent Right, although it could harass Right governments and at times help bring them down. The Marxist Left was a crucial factor undermining both Ovando and Torres and rendering the experiment in military populism vulnerable to the increasingly antipopulist Right.

This ideological conflict over models of the political economy reflected a kind of quasi class struggle. The Right model of antipopulist state capitalism was backed more and more by the bulk of the urban middle classes (both civil and military) and a new emergent national bourgeoisie rooted in the private sector. The Left drew support mainly from the lower middle class and organized labor (especially miners and factory workers). One study estimated the bourgeoisie, the middle class, and the lower middle class made up about 27 percent of the economically active population, with the working class forming about 30 percent of the EAP.[1] The big question mark was the peasantry, which constituted over 40 percent of the EAP. The traditional peasantry was split along a variety of lines, from those who avoided national political struggle, to those who backed Right caudillos, to those who backed the Left. In practical terms the traditional peasantry did not function as a piece because it did not perceive itself to be a coherent social class or act as such.

The confused picture in the countryside points to an important truth in Bolivia. Although class conflict is real and always present, it is far from being the only important conflict. At many crucial moments other kinds of conflicts and dynamics not only exist but blunt or override class conflict. Bolivian politics simply cannot be explained in purely class terms or any other singular analytical model for that matter.[2]

Another increasingly important line of division is regionalism. At the outset of the Banzer regime, the main line of division was between Kolla Bolivia (the Andean highlands), centered in La Paz, and Camba Bolivia, (the eastern lowlands) centered in Santa Cruz. This split had some classlike aspects but also embodied purely regional and to some degree racial aspects. By the end of the regime the regional impetus had divided Bolivia's departments among themselves in an increasingly intense battle to decentralize power on the one hand and extract privileges from the central state on the other.[3]

The state itself was a focal point of another crucial dynamic of conflict and competition, namely, intraelite factional struggles to control the largess of the state as a resource to elaborate a myriad of patron-client networks. Clientelistic politics has always been a primary dynamic in Bolivian politics, at times overriding ideological, class, and regional divisions. During the Banzer regime this competition if anything was intensified and became so widespread and primary that it undermined the very institutional fabric of public life.

At the beginning Banzer sought to assert control over the extremely complex and intensely conflictual reality of the nation by forming a broadly based civil-military coalitional regime. The regime was based on three pillars: the military, a grand coalition of political parties between the MNR and its oldest and most bitter rival, the Falange Socialista Boliviana (FSB); and a bloc of so-called independents drawn largely from the private sector. The military was obviously the linchpin, owing to the fact that force remained the ultimate arbiter of political outcomes. As a result, the military not only backed the regime but shared openly in the process of rule and in the control of key components of the state apparatus. It was the institution as such, not simply specific officers, that was a part of the governing coalition.

The ostensible masterstroke was the formation of the so-called Frente Popular Nacionalista (FPN) made up of the main-line MNR headed by Paz Estenssoro and the FSB headed by Mario Gutiérrez. The two were to share equally with the military in cabinet posts and in control of key components of the state apparatus. The independents also received some cabinet and subcabinet posts. Banzer sought the alliance for a number of reasons. The MNR, of course, brought with it the legitimacy of the party that had made the revolution of 1952, and the FSB stood for a Right alternative to the revolution. Together they seemingly not only conferred legitimacy on the regime but also provided institutional links into key sectors of civil society. Thus, they created at least the illusion if not the fact of a broad base of civil support for the regime, which gained further credence from the civilian independents. It was an impressive array and did give substance to the government's assertion to be a national and not purely military effort.

As Banzer labored to create a new governmental scheme, he also moved to crush the opposition. Violent repression began during the quasi civil war of August and was extended over the first weeks and months of the new government. Repression fell heavily on Left party activists, student leaders, labor leaders, church activists, and others. Actual numbers of the victims are hard to come by, but suffice it to note that scores were killed, others disappeared, hundreds that were imprisoned were later dispatched to detention camps located in some of the most insalubrious parts of the interior, and still others were forced into exile or underground. It was brutal and in the short term effective.

The repression operated mainly out of the Ministry of Interior, headed by Colonel Andrés Selich, but was supplemented by spontaneous summary actions by civil and military supporters of the regime. Components of the parties of the FPN also indulged the settling of some old feuds. Commentators on this period usually view it as one of violence on an unprecedented scale, surpassing even that of the Barrientos period. In our view, the significance of the violence lies not in the number of its victims but its nature. Under Barrientos large numbers died but these were in the main (by no means exclusively) workers killed in the heat of confrontations having to do with specific work and or political actions.

In the initial days of the Banzerato repression was much more organized. Moreover, the aim was not simply to "discipline" and control labor (that was to come) but specifically to break the back of the ideological Left and its sympathizers. Hence, the abuse spilled over onto the middle class and was directed at elite cadres rather than bases. Students for the first time were also a target for systematic repression; university autonomy was abrogated and the institutions of higher learning were shut down.

The transformation of the nature of repression under Banzer must be viewed in the context in which it occurred, for it was a harbinger of even worse things to come after Banzer, as well as an indicator of general political trends. Recall that a goodly part of the Left participated in and backed the coup of 1964. The falling out with Barrientos came only as the anti-populist nature of his economic policies became evident. As the rupture came, however, a deadly minuet of violence and counterviolence developed around the issues concerning Bolivia's future, and ideological divisions steadily moved toward polarization. In short, the stakes in the struggle steadily increased.

As ideological division and conflict escalated, both sides gained sharper definitions of who was who, and both came to view the other as a deadly opponent aiming at the other's elimination from the political scene, if not anihilation. Although each side blamed the other for initiating the process, both became more and more violent. The Left had its heroes and martyrs but so did the Right. The Left harked back to the invasions of the mines and the Noche de San Juan. The Right pointed to the guerrillas of Nancahuazú (Ché), the ELN, and the Teoponte guerrillas. Above all the Banzer regime harked back to the perceived threat posed by the popular assembly, particularly to the threat to the armed forces. By that point a good part of the military had developed a particular antipathy to the Left. By the early 1970s all sense of dialogue had disappeared from public life and hatred born of mutual righteousness poisoned the political air that all breathed.

The Struggle for Control

Although there was broad agreement in the Banzer regime on the need to control if not break the Left and on the broad lines of the political economy, there was also deep division, particularly over how to organize the new government. The internal battle over power began before the guns were silenced. Banzer had to claw his way into the presidential chair, just as he had to scratch and bite to stay there, for he was far from the only officer who wanted to wear the presidential sash.

At first a triumvirate made up of Banzer, Andrés Selich, and General Jaime Mendieta was formed. It was short-lived; Banzer was able to out-maneuver the other two, who were forced to acquiesce in his ascension. Mendieta was then appointed minister of defense, and Selich minister of interior. Selich never accepted his status and continually sought to create a public image of himself as the true leader of the "revolution." His open challenge led to his ouster from the ministry (after the brunt of the repression was accomplished), a brief stint as ambassador to Paraguay, and finally ouster from the army and formal exile. Then in late April of 1973, while the regime was in the throes of intense internal jockeying, Selich returned to Bolivia to attempt to organize a coup against Banzer. He was picked up, taken to the Ministry of Interior, and in a macabre and ironic twist was beaten to death by the very security agents he had previously commanded. The circumstances of his death and a botched cover-up caused a scandal that added to the divisions in the military, but Banzer was able to ride it out.

This minidrama was important and indicative of developments in the political situation. The fact that two colonels and one general made up the triumvirate and that one of the colonels (later made general) emerged as president, (Barrientos, Ovando, and Torres were all generals) was dramatic evidence of the breakdown of the chain of command in the army. Further, it was evident that the institution was not acting politically as a coherent force directed by its formal leadership. Along this line it is also significant that although Banzer had substantial partisans among the non-general officer staff, the more decisive element in bringing him to the presidency was the support he received from Santa Cruz and segments of the private sector. That is, part of his military backing may have originated in the perception of his ability to rule through key civil actors; he was not purely the candidate of the military, let alone the army. It was his personal abilities and outside connections that determined his rise, not the fact that he was of the military.

The observation points up the fact that unlike its counterparts in Brazil, Argentina, and Peru, the Bolivian military was not functioning as an institution with a corporate sense of a mission to rule; nor did it, as an institution, have any sense of vision to impose on Bolivia. It had a negative unity that arose from fear of the Left, not a positive sense of stewardship. As a result, in spite of its formal facade, the Banzer government quickly became a personalistic dictatorship and remained so throughout the seven years of Banzer's tenure.

The military's lack, in a corporate sense, of a governing mission was an outward manifestation of the deep division affecting the institution. As we noted, some of the issues were ideological and tied into the general conflicts racking the civilian political elite. At that moment, however, ideological divisions were temporarily overcome. A major source of fissure, however, was generational and tied up with when groups graduated from the military academy, which academy they had attended, and where they were in the career cycle relative to the revolution of 1952. Perhaps owing to the abrupt changes in the institution that came with the traumas of 1952, the formation of cohorts was based on membership in particular graduating classes (promotión), especially in the army. The primary identity of an officer was and is promocíon, and officers move through their careers not purely as individuals but as members of a cohort. This process had been disrupted by the introduction of ideological political criteria in promotions to higher ranks, especially during Ovando and Torres. Thus, there were many sensitivities as to who stood where in the formal rank system and in the class cohort system.[4]

At the time officers who had graduated from the army's Escuela de Comunicaciones (School of Communications), like General Mendieta, were resented by the bulk of officers, who came out of the Colegio Militar (Military College). Moreover, most of the general officers were loath to accept fully Colonel Banzer's authority over them, particularly in military matters. To assert his authority better, Banzer moved quickly to advance officers from his own promoción who would be more disposed to be loyal to him as one of their own. Although this move increased his control over the top command in the short term, it generated suspicion in the lower ranks, where officers began to look at the top command as more beholden to Banzer than to the institution.

This latter division was reflected most between the high command and the cohort of majors and lieutenant colonels who were advanced to the command of operating regiments. These cohorts were graduated beginning in 1954 from the new military academy, Gualberto Villarroel, and were advanced over older officers from the pre-1952 academy, Pedro Villamil. Most of the Pedro Villamil officers had been cashiered in 1952 only to be recommissioned by Barrientos after 1964. They were resented by the younger postrevolutionary officers, a cohort that saw itself as "nationalist" in a broad sense but as professionals identified first and foremost with the institution in a primary sense. They came, in fact, to call themselves institutionalists. Their concern was that Banzer and forces exterior to the military were endangering the institution by embroiling it in political matters and associating it with the brutal repression practiced by the regime. (Many of the recommissioned officers were also disturbed by this development, especially the relationship with the MNR.) These men not only irritated Banzer but also mounted at least one serious coup attempt against him.

The various divisions centered on an increasingly intense debate within the military over the role the institution should play in the new government, and particularly with regard to the FPN and its two political parties. Banzer and the civilian parties sought to present the FPN as the formal expression of the government (indeed as the government) and to define it formally as made up of the MNR, FSB, and the military as such. At the same time, Banzer and the party leaders wanted to keep military officers in governmental positions to a minimum. Many officers saw this, not incorrectly, as a move to use and control the military at the same time.

The military's unhappiness with the situation was open. Some officers resented the inclusion of the military in a political pact on equal terms with civilian political parties. Some feared that the military was coming to be viewed as little more than an armed political party or, worse, as the armed expression of the parties. These attitudes were compounded by the resentment of many of the association of the military with either the FSB or the MNR. The concerns were partly ideological, but for the disaffected the issue was more the military's association with a party like the MNR, which had humiliated the institution in the early 1950s; many were particularly resentful of Victor Paz, whom they saw as the author of that humiliation.

In the welter of charges and countercharges published in a series of communiques, it was never clear what the relationship of the military to the FPN actually was. At least two contradictory lines surfaced within the military. One was an institutionalist line backed by the younger majors and lieutenant colonels; it argued for no formal association with the FPN and called on Banzer to hold elections for a new all-civilian regime, as promised. Another, less clear view was associated with some more senior officers who were not only against formal affiliation with the FPN but also pushed steadily for an increase in the military presence in the government and a downgrading if not complete ouster of the civil parties.

Banzer tried to resist both groups in the military but was more successful resisting the former than the latter. Slowly but surely he was forced to distance himself from the civilian parties and bring more officers into the government, a process that culminated in July 1974, when he abandoned the civilian parties altogether and established an all-military cabinet. It was an extremely complex game, the intricacies of which are not fully evident, but a number of points can be stated.

Retrospectively, it seems clear that Banzer's primary aim was to consolidate his personal power. In forming the FPN, he wanted not only to build a general bloc of formal support but, more subtly, to play the civilian parties and the military against each other. He periodically would promise elections, partly because like Barrientos, he would have liked to legitimize his presidency, and partly to keep the military factions and the civil parties off balance and thereby buy time. One thing is now fairly sure: he did not want to rule as a creature of the military and be completely beholden to it. Thus, when forced by circumstances to bring more officers directly into the government, he chose men endebted to him. Likewise, even as he struggled to maintain the facade of the FPN, he did so more by manipulating the personally ambitious party subleaders than through top leaders, like Paz, who could rival him.

The multiple divisions within the military were mirrored in the civil component of the FPN. Aside from the obvious historic antagonism between the MNR and FSB, both parties, but particularly the MNR, were racked by internal splits. The reasons the parties had entered the FPN in the first place were involved and reflected ideological, strategic, and personalistic choices. In the months prior to the formation of the FPN the two most prominent leaders of the parties, Victor Paz and Mario Gutierrez, had worked toward an ideological and personal meeting of minds such that Paz was able to declare publicly that he saw a shift by the FSB to a more Christian Democratic view that was more acceptable to the MNR. There was, at the rhetorical level at least, a closer affinity between the two, which was probably helped along by the common perception born of the previous two years that the real threat lay to the left.

The public position of the two leaders was that the experience of the Torres period demanded a show of unity from the authentically "nationalist" political forces. It is relevant that both the MNR and FSB had always characterized themselves as nationalist movements and both, but particularly the MNR, had always attacked the Marxist ideological Left as bearer of an alien and nationalistically illegitimate ideology imported from inappropriate foreign sources. In this the MNR was like all populist parties throughout Latin America. Aside from the ideological threat, the Paz wing of the MNR in particular was convinced that the Left had demonstrated that it was an irresponsible melange of unrealistic ideologues who were leading the nation into chaos and backwardness. Moreover, Paz argued that a Left revolution was in practice impossible and that any attempt in that direction could provoke direct intervention by neighbors like Brazil and Argentina and thereby threaten the very existence of Bolivia. In this regard it is relevant that Brazil did show real concern over the Torres government, obviously welcomed the rising of 1971, and most probably aided the rising, at least indirectly.

Both the MNR and FSB saw a strong civil-military "nationalist" regime as a way to guarantee the control of ideological Left and perhaps deal it a destructive blow. Some military officers, in fact, argued that the civil parties backed and encouraged the violent repression aimed at the Left party elites of the early Banzer regime. It is probably not going too far to argue that old political hands like Paz and Gutierrez saw an opportunity to use the military as an instrument to contain and/or eliminate their long-standing political foes. Indeed, some institutionalist officers clearly saw it that way, and that view fueled their objections to any formal entry of the military into the FPN.

Endemic Factionalism

Other than such ideological and strategic considerations there were additional, equally strong motives at work. In the original formulation the Banzer government was to be short-lived; once "order" was restored, elections were to be held in 1972. The MNR, in particular, knew from the experience of its own twelve years in power that the best place from which to contest an election was governmental office. The grand design of the party chiefs was, then, to help crush the Left and at the same time position themselves for the expected elections. Paz, the ever-shrewd maneuverer in pursuit of this strategy, positioned his part of the MNR in the government but did not himself accept an office, thereby remaining free to campaign independently when the time came.

At yet a deeper level another important motive was at work. The FSB had never held governmental office, and the MNR, which had tasted the perks of office, had been kept out since 1964. The fact was and is that in Bolivia politics perceived as access to the patronage resources of the state is all but the only game in town, especially for most of the urban middle class. The formation of the FPN created the opportunity for the job-hungry cadres of both parties to tap into the mother lode of the state apparatus. The salience of this motive was made obvious when many of the key sectors of the state were carefully apportioned between the MNR and the FSB, and all jobs in those ministries, public corporations, and so on were doled out as patronage by party strongmen. For politicians like Paz, power within the FPN provided the means not only to reward party cadres but also to build personal power in the context of intraparty factional struggles.

Whatever the formal organizational facade, personalistic factionalism was still the name of the game in party politics. After a short period in power the FSB developed two major factions; however, factionalism was more rife and significant in the MNR. In a real sense it was factionalism that brought the party down in 1964, and in the intervening years it had worsened. Faction dynamics in the MNR continued to be driven by ideological or programmatic differences, personal ambitions, and old-fashioned clientelism.

By the 1970s the MNR had become like a great tree with myriad branches of various sizes springing from the trunk. The problem was that many of the branches had fallen off and the remaining ones were claiming to be the trunk. The original four major leaders of the party had long since fallen out, with two—Juan Lechín and Walter Guevara—forming their own parties, and Victor Paz and Hernán Siles battling over what was left. The factionalism obviously enervated the party but the MNR remained the largest party by far and continued to carry the mystique of the revolution of 1952. The mystique of the revolution itself had become all but consensus in Bolivia, and the bulk of the ideological issues were over differing interpretations of the revolution and alternative futures in which to take it. This was one of the reasons Banzer sought to identify himself with the revolution by integrating the MNR into the FPN.

The MNR formally split again along programmatic lines around the two towering figures of the party, Paz and Siles. From exile in Chile, Siles formed a "Left" MNR called the MNRI. Paz, in turn, gained control of the formal party apparatus and led it into the FPN. The split formalized the division of the MNR into a Right and Left interpretation of the revolution. Siles now stood for the basically populist wing of the MNR; Paz was firmly identifed with the "realist" wing that saw the need to curb populism so as to promote state capitalist development. This division encapsulated the real programatic differences in the party and the revolution and was to remain the major split until now. Other more patronage-motivated divisions were to develop between Paz and his principal subchiefs in the months to come.

The point is that the Banzer regime was at first an extremely complex coalition made up of a multiplicity of groups, factions, and tendencies that often had contradictory goals and purposes. Whatever unity the government had was born of the threat posed to all by the ideological Left as manifested under Torres. As the urgency of that threat receded, the fissures in the military, the parties, the FPN, and the government quickly came to the fore.

Discontent was manifested first in the military and took two directions. First was the many-layered concern about the makeup and organization of the FPN; the second was the concern about the clear intention of the Paz MNR to use the FPN to rebuild its political position. As early as March 1972 Banzer felt compelled to sack army Commander Federico Arana Serruto because he publicly complained about the composition of the executive committee of the FPN: the executive committee was weighted toward the parties—four seats apiece for the parties and two for the military. Top officers saw this as an attempt to submit the military to the control of the parties.

Military officers were more successful in their open attempt to bloc the Paz MNR from rebuilding its popular organizations, especially in the countryside. Although inchoate, the peasantry remained an important political factor. The traditional Indian peasantry made up the largest population group and therefore was crucial in any electoral politics, real or formal. Moreover, since the early days of the revolution peasants in some key areas of the departments of La Paz and Cochabamba had been organized into armed militias that had been deployed in various ways in national political struggles, including as a counterweight to worker militias. Also, peasants not only controlled a substantial part of the nation's food supply but could and often did back their demands by cutting off transportation to the cities. For these and other reasons, national politicians sought to bolster party and personal positions by forging links to peasant leaders and the blocs they controlled.

Until the 1960s the MNR had a monopoly in the countryside, and as the author of the agrarian reform of 1953, Paz himself was the major national personality among the peasants. The rise of Barrientos changed that dramatically. After 1964 Barrientos not only managed to project his image into the countryside but forged an important institutional tie between the peasantry and the military, formalized in the so-called pacto militar-campesino. After his death the military continued to maintain the idea of that special tie.

Not unexpectedly, Paz and the MNR moved quickly to rebuild their bases among the peasantry in anticipation of oncoming elections. Indeed, Paz counted heavily on his status among the peasantry to energize his and the MNR's comeback. In that context, the military, in spite of its protestations that it was apolitical, was in direct competition with the MNR for the support of the peasants. It moved with equal alacrity to bloc the MNR and to revitalize the military-peasant pact. An attempt to hold an MNR peasant congress in Cochabamba in February of 1972 was torpedoed by peasant leaders loyal to the military, and the military then all but formally prohibited the MNR from any organizing efforts in the countryside.

As 1972 wore on Paz became increasingly dismayed by developments in the regime. In addition to frustration for the party, his influence in policy-making was declining. In October 1972 Banzer decreed a devaluation that Paz had been opposed to, this despite the fact that the MNR was in control of the Ministry of Finance. Differences over this and other policy matters helped to foment division in the MNR between Paz and many former political lieutenants. Because of the effect of devaluation on prices, it spurred popular discontent that sparked renewed repression by the government. Aside from his own disagreement with the devaluation policy, Paz was distressed because MNR leaders in other posts, like the Ministry of Labor, were forced to sell the package to popular-sector groups like labor. From Paz's point of view, this was not a good way for the party to prepare for elections.

The issue of when elections would be held was at the time extremely tangled. Banzer would call for elections to keep his opponents off balance but would then postpone them, often at the behest of his supporters. Parties like the MNR wanted elections as a way back to power—but not immediately. They wanted time to prepare the ground as well as for the memories of the worst of the repression to fade. On the other hand, the military's efforts to bloc MNR's organizing efforts and the growing suspicion that Banzer intended to hold on to power indefinitely caused consternation within the party. The military men, in turn, were split on the issue of elections, with some wanting to forget elections and consolidate an authoritarian regime dominated by the military and others pushing for an orderly retreat from politics and an early return to civilian rule.

Late 1972 and all of 1973 were tense times and national political life was in a constant state of flux. Agitation born of popular reactions to the devaluation of October 1972 provided a focal point for the opposition and popular protest. The problems internal to the regime were also constant. Tension in the FPN, popular agitation, rumored coup plots, and purported subversive cabals created a climate within which Banzer reinstated in March the so-called law of national security, which provided a legal pretext for him to deal summarily with his opponents. The law, which had been abrogated by Ovando, had been originated by Barrientos as a way of dealing with popular opposition during that period. In dusting off the law Banzer not only gained a legal tool to control the situation but showed an affinity for the attempts at constitutional engineering that Barrientos had engaged in; earlier, for example, he had declared that his regime would implement the Barrientos constitution of 1967. These moves toward legalizing his regime's actions and building a constitutional base were clues that in attempting to give some institutional coherence to his regime, Banzer would follow a basically corporativist scheme.

Shift to the Military

Popular discontent and rising concern in the military provoked a cabinet crisis in April of 1973, the outcomes of which were rather significant. Bowing to military pressure, Banzer brought a number of midcareer officers into political positions, including cabinet posts. Two, Colonel Juan Pereda Asbún (minister of commerce and industry) and Colonel Alberto Natusch (minister of agriculture), were to go on to figure prominently in the nation's unfolding political life. To make room for the officers, two subchiefs of the MNR and FSB, Ciro Humbolt and Carlos Valverde, were separated from the cabinet, whereupon Valverde broke with the regime, provoked a split in the FSB, and began fomenting plots in Santa Cruz against the government. Just as important, the changes marked a decline in the role of the civil parties and the FPN in the government and the inexorable rise to dominance of military officers.

Even at that stage, however, Banzer was resisting the maneuvers of military men. At the same time that he increased their role in the cabinet, he installed civilian Alfredo Arce Carpio as head of the crucial Ministry of Interior, a post that usually had been held by a military officer. The military had been particularly interested in the post because of its strategic power and also because since the overthrow of the MNR in 1964 it had given the military control of the national police *(carabineros),* which was considered to be an armed instrument of the MNR. Banzer's appointment, though, came to naught as a result of the Selich affair in May. The military seized upon the grisly circumstances of a brother officer's death and the subsequent coverup as indicative of Banzer's disdain for the institution. Simmering discontent in the officer corps quickly rose to a boil. Banzer found himself in a situation wherein, to buy peace with the military, he had to oust Arce Carpio and return the ministry to a military man, Colonel Walter Castro Avendaño.

Backpedaling all the while, Banzer announced that elections would be held in 1974. At the same time he again moved to assert some control over the fractious officer corps and assuage the civil parties by intervening in the all but open dispute between the armed forces commander, General Zenteno Anaya, and the party leaders, especially of the MNR. Specifically, he relieved Zenteno and assumed the command personally. Symbolically, the clear message was that his claim to rule was now based on his dual position as president of the republic and commander of the armed forces.

As 1973 wore on the discord and division in the FPN proceeded apace. The division in the FSB was manifest. At the same time Paz, who had begun to distance himself from Banzer and his economic policies, also began to split with his subchief Ciro Humbolt and other party stalwarts, like Rubén Julio, who remained committed to Banzer. Things started to move quickly when a rump FSB faction led by Gutierrez in August sought to nominate Banzer as the FSB candidate for the projected elections in 1974. The high command of the military was most distressed by that turn of events and put pressure on Banzer to refuse the nomination.

By that point the military was attacking the civil parties of the FPN, accusing them of corruption and of converting the ministries under their control into their own "feudal" domains. Calls were simultaneously made for the establishment of a completely military government. In November Banzer bowed to military pressure and declared that he would not be a candidate at all in 1974. Shortly thereafter the high command called for rescheduling the elections for 1975.

These actions precipitated another political crisis, which for all practical purposes put an end to the debilitated FPN as an effective governmental entity. Gutiérrez left the cabinet and was later named an ambassador. More important, Paz announced that the MNR was leaving the FPN to follow its own course. Interestingly, he attacked the government as being dominated by and beholden to private-sector entrepreneurs. This charge probably reflected some accurate analyses of the makeup of influence in the government as well as the old-time politician's attempt to regain popular support by attacking the private sector. Be that as it may, party subchief Humbolt broke with Paz and declared that the MNR was still in the government. The MNR was now formally split again.

Even as he bowed to military pressure, Banzer continued to try to avert becoming completely reliant on the officers of the high command. Again he sought to gain some control over the military by reorganizing the command structure. Specifically, he abolished the post of commander in chief and created a joint command, which rendered the separate branches easier to control. The military never liked the scheme and three years later forced a return to the old arrangement. Meanwhile Banzer publicly continued to insist that the FPN was still viable and the base of his government.

To give some substance to his assertion, Banzer, January of 1974, attempted to gain some mastery over the parties of the FPN, especially the MNR. The government accused Paz of a series of "political" crimes and forced him into exile. At the same time Humbolt, now clearly Banzer's man, used a convention of the rump MNR to excommunicate Paz from the party and have himself declared chief. Still, Banzer knew that what was left of the MNR and FSB hardly constituted the civil political umbrella that he sought from the FPN, so to bolster its image he brought in other civilian elements. The most important were politicians associated with Barrientos and now operating as the Fuerza Revolucionaria Barrientista (FRB). The group was small and added little, but it did bring into the regime some individuals like Edwin Tapia Frontanilla who were to have substantial influence on Banzer's later strategy.

January 1974 was a month of some consequence for the Banzer government. The FPN continued to unravel and Banzer was swimming hard to keep on top of the fluid political situation. His concern for his hold on power showed up in his minister of interior, who began to warn of various coups, often being said to be plotted by unlikely alliances of political groups and personalities. In this context the government's economic team at mid month announced a series of measures that had the effect of raising the price of many basic consumer goods by as much as 100 percent. The measures were part of the program begun in 1972 to curb popular consumption so as to generate investment capital. The measures of 1972 had sparked popular protest that the government had moved to repress. The measures of January 1974 provoked protest and brought on a violent confrontation between the government and one of its ostensible support groups, the peasants of the politically salient Cochabamba Valley.

The peasants reacted strongly to the measures mainly because, unlike some groups, they received no offsetting bonuses for the goods they had to buy and yet were prohibited from raising the prices of some of the food they marketed. Banzer sought to defuse the situation in the countryside by taking a leaf from Barrientos's book: he called on the peasants to fight the "communist" threats to his government. The official peasant confederation tried to mobilize the peasantry behind the call but it was quickly apparent that these Banzer proteges were speaking into the wind. Moreover, other groups and organizations from both the countryside and outside it urged direct peasant action against the measures. The mounting peasant protest coincided with a strike by workers (of peasant origin) in the Manaco shoe factory located in the Cochabamba Valley town of Quillacollo, which had long been a center of powerful peasant unions. By late January the peasants in key localities of the valley joined with the Manaco workers in demonstrations, using the peasants' favorite political weapon, roadblocks.

On January 28 the government responded by declaring a state of seige and dispatching army troops. During the tense negotiations in the ensuing hours Banzer showed that he was no Barrientos when it came to dealing with the peasants. He refused to go to the scene, demanding that the peasant leaders come to La Paz. And, he showed his disdain for the peasants by declaring that their protest had been bought with money and liquor by communist agitators. Confrontation was all but inevitable.

It is not entirely clear how the first clashes occurred. Once they did, however, the government called in air support and a bloody battle took place. When it was over scores lay dead and wounded and hundreds had been arrested. The government survived, but the opposition had another doleful symbol of popular resistance to antipopulist policies: the Massacre of Tolata.[5] The bloody confrontation was indicative of some important changes in the political scene since the days of Barrientos. Foremost, the pactomilitar-campesino was a dead letter. Then, in certain areas at least government could no longer manipulate peasants by means of organizations whose leaders were bought and paid for by the government. Finally, it indicated that new forces as yet dimly understood by outsiders were at work in the countryside.

In subsequent weeks Banzer sought to pour oil on troubled waters by offering indemnities to the families of the slain. Again he blamed the whole episode on outside communist agitators, and in one bizarre speech in effect gave the peasants license to kill such agitators by offering bounties. In addition, the government sponsored the first national meeting of the Confederation of Bolivian Peasants. Under the control of Banzer loyalists, the conference ratified the pactomilitar-campesino and restated the peasants' loyalty to Banzer as their leader. These were, however, staged events that bore little connection to the new political reality in the countryside.

The Tolata action fed into the already charged political atmosphere and helped set off further wrangling within the regime. At least one real coup attempt occurred. It was followed by another cabinet crisis that was resolved by Banzer's seeking to amplify civil participation in the government and the FPN. Now, though, Banzer was turning from the rump factions of the MNR and FSB to the civil groups that had formed around Barrientos. These Barrientistas became full members of the FPN, and one of their leaders, Edwin Tapia Frontanilla, gained the president's ear as secretary to the presidency.

Ever bobbing and weaving, Banzer then sought to divert attention from his internal troubles through the classic maneuver of mobilizing nationalist feelings around a foreign policy issue. That meant above all wrenching from Chile an outlet to the sea, which Bolivia had lacked since 1879, in the War of the Pacific, when Chile bested the combined forces of Peru and Bolivia. Ever since the issue, fueled by anti-Chilean feeling, had been a major nationalist symbol, particularly for the armed forces, which were always smarting over their humiliating record in foreign engagements. Playing upon these sentiments, Banzer traveled to Brazil in 1974 to meet the new Chilean strongman, General Augusto Pinochet. As a result of their talks, negotiations on an outlet began and an air of optimism swept the country.

The government lost no opportunity to make the point that a solution was possible because Banzer was talking to another authoritarian antipopulist leader through the good offices of authoritarian Brazil. Indeed,

Banzer's regime was beginning to look like it was a part of an authoritarian wave of the future, particularly in the southern cone of Latin America. Seizing on the foreign policy initiative, the military high command (not Banzer) in April issued a communique that stated that because of the need for national unity during the delicate negotiations with Chile, the elections pending for 1975 were to be suspended indefinitely. The military was clearly capitalizing on recent events to downgrade even further the civilian factions of the FPN and to consolidate its power around Banzer.

Whatever the ability of the high command to assert its influence over Banzer and downgrade the civil parties, it was not in firm control within its own house. Since the first days of the regime, officers graduated after 1952 had been coalescing into what came to be known as the "generational" group. The group increasingly made it known that it objected to both Banzer's and the older officer generation's use of the armed forces as a political tool for their own ambitions. Responding to the recent political trends and especially the high command's indefinite suspension of elections, the cohort of "institutionalists" mounted a serious coup attempt on June 5, 1974. When the coup failed, prominent members of the group, such as Lieutenant Colonel Raúl Lopez Leytón and Major Gary Prado, were forced into exile in Paraguay.

The coup was significant for many reasons. It revealed the generational split in the military and showed that issues other than ideology, specifically the role of the military in politics, were pulling at the institution. It also marked the coming of age of the generational group as a permanent force in the military and in national political life. Although the officers were exiled and formally separated from the army, they maintained important contacts in the military, especially among the full colonels. Indeed, these colonels continually sought to mediate between Banzer, the high command, and the generational group, and over Banzer's objections, many implicated in the coup were later reincorporated into the army in January 1975.

While that little drama was being played out, the generational group issued a long communique from Paraguay on June 17 in which it laid out a lengthy justification for its action. The document is revealing not only because of the political position taken by the officers but also because of its description of how the action of June 5 developed.

Substantively, the group stated that its aim had been the immediate resignation of Banzer, charging that he failed to interpret correctly the national spirit, that his government was rife with nepotism, and that he had surrounded himself with mediocre people who were threatening the integrity of the armed forces and the nation. In his place the officers had demanded a military government that would take precedence over the political parties, institutionalize the country, and call elections at a fixed time and in which there would be no official candidate. In addition, they had wanted a solution to the problem of the universities, summary judgment in cases of corruption, and the identification and punishment of political crimes and assassinations during the Banzer years. The action had been taken mainly to get the attention of the high command, which had not responded to repeated statements of concern expressed within the chain of command. Once the coup had been mounted, they immediately had offered to negotiate so as to avoid a split in the military and the "spilling of fraternal blood." Most interestingly, the officers asserted that a full colonel, Miguel Ayoroa Montaño (actually minister of industry and commerce), had acted as a go-between with the high command. They further declared that because key general officers had accepted their demands, they terminated the action. It was then, according to the document, that they had been betrayed, arrested, and exiled.[6]

The generational group's communique then raised institutional concerns along two lines: the military was being used by Banzer as an instrument of the FPN and its ineffective and corrupt civilian parties; and the high command was dominated by Banzer's henchmen who put their and his personal interests ahead of that of the institution. The generational divisions were manifest in the fact that officers of the colonel generation were brokering between the major and lieutenant colonel ranks and the general officers. However, the chain of command was now all but inoperative.

Although the rising of June 5 failed, its message was not missed. Indeed, in some respects it gave the high command the excuse it had been seeking for some time for asserting its predominance in the regime. Bowing to the realities of military politics, Banzer in early July formed an all-military cabinet. Then, as if acceding to the demands of the generational group, he announced elections for 1975 and pledged that he would not be a candidate. These actions all but ended the FPN as a practical reality.

The rump factions of the MNR and FSB responded by calling for immediate elections. They were joined by other parties that had had some relations with the government in the intervening months, like the Christian Democrats (PDC) and the Partido Revolucionario Auténtico under Walter Guevara Arce (another old MNR leader). Banzer responded by sending Guevara Arce and Benjamín Miguel, the leader of the PDC, into exile. Banzer then turned on Ciro Humbolt who was accused of complicity in the coup of June 5; by July he was also in exile. In spite of all, an even smaller rump of the now decimated MNR tried to maintain its alliance with Banzer. It seemed that no matter how many times Banzer purged MNR leaders he could always find a few more to help maintain the fiction of an MNR allied with his government.

By that point Banzer's main civil allies were the Barrientistas led by

Edwin Tapia. Again taking a page from the book of the generational group, Banzer announced at the installation of his new cabinet his intention to construct a new set of national institutions. To this end he created the National Council for Structural Change (CONARE), which was to be headed by Tapia Frontanilla, who continued as secretary to the presidency as well. It is interesting that unlike an earlier council to restructure the state, CONARE was to be made up of thirty citizens of proved ability and patriotism; no political parties as such were represented. In reality, CON-ARE harked back to Barrientos and showed a predilection of Banzer and his Barrientista supporters to create essentially corporatist political structures based on the representation of officially recognized functional groups. In addition, CONARE projected a weak legislature and a strong executive power. Also, in discussing electoral reform it pondered schemes that would all but outlaw the ideological Left from political participation.

The political waltz, however, was far from over. In September Banzer allowed that although he would not run in 1975 on his own, he was open to the persuasion of the people. The center Right civil parties, sensing an about-face, reacted with rage and dismay. As a result, all the parties that at one point had supported Banzer were now arrayed against him. These developments were given heightened significance by a scandal that suddenly exploded. Tapia Frontanilla was forced to resign his position when it was revealed that he had arranged a diplomatic passport for the head of the Barrientos youth group, who had been arrested in Canada on charges of cocaine trafficking. This and the rumored involvements of relatives of Banzer in cocaine led many to charge Banzer's complicity as well. Although the charges led to no action and Tapia Frontanilla was publicly cleared, it marked the first time that members of a government and the military were associated in the public eye with cocaine. It was not to be the last time.

Banzer's last civil political card had been played, and his plan to create a set of institutions that would constitutionalize his presidency à la Barrientos had also come to naught. The political situation was in complete disarray and Banzer had few resorts other than the military to which to turn. In the language of Bolivian public life, there was a complete *desgaste* (exhaustion) of center Right civil politics.

On November 7 a coup was mounted in Santa Cruz by elements of the 19th Manchego Battalion together with Carlos Valverde of the FSB and officers associated with the Paz MNR. This has often been referred to as an *auto golpe* (self-made coup) by Banzer to justify the actions that followed. That may be so. On the other hand, there is evidence that the action was a real coup by the Paz MNR, Valverde FSB, and dissident officers to regain control of the process. In any event, Banzer had to turn to the armed forces to put down the coup. In the aftermath some cabinet members as well as numerous members of the MNR and FSB and implicated military officers were arrested and exiled.

November 9, 1974, was a turning point in the Banzerato. A dramatic formal regime shift occurred: all pretense at ruling through the FPN and the traditional civilian parties of the center Right was dropped. By decree the military assumed full political and administrative control of the state and the government. The decree declared that the military was to exercise that control legally until 1980, and in the interim was to oversee a complete reorganization of the political system so as to realize a "new Bolivia." It also declared the military's intention to carry out a structural transformation of state-society relations and to create a new set of governmental institutions.

Search for a Political Formula

In response Banzer returned to some of the political themes he had introduced when setting up CONARE some months before. Specifically, he continued to attack the major institutions of liberal parliamentary democracy as roadblocks to establishing effective government. As before, he noted that parliaments acted mainly to thwart the will of the executive; an executive that spoke for Bolivia as a whole while parliaments represented particularistic interests. Given that no parliament existed during his tenure, the allusion here was to some of Barrientos's problems with his legislature. Behind the problems of parliament were the political parties.

Banzer turned completely on his erstwhile civil allies of the FPN. The parties, according to Banzer, were merely fragments of civil society dedicated to the furtherance of personal and sectarian ambitions. They were bloated with job-hungry cadres who served only to inflate public employment even as they sowed particularistic discord in society. What Bolivia needed more than anything else was "national unity" and political stability.

The decree of November 9, 1974, was dubbed the Plan for a New Bolivia (Plan Nueva Bolivia). It signified not only a new government in Bolivia but also a new regime, a regime based on a more monistic, centralized, and authoritarian vision of state-society relations that was juxtaposed to the pluralistic model of Bolivia's formal constitutional tradition. The regime moved quickly to overhaul some of the infrastructure that mediated between state and society, namely, political parties and labor unions.

By decree all political parties were declared to be in indefinite recess and all their activities were banned. The de facto suppression and control of labor unions more or less in effect since 1971 was restated, broadened, and legalized. Actually, all the officers of all major civic associations were declared to be subject to government review and appointment. In practice, the main target was the unions, their offices were intervened and all job actions, such as strikes and work stoppages, were banned.

At the same time the government declared its intention to reorganize the state, and in particular rationalize and modernize the civil service. To this end, an interesting decree gave the government the power to "draft" all citizens into the service of the state and subject them to military discipline. The decree had little real effect on the civil service but it did give the government a lever to control labor leaders by drafting them as government-controlled "coordinators." Moreover, the government used it as a kind of cover to appoint politically "independent" members of the private sector to key policy posts, especially in the economic area. Indeed, the new regime, although formally a military one, openly moved to a quasi-official but personalistic alliance with the private sector. Prominent entrepreneurs were placed in a variety of key positions and civilian "technocrats" from the private sector were put into numerous important staff positions. All of these civilians were presented as apolitical individuals appointed because of their technical abilities, not their political affiliations.

Thus, in formal terms, Bolivia was subjected to a new military regime that more or less openly mimicked some of the new bureaucratic authoritarian regimes that had proliferated in South America since the Brazilian coup of 1964.[7] The November 9 decree projected a state-centric regime oriented toward asserting authoritarian control over the civil society and expressing itself in a government based on a Bolivian version of the military-civil technocrat alliance said to be characteristic of the bureaucratic authoritarian regimes. As we will see shortly, this resemblance was superficial and masked a fluid personalistic regime that is better characterized as a neopatrimonial regime.

The consolidation of the openly military regime seemed to give the Banzer government some internal coherence and stability. It was needed, for almost immediately thereafter popular opposition to the regime became resurgent. Bolivia was about to demonstrate a lesson learned in other authoritarian situations in Latin America as well: complete exclusion of the popular sectors of society is at best a temporary expedient that cannot be maintained indefinitely. The fact is that long-term stability is predicated on finding some viable way to incorporate the popular sectors, especially organized labor, into the system of governance.

Over the next three years opposition to the regime was centered in organized labor, especially the miners and dissident sectors of the urban middle class. A substantial portion of middle-class opposition came from what was for all intents and purposes a "political class" whose economic well-being depended on its ability to penetrate the state as a source of jobs, fees, contracts, concessions, and the like. This political class was large and found articulation through the myriad of political parties. For this group, ideological considerations and programmatic platforms often masked a more fundamental dynamic of "ins" and "outs." Given the monopoly of the military and its civil allies from the private sector on patronage, the bulk of the political class and the political parties were perforce in confrontational opposition to the regime, if for no other reasons than access to the resources of the state.

Another critical source of mainly middle-class opposition was the Catholic church. As in other countries of Latin America, a substantial portion of the church had become directly involved in politics as a result of theologically focused concerns with social justice and human rights. The intensity of political conflict in Bolivia since the 1960s had helped radicalize numerous church people, who had become deeply committed activists on behalf of the popular sectors. Owing to the attempts of authoritarian regimes to exclude, repress, and control secular modes of political expression, the church remained one of the few institutions that could still function openly. Under Banzer, in particular, the progressive sectors of the church acting through organizations such as the Comisión de Justicia y Paz, became the de facto spokesmen of the repressed popular sectors. Hence, the church was on a collision course with the regime.

The other largely middle-class sector of opposition originated in the universities, especially the University of San Andrés in La Paz. Traditionally the source of opposition to the government, the universities became bastions of resistance to the regime. Throughout its tenure the Banzer government often closed the universities and struggled to come up with some plan of reorganization that might depoliticize the university system. Its efforts came to naught, and university student organizations openly entered into pacts and alliances with banned trade union organizations like the Confederation of Bolivian Workers (COB) and the mine workers' federation (FSTMB).

There were two major government clashes with the miners. The first occurred in January 1975 when the government seized four church-run radio stations in the historic mining center of Siglo XX. That takeover escalated into a battle with the church and the parties, and led to the arrest and exiling of many priests and political figures, most notably Hernán Siles. The regime sought to contain the affair by isolating the mining camps and closing the University of San Andrés. The dispute was brought to a negotiated solution when the miners returned to work and the government allowed the university and the radio stations to reopen.

A more dramatic clash came in May and June of 1976. Government attempts to repress a revived FSTMB provoked a miners' strike that lasted for over four weeks. As in the earlier conflict, the strike spilled over into conflict with the church and the university. This time the army occupied all of the major state-owned mines. The strike was resolved when the government, which would not yield to the miners' wage demands, agreed to recognize the base committees set up by the FSTMB. This constituted a kind of organizational victory for the miners, who then returned to work, but the military continued to occupy the mines for the remainder of the Banzer period.

A very significant phenomenon throughout this period was that in the face of the government ban on unofficial unions, miners were able repeatedly to organize and to hold their own elections for their union leaders. Invariably, they elected people from the FSTMB and COB, and particularly longtime union leader Juan Lechín Oquendo. In spite of the government's efforts to impose controlled unions, the workers demonstrated over and over their ability to maintain their own parallel organizations. This fact plus the need for the government to militarily occupy the mines on a semipermanent basis demonstrated most eloquently the vitality of the workers' movement and the complete ineffectiveness of the government's labor policy. Again it was shown that labor could be repressed in the short term but not coercively controlled in the long term.

Throughout this period Banzer continued trying to divert political opposition through negotiations with Chile over an outlet to the sea. The new Pinochet regime in Chile at first seemed to send signals that a successful solution could be achieved. It also made available to Banzer the inhospitable climes of Tierra del Fuego as a dumping ground for dissident politicians and labor leaders who were arrested and exiled during the mid 1970s. In the end Chilean nationalism overcame any affinity between the two authoritarian regimes, and for many other, complex reasons the deal fell through. Banzer was able to use the issue to buy time but in the end his failure to achieve his objective hurt him, especially among his colleagues in the military.

While problems with the extra governmental opposition mounted, Banzer and the military worked hard to give the regime an image of coherence and purpose similar to that which was attributed to many of the other "new authoritarian" regimes that dominated most of the region. The image was promoted by a national development plan published by the government in October 1976, Plan Quinquenal. It presented the military government as a legitimate regime charged with overseeing the long-term transformation of Bolivia. Taking a lead from Brazil, it portrayed the armed forces as a national institution above the political fray that would contain interest groups, factions, and parties in the name of the national interest. The military was to hold power indefinitely, that is, until its entire task was completed. The sense of coherence and permanence projected by the plan was, as in the past, to prove most illusory.

The veneer of military unity was shattered when in rapid succession two general officers associated with opposition to the regime were assassinated outside Bolivia. In May General Joaquín Zenteno Anaya, who because of his opposition to Banzer had been sent into golden exile as ambassador to France, was gunned down in Paris. The act was imputed to a leftist group avenging Ché Guevara, but rumors persisted that its origin lay in the political infighting in the Banzer regime. In June General Juan José Torres was kidnapped and murdered in Buenos Aires. The deaths and the ways in which they were handled by the government (for example, it refused to allow Torres to be buried in Bolivia) revived many of the long-simmering disputes in the armed forces.

A critical moment in the Bolivian drama came with the election of Jimmy Carter as president of the United States in November of 1976. Bolivia has always been more vulnerable to external pressures than most of the larger, more developed countries of Latin America. This fact plus the policy thrust of the revolution after 1956 gave the United States in particular a great deal of influence over governmental behavior in Bolivia, particularly that of "right" governments pursuing some version of state capitalist development. Thus, the new focus on human rights of the Carter administration quickly came to loom large in Bolivia. The Carter State Department listed the Banzer government as one that had regularly violated human rights, notably in the Tolata action of 1974 and the occupation of the mines in 1976. The damning document and a policy statement were officially handed to the Bolivian government by Under Secretary of State for Latin American Affairs Terrence Todman in May of 1977.

By 1977 Banzer was under pressure from elements within his government and the military, from outsiders, and from the United States. And, the economy had also begun to turn sour. Ever the realist, he began to bob and weave, seeking a way out. Although he defended the role of the military, he also sent out signals of a possible political opening and a restoration of "full participation and pluralism." In retrospect it seems clear that in bowing to the pressures, Banzer was trying to organize a controlled political opening that would culminate with him elected as a constitutional president.

In July 1977 Banzer unveiled a step-by-step return to civilian rule by 1980. At the same time, following again the example of his defunct mentor Barrientos, he sought to mobilize a peasant base in anticipation of his eventual candidacy. On August 2 the official peasant confederation, meeting in the historic town of Ucureña, site of the signing of the 1953 Agrarian reform, declared Banzer to be the peasant candidate. Banzer responded by declaring his intention to make the indigenous languages of Aymara and Quechua official languages that would be compulsory in schools by 1979.

Banzer's plan did not lessen U.S. interest nor call off the opposition, both of which continued to push for an earlier timetable. President Carter put pressure on Banzer in September when he traveled to Washington in connection with the signing of the Panama Canal Treaty. Banzer finally announced plans in November to hold elections in July of 1978. At the same time he lifted the ban on political parties but let stand the ban on union activity. He again clearly aimed to run and win, thus constitutionalizing his hold on the presidency. But as we shall see, the announcement of November 9, 1977, quickly led to Banzer's losing control of the political situation completely, which merely ratified the fact that his control had been rather tenuous all along.

State Capitalism

From the outset the economic policy of the Banzer government was designed to put Bolivia back onto the path of a state capitalist development strategy. To do so, the government rearticulated an approach that had grown directly out of the revolution of 1952 and had been articulated by the center Right of the MNR since the late 1950s and early 1960s. It is not surprising, therefore, that in the early going of the FPN, the Paz MNR held the main economic posts in the cabinet.

In the Bolivian context the thrust of the state capitalist model has always implied at least two politically charged dimensions: (a) an emphasis on capital accumulation, and (b) a substantial shift of resources into the modern components of the private and public sectors. Since the late 1950s the costs of the approach have always fallen most directly on organized labor and somewhat less directly on the traditional peasantry. The resistance of organized labor to the costs increasingly pushed the state to impose the costs coercively. These tensions within the political economy helped lay the MNR low in 1964 and bring about the military-backed authoritarian government of René Barrientos and, later, Hugo Banzer.

In Bolivia, as elsewhere in Latin America, the state capitalist model thrust the central state to the forefront, where it was in a sense charged with at least three major roles. First, the openly political role of "disciplining" labor through a forceful imposition of costs; in a populist context like Bolivia this meant a shift from a strategy of seeking to incorporate labor through co-optation to one of excluding labor. Second, the role of primary generator of capital and the mechanism to mediate and direct the flow of capital into the private sector. Third, through the public sector and especially public corporations, the role of entrepreneur in its own right. The three roles were pulled together most fully during the Banzerato. In a very real sense the period saw the culmination of the logic of state capitalism in Bolivia.

Thus, once the ideological Left was repressed after the rising of August 1971, the government remained on a collision course with labor as it sought to reverse the populist thrust of the Ovando and Torres governments and set in place the state capitalist model. Throughout its seven years the Banzer regime was locked in conflict with labor, which it was able to repress but never fully control. Moreover, as we saw, the conflict with labor was generalized to a clash with the peasantry as well when the costs of this new round of state capitalism began to fall more directly on the traditional agricultural sector. The manipulation and domination of labor and other popular sectors was central to the economic policy of the period.

The state under Banzer was used to create a "climate of order" (read: manage labor) that would encourage the private sector as well as international supporters of capitalist development. To do so, it lowered general levels of consumption by keeping a rein on wages while prices rose. Other mechanisms for keeping consumption down were set forth in the decrees of October 1972 and January 1974, which devalued the peso, removed subsidies from basic goods, and mandated price rises of up to 100 percent without compensatory wage increases. In addition the Banzer government revived the pro-private-sector policies set in place by Barrientos and put a number of its own on the books. Most important among them was a general investment law and a law on hydrocarbons designed to stimulate foreign and local direct investment, which had been decreed in October 1971, along with creation of a national investment institute (Instituto Nacional de Inversiones, (INI)) that was charged with fostering private sector investment, both national and international. From the outset INI was dominated by people from the local private sector who used it as a base to build influence in the government over the suceeding years.

One of the most important tasks that fell to the state during the Banzerato was to generate and direct the flow of capital investment. This role developed de facto until 1976, when it was formally assigned to the state in the new five-year plan (Plan Quinquenal) decreed by the government in October of 1976. The fact is that the state, through infrastructure projects, public corporations, and credit policies, became the largest source of investment. Over the period the public investment accounted for 9 percent of GNP, and fully two-thirds of total investment flowed from the state. A large part of that investment involved direct transfers into the private sector.[8]

Since the revolution of 1952 state capitalism in Bolivia has always been a kind of hothouse capitalism in which the private sector has developed under state nurturance. The reasons for this are many, some specific to Bolivia and others common to the South American pattern of dependent capitalist development. Prior to 1952 Bolivia did not possess a modern capitalist bourgeoisie of a size and capacity that enabled it to act as a class. To the extent that a modern capitalist class exists today, it is a product of the revolution of 1952, the policies pushed by the center Right of the MNR and subsequent state capitalist regimes, and by the stimulation of the central state. Modern capitalism in Bolivia was largely state induced and the local national bourgeoisie was largely dependent on the state.

The role of the state in the recent development of Bolivia stands out in many ways that we will highlight as we move through the narrative. In the 1970s the work of generating investment capital fell to the state largely by default. The fact is that in spite of the government's pro-private-sector investment policies, neither the international nor the Bolivian private sector responded. Very little direct foreign investment entered the country during the 1970s, and domestic private sector investment was limited. The state's central investment role was ratified in the 1976 five-year plan, which projected that the state would provide some 71 percent of investment over the period.

How was the state to finance its role as chief investor? One source was external aid, especially from the United States. Since the mid-1950s the United States had consistently backed Bolivian governments that pursued antileftist policies and pushed some variant of the state capitalist development model. However, over those years total aid, although high, had declined and changed in composition; there had been a steady shift from direct budgetary assistance to other forms of assistance, most particularly military aid, and the trend was continuing.[9] In the end the state's investment was principally financed from three sources: (a) indirect taxes, especially on primary export products like minerals; (b) mounting government deficits (including public corporation deficits) met increasingly through printing currency; and (c) foreign borrowing. The results of this approach were an undercutting of the mining sector, the stimulation of inflation, and a massive foreign debt.

Shifts in Economic Structure

By the mid-1970s Bolivia was experiencing annual growth rates of 5 percent which led many to take their cue from Brazil and dub Bolivia an economic miracle. But, even within the Bolivian context such rates, while respectable, were really nothing new. More important, behind the growth were some important structural shifts in the economy that were to call into question the ability of the economy to sustain economic development. The most notable shift was the decline of the role of the productive sectors in the economy that began in the 1960s and accelerated in the 1970s. In the 1950s the productive sectors had contributed 60 percent of total GNP; in the 1960s, the figure was 58 percent; and in the 1970s, 46 percent. Most significant in this regard was the drop in agriculture's share from 29 to 20 percent, and that of mining from 16 percent to less than 9. Manufacturing, energy, transportation, and communications remained roughly constant over the period. Increased shares were posted mainly by hydrocarbons, construction, commerce and finance, government and other services.

Two factors among the many behind the shifts were the fundamental biases built into the variant of the state capitalist model pursued in Bolivia since the late 1950s. The first was the marked tendency to favor large, seemingly modern corporate enterprises in both the public and private sector to the detriment of smaller traditional activities, like those of artisans and above all traditional peasant agriculture. The second was the firm goal to pursue national integration by marching to the East.

The Banzer government reflected and consolidated these previous policies. Hence, one of the highlights of the 1970s was the economic and political emergence of the eastern lowlands, especially the department of Santa Cruz.[10] Santa Cruz and the East had long benefited from the state's investment in roads and other infrastructure. Another important policy was the development of hydrocarbons and the fact that the central government had ceded to producing departments the right to control directly 11 percent of associated tax revenue. Also, under Banzer, Santa Cruz in particular benefited from a government-directed flow of all but concessionary credit into the region.[11] The credit fueled a boom in agro-industrial enterprises developing commodities for export and some manufacturing. Eastern agro-industry surged in this period, which meant that the overall decline of agriculture in GNP reflected mainly the fortunes of the massive traditional peasant sector.

Behind these patterns stood some important trends, again these were trends that came to fruition under Banzer but had been set in motion earlier. In retrospect we can see that the state had been mediating some important capital transfers in Bolivia for over twenty years. Specifically, there had been shifts from the traditional sector to the modern sector, and especially from the traditional agricultural sector to the urban sectors. At another level, a massive shift was taking place from the Andean region's mining and traditional agriculture to the less populated East and particularly Santa Cruz. These economic patterns were to have important political effects.

One key to the boomlet of the Banzer years was the increased revenues the state was able to capture from the export of minerals and hydrocarbons, but the performance of these commodities also sheds light on the superficiality of the boomlet. The higher revenues were a consequence of the sharp rise in prices that these commodities commanded in the world market. The money paid for minerals, however, was not matched by greater output; in fact, the production of most went up only slightly while that of the historically important tin actually declined. Petroleum production rose but at the cost of using up reserves; by the end of the decade proven oil reserves were all but gone and the nation was threatened with the possibility of becoming an oil importer. As had been so often true in the past, Bolivia was using up nonrenewable, primary-product resources to finance a development boom that was to prove to be more flash than substance.

A factor of consequence in the political economy of the period was the steadily growing deficits of the central government. The deficits were the result of public spending that between 1971 and 1975 alone grew 16.5 percent or more than twice the rise in GNP. The burst in spending in turn demonstrated the preponderant, enlarging role of the state in the economy.

As we have noted over and over, the revolution of 1952 produced a dominant model of development that is best termed state capitalism. In Bolivia the state component of the model has been primary from the beginning. During the MNR years the state was made the dominant actor in the economy. Under Barrientos the private sector prospered and the size and function of the state stabilized but remained large and preponderant. During the Banzerato there was a definite attempt to stimulate the private sector but at the same time the size of the public sector grew tremendously and the overall role of the state in the economy markedly increased. Indeed, under Banzer the state dimension of the state capitalist formula reached its zenith. By the late 1970s the state was accounting for some 70 percent of the economy (exclusive of traditional peasant agriculture) and, as we saw, fully two-thirds of total investment. Behind this was the tremendous expansion in the 1970s of state agencies and public corporations, for by then the central state had 120 public agencies and over 50 public enterprises and financial institutions. The significance of these entities stands out in the fact that three state enterprises alone (mining, COMIBOL; smelting, ENAF; and hydrocarbons, YPFB) accounted for 75 percent of exports.

The Banzer government created at least twenty-four public agencies and corporations. One of the more important was the state-military enterprise COFADENA, which emerged as a highly diversified industrial corporation that turned out products like bricks and leather goods and assembled trucks as well. COFADENA reflected not only the increase in the role and size of the state but—just as important—the melding of the military into the economic functions of the state, not to mention lucrative public employment.[12]

One of the crucial aspects of the weight of the state under Banzer was the dramatic rise in public employment. Again, this was an acceleration and a culmination of a trend started in the 1950s under the MNR. Between 1971 and 1975 government employment grew at an annual rate of 9.9 percent, or three times the growth in the total labor force. In fact, under Banzer total central government employment doubled. A large portion of that was in state enterprises, but the number of employees in the components of the central administration alone went from 49,127 in 1970 to 88,811 in 1978. We will return to this subject below.

The size and role of the state produced steadily expanding deficits that could not be offset simply by taxes or by printing money, or by foreign direct budget support. Hence, to help finance its own weight as well as public and private sector investment, the government turned to foreign borrowing. Like the rest of Latin America, Bolivia financed a substantial portion of its growth in the 1970s through state-guaranteed loans from private commercial banks in other countries. By the time Banzer left office, the Bolivian state was liable for over $2.5 billion, an enormous debt for a country of some 5 million people. The debt not only mortgaged the country's economic future but saddled the treasury with a debt-service burden. In short, the state had become an economic engine that was more and more expensive to keep going.

An important element in the level of public debt was the public enterprises that ran huge deficits throughout the 1970s. The shortfalls reflected shifts of capital into the private sector as well as the cannibalization of state corporations like COMIBOL to finance the expansion of the state's own apparatus. In a complex game of robbing Peter to pay Paul, the government had to subsidize state agencies that had previously been plundered for the benefit of the state apparatus and the private sector. Between 1975 and 1977 fifteen major entities were subsidized to the tune of $200 million. In 1978, despite high mineral prices, COMIBOL alone lost $60 million.

Perhaps nothing illustrated the complex relationship that developed between the state and the private sector more than policies toward the development of agro-industry in the eastern lowlands. This sector grew rapidly during the 1970s largely because of massive infusions of credit provided by the government at concessionary interest rates. Indeed, the terms were so generous and the enforcement of loans so lax that most economists agree that a sizeable proportion of the credit passed through agro-industry into other activities, such as construction, foreign investment, and flat-out capital flight.

Government investment stimulated a boom in agro-industry and a brief rise in nontraditional agricultural exports. Cotton is illustrative. Credit and rising world prices pushed cultivation from 16,600 hectares in 1970 to 50,000 in 1975. When world prices turned downward, the bottom fell out, and by the late 1970s, only 15,000 hectares were under cultivation. The boom-bust cycle in agro-industry left behind millions of dollars of bad debts that, among other things, led to the bankruptcy of the Bolivian agricultural bank.[13] In some ways agro-industry was symbolic of the period. Billions in investment capital funneled through the state created a superficial level of growth quickly erased in a classic boom-bust, primary-product cycle. A substantial proportion of wealth created went into upper-income construction projects and the enabling of luxury consumption, mainly of imported products. When the bottom fell out, Bolivia was left with anemic mines, empty oil wells, reduced crop acreage, and a staggering debt that fell squarely on the state.

Winners and Losers

A major point that we have emphasized is that the state capitalist model has carried a very clear set of implications regarding who would win and who would lose economically in the short term. These cost allocations have been a major source of political struggle in Bolivia since the revolution of 1952. They were a factor in the rising that brought Banzer to power in 1972, and throughout his term the issue of defining and imposing costs structured the relationship of the state and key social groups and set much of the tone of the regime. Given its state capitalist development strategy, the Banzer regime revived, consolidated, and in some senses increased the cost allocations inherent in the state capitalist model since the early 1960s.

The major direct loser in periods of the antipopulist state capitalist approach has been organized labor, particularly factory workers and above all miners. Indeed, since the 1960s labor has pitched its political struggle mainly to regain wage, salary, and benefit provisions achieved in the early days of the revolution, and to prevent further deterioration of its position. As we saw, labor lost badly under Barrientos but was able to use its influence under Ovando and Torres to regain roughly the wage position held in 1965. Under Banzer pressure on labor began again, and over the seven years its position deteriorated markedly.[14]

The main state mechanism to impose costs on labor was wage and price policy. In the simplest terms the government held most wages in check even as inflation, averaging 25 percent a year, pushed prices steadily upward. The result was a steady decline in the real income of most categories of workers which translated into an overall decline of real wages in the economy. The allocation of costs to labor sectors did not fall equally, however, and the distribution reflected the particular biases of the state capitalist model in Bolivia. The hardest hit wages were in mining, manufacturing, and construction. Workers in petroleum, commerce and finance, and banking held their own or in some cases improved slightly. The differential allocation helped undercut unity in the labor movement and fostered pursuit of specific group benefits among the more privileged workers, like those in petroleum. In any event, favoring some workers over others helped assure that even though Banzer clashed with certain worker cohorts, especially miners, he did not confront an effective class-based challenge to his rule.

As we argued above, the state capitalist model in Bolivia was also clearly biased against traditional agriculture, hence one of the losers was the traditional Indian peasantry. The peasants had been among the biggest gainers of the revolution, largely because of the agrarian reform of 1953, which converted most peasants from *colonos* to small landowners. In the early 1960s they began to lose, mainly because of the neglect of the traditional sector in the investment priorities of the state capitalist development model. Up through the Barrientos period the losses were mainly indirect because of the general decline of investment and credit in the agricultural sector, which was in turn reflected in the sector's declining share of the GDP. The relative prices of traditional products had held, and therefore immediate family income at least had not deteriorated.

During the Banzer period the peasants' situation worsened. The investment biases of the development model continued, the traditional sector's share of agricultural investment dropped further, and more direct cost allocations began to be felt in the countryside. Specifically, the relative prices of traditional agriculture products were held to levels lower than the prices to which nontraditional products had risen, and relative to the increase in prices rural families paid for their necessities. The upshot was a marked decline in the production of the traditional agricultural sector relative to the modern agricultural sector, and a marked decline of the terms of trade of the traditional agricultural sector with the urban sector. Thus, from 1965 to 1979 the share of production of the altiplano (traditional) declined from 21.0 percent to 17.5 percent, and that of the eastern lowlands (modern) increased from 24.3 percent to 32.0 percent. At the same time, according to one study, the index of prices for agricultural products rose from 100 in 1972 to 262 in 1978, and the index of a typical family basket of products went from 100 to 327.38 in the same period.[15]

It seems clear that Banzer sought to keep the urban sector somewhat quiescent with cheap food at the expense of the traditional rural sector even as he continued to shift capital from the traditional sector to the modern sector. This escalation of the costs imposed on the peasants undercut Banzer's attempt to manipulate the pacto militar-campesino and provoked a peasant disaffection, manifested in incidents like the violent clash in 1974.

The big gainers under the state capitalist model were those who controlled the dominant organizations of the economy in both the private and public sectors, namely, private sector entrepreneurs and the top techno-bureaucratic managers (civilian and military) of public and private enterprises. In general, the urban middle class benefited, as did components of the petty bourgeoisie in activities like commerce and transport. The pattern of winners and losers was set in the early 1960s and ratified and consolidated in the 1970s. It was generally similar to the rest of Latin America, which saw a marked trend in the income distribution profile toward concentration of income at the top levels of the scale. Most would agree that the regional pattern reflected the cost allocation patterns implicit in the reorganization of dependent capitalist economies, especially under the modernizing authoritarian regimes that proliferated after the mid 1960s.

Bolivia by the mid-1970s had one of the more unequal income distribution profiles in the region. Data are extremely difficult to obtain, but according to one mid-1970s study earners in the lowest 40 percent received only 13 percent of all work income; the next 40 percent received 26 percent; and the top 20 percent received 61 percent of the total. Another study, produced by the central bank, not only confirmed the unequal distribution (although in less harsh terms) but noted that the trend toward income concentration at the top was accentuated during the Banzer years. In that study the lowest 40 percent saw its proportion fall from 22.1 percent in 1975 to 19.4 percent in 1978; the upper 20 percent increased its share from 41 percent to 46 percent; and the middle 40 percent declined from 36.9 to 34.6 percent. However measured, the clear trend was there.[16]

It is important to disaggregate the gross figures somewhat so as to discriminate within general groupings. As we saw, for example, although the working class as a whole lost, certain categories of workers—especially in oil and financial circles—actually did fairly well. In the area of winners similar discriminations are relevant. First, the upper reaches of the private sector benefited, but so did the upper reaches of the state apparatus. This fact points up that the peaks of the economy and income are controlled not by a single capitalist class of entrepreneurs, which is less than 1 percent of the EAP, but by a combination of entrepreneurs and high-level managers in the public and private sector who according to one estimate together make up around 1.5 percent of the EAP. This stratum shares operational control of the economy with a stratum of upper-middle-level techno-bureaucrats in the public and private sectors and together they constitute somewhere around 7.5 percent of the EAP.[17] Thus, in Bolivia, the dominant income and control strata are not mainly those who own the means of production but also those who hold techno-managerial positions. Moreover, control of the economy is based not exclusively or even mainly on control of the private sector but in a fusing at the techno-managerial level of the public and private sectors.

This analysis calls into question the view advanced by some that during the 1970s Bolivia experienced the emergence to political and economic dominance of a private sector class of entrepreneurs or a national bourgeoisie. Moreover, even within the private sector the gains were unequally distributed. As we saw, throughout the 1960s and 1970s there was a steady shift from the productive sectors toward commerce, finance, and services; most marked in that shift was a decline in mining. Again, all of these sectors had public and private components.[18]

The trend clearly continued and was reinforced under Banzer. In fact, gains cut along three lines. First, there was a continuation of the rise of the modern, urban, capital-intensive dimensions of the economy; the groups in control of these advanced. In sectorial terms the big gainers were agro-industry, finance, commerce, hydrocarbons and to some extent construction. Finally, there was an obvious regional bias toward the eastern provinces and especially Santa Cruz.

In some ways, the outstanding fact of the 1970s was the decline of the mining sector. There were many factors at work but one of the most crucial was the state's fiscal policies. As we mentioned above, for over twenty years the central state had been draining resources from traditional agriculture and mining. The critical factor in regard to mining was, as we will show below, taxes. The point for now is that neither the state nor the private component of the mining sector was a big winner in this period. This calls further into question the common view that within the dominant capitalist class the lead group was the cohort of private mine owners who in Bolivia are referred to as the owners of medium-size mines. Although this group gained relative to workers and peasants, it did not fare so well relative to other sectors of the economy.

The Banzer Regime in Perspective

It would be useful at this point to try to bring the preceding political and economic narratives together in an interpretation of the Banzer regime and its significance in the developing pattern of the contemporary Bolivian political economy. Throughout this chapter we have presented the period as one that saw both a culmination and exaggeration of some basic tendencies built into the process of the political economy set in motion by the revolution of 1952.

From our perspective a key point is that although the process has both a political and an economic face, the principal problem since the revolution has been political. Specifically, it has been a problem of forging and institutionalizing a political formula or regime that could sustain a particular model of development and the cost allocations inherent in it, as well as provide stable links between the society and a state that is the central manager of the development process. In this sense a political formula has two dimensions: a pact of domination or organization of social forces to sustain particular governments and their policy strategies; and a regime-type or institutionalized pattern of interactions between state and society that confers legitimacy on the state, the governments that speak for it, and broad models of development.

In the revolutionary process the original, main-line MNR projected a development model based upon a broadly distributionist state-led capitalist pattern, e.g., populist state capitalism. At the same time it projected and partially implemented a political formula based upon a reading of the Mexican experience. It sought to ground governmental and state power in a pact of domination formed by a multiclass coalition of the urban middle class, workers, and peasants. The populist pact was to be given institutional coherence in a corporatist regime based on a single hegemonic political party that would simultaneously link state and society and incorporate on an ongoing basis the key social sectors of the pact into the regime so as both to legitimate and sustain it.

By the late 1950s it was evident that the MNR's political formula was unraveling. The reasons were many, but two stand out. First, the cost allocations inherent in the state capitalist model rent the unity of the populist coalition. Labor was alienated from the process and the MNR was increasingly incapable of serving as a vehicle to incorporate labor into a new regime type. As a result, labor—led by the miners—came to focus primarily on the COB, which in turn adopted an aggressively defensive posture toward the MNR and subsequent governments bent on pushing an antipopulist state capitalist model. Second, at the same time the MNR began to fragment into a congeries of personalistic factions led by ambitious party subchiefs. Behind that was a political dynamic that has been crucial in Bolivia for most of the century, namely, job-faction politics. This reality is rooted in the peculiarly dependent urban middle class (dependent on wages, salaries, and fees) produced by the primary-product export pattern of delayed development in Bolivia, and in the fact that because a broad spectrum of job-producing private sector firms was lacking, the state has been the main source of economic and status support for the urban middle class. As a result public employment has always been a commodity circulated mainly through a dynamic of intraelite "ins"-and-"outs" politics.

This underlying dynamic was actually heightened by the MNR, owing to the increase in the salience of the state after the revolution and by the fact that given its hegemonic ambitions, the MNR converted itself into the "only game in town" as far as job and patronage distribution was concerned. Furthermore, the MNR did not constitute itself as an elite vanguard party but opened its doors to all willing to profess party loyalty. The upshot was that the party absorbed the intraelite-faction dynamic into itself, undermining the capacity of the top leadership to control the organization. Whatever else it was, the MNR (as other parties before and since) became an organization with the instrumentalist purpose of distributing the resources of the central state among its members. This function all but forced the organization to divide into a loosely knit farrago of personalist factions formed around party chiefs, subchiefs, and their respective party clienteles.

This dynamic had other long-term consequences. First, it built into the system a party-mediated stimulus toward steady expansion in the size and functions of the state so as to add to the store of distributable patronage. This in turn pressed the state to increase its extraction of resources to maintain and expand the state apparatus. At the same time the centrifugal tendencies introduced into the MNR were imported into the state, pieces of which were captured by competing personalistic factions within the party. This situation began to undercut the capacity of the state to govern. Moreover, because the state's capacity to grow enough to meet the patronage demands of all the factions was limited, the logic of "ins" and "outs" assured that the party began to generate anti-MNR government opposition from within itself.

The cost allocation realities of the development model destroyed the populist coalition and all but negated the ability of the MNR to realize its corporatist project of incorporating key social sectors into a party-mediated pact of domination. Simultaneously clientelistic faction politics undermined the ability of the MNR to support MNR governments charged with administering a managerial state, and converted the party into an instrumentality to assault the state's resources. Both dynamics came together in the 1960s to diminish the MNR-controlled state's capacity to govern, and in 1964, led to the overthrow of the Paz government, which by that time was mainly based on factions.

The coup of 1964 was, in our view, a result of the multiple political failures of the MNR, failures that created a vacuum at the level of the central state, which all but forced the military to become the political pivot between the state and an increasingly fragmented civil society. The Barrientos government continued to push the state capitalist model. Barrientos also sought to reconstitute a panoply of political institutions to legitimate a new regime and to build a new party-focused coalition to undergird his regime. Barrientos, however, was unable to institutionalize his regime and his civil party front turned out to be little more than a degenerated version of the same faction politics that plagued the MNR. Lacking support links to civil society, Barrientos was forced to rely more and more on the military both to underwrite his hold on power and to enforce the policy implications of the state capitalist model. In spite of the 1966 elections his government ended up as little more than a personalistic military-based authoritarian regime.

Like the MNR before, the Barrientos regime was to a degree successful in pushing an economic strategy but a failure in terms of finding a stable political formula. Indeed, we argue that during his tenure a crucial process of institutional decomposition took hold at the level of formal governmental institutions and at the level of party infrastructure. Under Barrientos the state was being detached from and set against civil society. A most important development was that the more the military became central to governance the more it began to be penetrated by the factionalistic politics of civil society. This reality began to eat away at the institutional coherence of the armed forces and turn the military into a set of factions, each aimed at controlling and distributing to itself the resources of the state.

The Banzer regime was in a sense a direct descendant of the Barrientos and the later MNR governments. Again under Banzer we see a forceful imposition of state capitalism, with a notable failure to create a viable political formula. Politically, the tendencies of the previous governments were reasserted and exaggerated during the 1970s. The results were to have even more serious consequences for the coherence of both the state and society in Bolivia.

At first, Banzer sought to create a mixed civilian and military government pointed toward some ultimate constitutionalization of central authority in an executive-focused corporatist regime. He wanted to undergird his regime with a pact of domination built around an alliance of private sector business interests, the urban middle class, and in theory the peasant groups that had backed Barrientos. Owing to the cost implications of the state capitalist model, the emerging authoritarian regime was oriented toward the repressive exclusion of organized labor and, as it turned out, the traditional peasantry as well. Although the government was able forcefully to target exclusions, it was again unable to organize its putative support groups in a manner sufficient to sustain a formalized regime.

In many respects, the Banzer regime was part of the general trend toward Right-oriented authoritarian regimes that developed in Latin America during the 1960s and 1970s. Moreover, the regime at some levels had some of the characteristics of what many analysts viewed as a new type of authoritarianism dubbed the bureaucratic authoritarian regime. The regime was based at least in part on an alliance between a development-oriented military and young technocrats drawn from civil society. Under this group Bolivia was set firmly back on the state capitalist path. As in Brazil and other countries, the regime assured the state capitalist model by forcefully excluding the Left and organized labor from political participation and by less-than-gentle imposition of the costs of the model on labor and the huge traditional Indian peasantry. At the same time private sector entrepreneurial interests had enhanced access to the regime; they and the urban middle class were the main beneficiaries of the development that occurred.

The resemblance to the bureaucratic authoritarian regime type, however, was superficial. One of the hallmarks of such a regime is that it develops as a bureaucratized entity based on an institutionalized military, and has a relatively coherent sense of mission. This was hardly the case in Bolivia under Banzer. Indeed, one of the ironies was that even as Bolivia experienced economic development, it simultaneously regressed politically. If political development, at the least, involves the articulation and coordination of a variety of modern institutions, Bolivia in the 1970s actually went through a process of political decay. In a sense that process, which began in the early 1960s, was completed in the 1970s under Banzer—a fact that is crucial to understanding the immense difficulties Bolivia faces now in trying to build a democratic system.

At the beginning Banzer sought to base his regime on three pillars of support: the private sector represented by key appointments to his cabinet; the military; and a seemingly grand alliance between the center Right of the MNR, led by Paz, and the party's oldest and most bitter rival, the Falange Socialista Boliviana (FSB). Aside from the military, the coalition seemed to give the regime a stable set of links into the civilian society through the nation's two most important political parties.

By 1974 Banzer had ousted both parties and was basing his regime on the military. Behind the collapse of the coalition were some important realities. In dealing with the parties, Banzer discovered that they were rump factions that represented little more than cliques whose primary purpose was to lay claim to public sector jobs. Moreover, in those circumstances, the party elites were the intermediaries in the patronage flow and thereby built their own support, which was then rendered to Banzer only indirectly. As always, party factions not cut into the action split from the main body and went over to the opposition. In sum, while they drained resources, the parties offered little by way of support and actually helped produce opposition.

In ousting the parties, Banzer eliminated the middlemen and centralized in his own hands the patronage flow. In so doing, he affirmed that beneath the surface the primary mode of rule in Bolivia lay in the Byzantine manipulation of clientelistic networks, networks that were rooted in the fundamentally dependent urban middle class, which continued to look to the state as the primary base of its well-being.[19] The logic of clientelism was such that the Banzer regime, despite its modern veneer, was for all practical purposes a contemporary version of the traditional mode of rule that Weber called patrimonialism.[20]

Bolivia during this period could well be described as a neopatrimonial society pursuing economic growth in a state-centric neomercantilistic economic model. The point is that both political and economic life came to revolve around the central state, not as a public sector expressing some abstract concept of nationhood but as the particularistic extension of an executive power expressed through a modern quasiprince, Banzer.

Neopatrimonialism brought with it a set of political dynamics and pattern of cleavages that cut through and at times subsumed more modern dynamics, specifically, personalistic patron-client dynamics that often were more important than the modern dynamics of group, class, and ideology—or at least as important. This is not to say that modern dynamics did not exist but, rather, that Bolivia epitomized the so-called living-museum effect wherein modern and traditional are blended into dense and complex patterns of cleavage and conflict. Under Banzer traditional neopatrimonial dynamics more often than not provided the core logic and set the tone for the entire system.

The complexities of the situation stand out in Banzer's relations with the private sector and the relationship between the state and civil society in the state capitalist formula. In the first instance it is clear that Banzer in a sense guaranteed some mode of capitalism in Bolivia, and the private sector surely benefited during his tenure, but it would be inaccurate to see his regime as dominated by some bourgeoisie of national and international interests or as expressing the coherent interests of any real capitalist class in Bolivia. The fact is that at that stage a capitalist class in Bolivia was at best incipient. And, Banzer built relations not with a class as such but with individuals and groups who became his personal retainers. Elements of the private sector profited because of their personal access to the executive and/or by paying bribes, commissions, and other patrimonial "fees" for contracts, concessions, low-interest loans, and so on. As the years went by Banzer engaged somewhat less than the enthusiastic support of the "capitalist class" as such; first, because his style of rule undercut the ability of the private sector to form and act as a class, and second, because the private sector elements not tied into the patronage nets came to resent and oppose Banzer. In the relations of the state to the private sector the theme was similar to that which came to pervade all aspects of Bolivian society; modern abstract modes of binding large numbers into entities capable of acting as units gave way to division and particularism that reflected the dynamics of personalized patron-clientelism.

Owing to his neopatrimonial style of rule, Banzer continued the process of deinstitutionalization. Most particularly, clientelism continued to invade the military, sapping its institutional vitality and undermining its organizational coherence. In a sense the military paid dearly for its role of repressing politics in civil society by importing societal politics into the institution. The point is that by the mid-1970s Banzer ruled almost exclusively by manipulating alliances of civil and military cliques. As a result, his hold on power was always tenuous, and he constantly had to fend off the coup plots of rival civil-military factions.

The neopatrimonial mode of rule also engendered contradictions in the state capitalist economic model. What developed in Bolivia was a kind of prebendal capitalism wherein, although individual capitalists benefited, the state was increasingly out of sync with the logic of modern capitalism.

Given the clientelistic dynamics of neopatrimonial rule, internal logic pushes any such regime in two directions: (1) the ruler must constantly expand his support networks, and, therefore, constantly expand the pool of patronage resources; and (2) the central state becomes the main patrimonial resource, and increasingly the executive tends to view the state not as a public phenomenon but as a personal resource to maintain his rule. Hence, there is a built-in tendency for the state to expand in size and increase the range of functions it performs, and at the same time the behavior of the state comes more to reflect the personal political needs of the ruler and his entourage than to conform to any modern framework of rational legal norms.

Thus, although the state in a real sense guarantees the possibility of capitalism by "disciplining" labor and imposing the costs of capital accumulation on it and the popular sectors, the state's own maintenance needs inevitably bring it into conflict with the capitalist sector over appropriation of the surplus produced. Moreover, the irrationalities introduced into the behavior of the state by the logic of neopatrimonial rule create problems for the capitalist sectors because they introduce unpredictability into the system and raise the costs of doing business in a variety of ways.[21]

The central point is that owing to the voracious maintenance needs of the neopatrimonial mode of rule, the state all but of necessity comes to be a parasitic reality in relation to the productive capitalist sectors and civil society as a whole. Moreover, the components of the capitalist sector and civil society that receive the prebends of the state likewise become part of the parasitic weight of an increasingly arbitrary state. In a context like

Bolivia neopatrimonialism introduces a predatory dimension into the behavior of the state by way of the demands on societal largesse by the patrimonial ruler and his ever-growing entourage.

This pattern came to pervade the relationship between state and society during the seven-year rule of Hugo Banzer. Under Banzer the state grew in size, weight, and economic impact to a degree unprecedented in Bolivian history. The public bureaucracy swelled from some 66,000 employees in 1970 to close to 171,000 by 1977. At the same time new agencies and public corporations proliferated rapidly to some 120 central government agencies and some 50 public enterprises. The state came to dwarf all other sectors and activities combined.

The conflict between the state and the private sector was manifested first in the area of mining. A number of important medium-sized private mine companies complained of a confiscatory tax system through which mining (a key productive sector) was in effect subsidizing the state and other components of the private sector, particularly banking, commerce, and agro-industry in the eastern lowland departments, such as Santa Cruz de la Sierra. In 1974 the tax system had shifted against the medium-sized miners because of a tax formula based on the companies' presumed costs as defined by the state. Studies of the sector by outside experts have confirmed that indeed the tax system was confiscatory and discouraged reinvestment in the sector.[22] The tax issue drove a deep wedge between Banzer and many of the medium-sized mine owners, who began to oppose him and raise question about the viability of a military-based state capitalist model. The issue raised by the mining sector spoke to even deeper dynamics at work during this period.

Since the early days of the revolution Bolivian governments had pursued a strategy of national integration, which mainly meant integrating the eastern lowlands into the nation. One effect of this was the shift of economic and political power away from the more highly populated western highlands, which were home to traditional peasant agriculture and mining, to the eastern lowlands, which were increasingly home to modern agro-industry and hydrocarbons. Indeed, one could argue (many have) that the policies of state capitalist national development in Bolivia involved a shift of capital and resources from the highlands to the lowlands tantamount to a predatory decapitalization of the former in favor of the latter.

In any event, in the 1970s the East, and especially Santa Cruz, emerged as a potent economic and political force. It is not at all coincidental that the uprising of 1971 began in Santa Cruz and that Banzer himself was from Santa Cruz. Moreover, a substantial amount of investment flowed to the region, especially in the form of all-but-concessionary loans. In addition, Santa Cruz, led by a powerful private-sector-based civic committee, was able to capture directly a significant amount of the profits generated by hydrocarbon production in the department, thereby diminishing the resources going to the national coffers.

Whatever the complex realities of transfers among regions, the rise of Santa Cruz introduced a powerful and discordant strain of regionalism into the national political scene. Furthermore, the Santa Cruz civic committee became a potent example for other departments, whose similar committees were soon pressing their own demands on the central state. The neo-patrimonial ruler sought to manipulate and contain the new regionalism through the same prebendal clientelism he used to deal with the myriad other particularisms pulling at the national core.

The Banzer regime, then, was not simply a derivative phenomenon of a pact of domination having to do with a powerful, singular capitalist class of national and international interests rooted in the private sector. There was no singular hegemonic class in Bolivia, nor has there been one since the revolution of 1952. Indeed, we argue that class dynamics was not the singular force of Bolivian politics in this period. Class conflict dynamics existed but alongside and often submerged in the dynamics of competition among shifting patron-client networks and an emerging layer of racially tinged interregional conflict. The layers of conflict overlapped and created an extremely complex reality, but all increasingly viewed the central state as an alien entity to be penetrated and used, and/or to be defended from.

Because of the decomposition of the central institutions of Bolivian public life as well as of the infrastructure of political parties, the state came to revolve around an executive apparatus that was set apart from and above civil society, which itself was much fragmented. The main mode of linking society and the state was the extremely fluid lines of personalized patron-client links that emanated from the neo-patrimonial executive, who spent most of his time and energy trying to hold onto office. The result was a large and quasi-parasitic state that in practical terms was weak and incapable of giving direction to a society that itself was suffering from the debilitating effects of multiple centrifugal tendencies. In sum, Bolivia had arrived at a point where a weak state was antagonistically set off against an equally weak society, a situation that was to call into question the capacity of Bolivia to create a central decision making center capable of maintaining national cohesion. This lamentable reality was to become more than evident in the next few years.

Notes

1. José Medardo Navia, "Análisis de la estructura social en Bolivia," *Revista de Cultura*, no. 7 (Cochabamba, 1983): 86.

2. Most analysts of Bolivian politics tend to view the process in purely class terms. We argue here that class is only one tendency in a more complex process. For one recent example of a class perspective, in English, see James Dunkerley, *Rebellion in the Veins* (London: Verso Editions, 1984).

3. The issue of regionalism has recently become a major topic in Bolivia. The principal original work remains José Luis Roca, *Fisionomía del regionalismo boliviano* (La Paz: Los Amigos del Libro, 1980). An excellent recent discussion of the issue is Fernando Calderón G. and Roberto Laserna, *El poder de las regiones* (Cochabamba: CERES, 1983).

4. The complexities of the internal dynamics of the military are treated at length in Gary Prado Salmón, *Poder y Fuerzas Armadas, 1949-1982* (La Paz: Los Amigos del Libro, 1984).

5. A presentation of the facts from the protestors' point of view is *La masacre del valle*, 3rd ed. (La Paz: Asamblea Permanente de Derechos Humanos de Bolivia, 1979).

6. These texts are republished in the rich and revealing book by one of the leaders of the generational group: Gary Prado, *Poder y Fuerzas Armadas, 1949-1982* (La Paz: Los Amigos del Libro), pp. 370-73.

7. The concept of bureaucratic authoritarianism was developed in the important works of Guillermo O'Donnell, like *Modernization and Bureaucratic-Authoritarianism: Studies in South American Politics* (Berkeley: University of California, Institute of International Studies, 1973), and "Corporatism and the Question of the State" in *Authoritarianism and Corporatism in Latin America*, ed. James M. Malloy (Pittsburgh: University of Pittsburgh Press, 1977), pp. 47-87.

8. The best source in English on economic policy in this period is the essays in Jerry R. Ladman, ed. *Modern-Day Bolivia: Legacy of the Revolution and Prospects for the Future* (Tempe: Arizona State University, Center for International Studies). A hostile but very good analysis in Spanish is Pablo Ramos Sánchez, *Siete años de economía Boliviana* (La Paz: Editorial Puerta del Sol, 1982). See also Susan Eckstein, "Transformation of a Revolution from Below: Bolivia and International Capital," *Comparative Studies in Society and History* 25 (January 1983): 105-35.

9. James W. Wilkie, "U.S. Foreign Policy and Economic Assistance in Bolivia, 1948-1976." in *Modern-Day Bolivia: Legacy of the Revolution and Prospects for the Future*, ed. Jerry R. Ladman (Tempe: Arizona State University, Center For Latin American Studies, 1982).

10. G. Richard Fletcher, "Santa Cruz: A Study of Economic Growth in Bolivia," *Inter American Economic Affairs* 29, no. 2 (Autumn 1975): 23-41.

11. Jerry R. Ladman and Ronald L. Tennermeir, "The Political Economy of Agricultural Credit: The Case of Bolivia," *American Journal of Agricultural Economics* 63 (February 1981): 66-72.

12. The "achievements" of the state in this period were celebrated in a vanity publication by the Banzer government: *Libro blanco de realizaciones del gobierno de las Fuerzas Armadas: Bolivia, 1971-78* (La Paz, 1978).

13. José Romero Loza, *Algodón en Bolivia* (La Paz: Los Amigos del Libro, 1978).

14. For a general discussion of questions of income distribution, see Susan Eckstein, "The Impact of Revolution on Social Welfare in Latin America," *Theory and Society* 10 (January 1982): 43-94.

15. Flores C. Gonzalo, "Estado, políticas agrarias y luchas campesinas: Revisión de

una decada en Bolivia," in *Bolivia la fuerza histórica del campesinado*, ed. F. Calderón and J. Dandler (La Paz: Centro de Estudios de la Realidad Económica y Social, 1984), pp. 447-545.

16. Richard A. Musgrave, *Fiscal Reform in Bolivia* (Cambridge: Harvard Law School, 1981), ch. 5.

17. José Medardo Navia, "Análisis de la estructura social en Bolivia," *Revista de Cultura* (Cochabamba, 1983), p. 86.

18. The relevant chapters in Jerry R. Ladman, *Modern-Day Bolivia: Legacy of the Revolution and Prospects for the Future* (Tempe: Arizona State University, Center for Latin American Studies, 1982), and Susan Eckstein and Frances Hagopian, "The Limits of Industrialization in the Less Developed World: Bolivia," *Economic Development and Cultural Change* 32 (October 1983): 64-95.

19. For an excellent discussion of the middle class and the state bureacracy, see María Isabel Arauco, "Acción social de los sectores medios: El caso de la burocracia estatal," in *Crisis, democracia y conflicto social*, ed. Roberto Laserna (Cochabamba: CERES, 1985), pp. 165-202.

20. Max Weber, *Economy and Society*, edited by Günther Roth and Claus Wettich, (New York: Bedminster Press, 1968), vol. 3.

21. The later dissatisfaction of the private sector with the weight and role of the state was articulated by the CEPB in numerous publications. For a compilation, see Confederación de Empresarios Privados de Bolivia, *Pensamiento de la empresa privada Boliviana* (La Paz, 1981).

22. Malcolm Gillis et al., *Taxation and Mining: Nonfuel Minerals in Bolivia and Other Countries* (Cambridge, Mass.: Ballinger, 1978).

4

The Tortuous Transition to Democracy

As a result of Banzer's call for elections in July of 1978, Bolivia again moved with the tide of the region and began a transition from a de facto authoritarian regime toward a formalized democratic system.[1] The transition turned out to be a tumultuous process of lurching from elections to coups d'état to elections that lasted for four years. Behind this tragic spectacle was the fact that once initiated, the transition set off such a rapid and dramatic decompression of power that the capacity to invest the state with an effective decision-making capacity all but disappeared. There existed no group, class, or institution that could step into and fill the power vacuum at the center. Over the next few years the chief political problem was to find a formula to reconstitute some mode of decision making such that the myriad economic problems facing the nation at the least could be confronted if not resolved.

The patrimonial nature of the system was confirmed when, after Banzer announced his intention to call elections, the situation got out of hand. Neo patrimonial rulers have power only when they actively monopolize it; a patrimonial lame duck is extremely lame indeed. Over the years Banzer had slowly lost the ability to manipulate the levers of power, a fact that was ratified when he called elections under pressure. The immediate reason was that he had no effective control over the military. However, the military itself also quickly demonstrated that as an institution it was not capable of filling the vacuum and mastering the situation. Unlike the military sectors of Brazil and Peru, which largely orchestrated the transitions to democracy, the Bolivian military could neither set the rules of the game nor influence the outcome.

As power decompressed at the patrimonial center, it dissipated into the myriad factions, parties, regional committees, and classes trying to achieve some formal control of the state. None, however, was able to provide a base sufficient to underwrite a decision-making center capable of defining new policy initiatives. Indeed, the logic of the situation quickly forced all groups into a defensive stance more oriented toward blocking and vetoing any policy initiatives that might spring from rival groups or coalitions. This dynamic created immobilism at the center, especially with regard to economic policy.

Over the next few years Bolivia's political leaders dreamed up a bevy of legal and constitutional formulas to rationalize various temporary solutions to the power impasse. Aside from any long-term ideological matters, the issue of democracy was bound up with the more immediate but difficult questions of who was going to hold power and how. Formal democracy represented but one potential procedural answer to the question of how. For most of the key groups and individuals the main issue was not democracy but access to power.

The dynamics of the years between 1978 and 1982 demonstrate some important aspects of the values and behavior of Bolivia's political elites of all stripes. The political elites backed democracy not out of any positive commitment to democracy as a system in itself but as a way, perhaps temporary, to open up access to power and the circulation of state patronage after seven years of authoritarian monopoly by Banzer and his entourage. For some, access meant solidifying class and group gains or the lifting of imposed burdens; for others, it meant pressing the interests of specific regions or economic sectors; for still others, it meant circulating jobs and patronage by substituting one central patrimonial patron for another.

Although a democratic electoral procedure opened up and theoretically rationalized the distribution of power, it was for most, if not all of the players, a second-best option.[2] Over the next four years just about every main faction and group demonstrated its willingness to back a coup if to do so seemed a quicker, surer way to power, or if it was likely to lose in a democratic contest. Votes were still only one political currency in Bolivia, and far from the most valued; all sides were inclined at a moment's notice to switch to the currency of bullets.

Fragmentation in the military was due to many factors. During the 1970s the Bolivian military, like other Latin American militaries, sought to assert the control of the state over civil society by actively repressing the traditional political dynamics of civil society as expressed in interest groups, class organizations, and political parties. The price paid by the military for such activities was to import into itself those conflict dynamics, dynamics that were fundamentally subversive of its hierarchical structure.

In addition, the military had grown fat during the 1970s as the officer corps directly benefited from the expansion of the role and functions of the state and the prebendal logic of Banzer's neopatrimonial system. Officers became accustomed to the powers and perquisites of state offices and managerial positions in public corporations. Many had come to expect at least one salary-generating position other than their military position. This fact brought petty jealousies and rancors over job politics into the officer corps as well as the rest of the bureaucratized middle class.

The most discordant element introduced into the military throughout the 1960s and 1970s was the corruption bred by prebendal patrimonialism. Patrimonialism generates a system of distribution within the state that has a marked tendency toward the private appropriation of public office and the surplus-extracting capabilities of the office, both legal (taxes, fees, etc.) and illegal (bribes, kickbacks, etc.) From the patrimonial ruler on down the modern distinction between private and public, which is the basis of modern notions of corruption, is blurred and distorted. Indeed, in the modern version of tax farming the attraction of public office becomes not the salary and formal perks (which are often small) but the potentiality for converting the extractive capabilities of the office into private gain. As one Bolivian politician once put it: public office becomes a license to steal. Be that as it may, corruption was a part of the military during its long dominance of national political life and particularly during the Banzerato.

The collapse of coherence within the military was the final manifestation of the decomposition of the entire institutional structure of Bolivian public life. The collapse came at a time of renewed social and political mobilization that posed the recurrent problem of fashioning institutions capable of shaping the new demands and energies surging toward the state from civil society. Bereft of a coherent institutional structure and lacking an organized capacity to deploy force, the central state was at that point extremely weak in relation to civil society. As the Banzer system ended, the political initiative shifted to the inchoate forces stirring in civil society after seven years of coerced quietude.

In Bolivia, as elsewhere, the transition from military-backed authoritarian rule was complicated by the economic context, which was fast becoming extremely problematic. The economic difficulties that came to the fore in the late 1970s were a product of the Banzer policies, aggravated substantially by the looming world economic crisis. The main crunch came because the exhaustion of petroleum reserves and decline in the prices for Bolivia's commodities, especially minerals, undercut the ability of the state to finance itself, supply the economy's capital needs, and service the large foreign debt.

The economic crisis demanded decisive action by the government. Moreover, the logic of state capitalism—reinforced by the policies of the International Monetary Fund and other international actors like the government of the United States, upon whom Bolivia was extremely dependent—dictated that any would-be government deal with the crisis through state-enforced austerity, which would of necessity impose hefty costs on civil society, especially the middle class, workers, and peasants. These requisites of state-centered economic management were clearly contradictory to the opening of the political system after seven years of exclusion and forced allocations of costs.

To the popular sectors of Bolivia, democratization meant first and foremost an opportunity to make up for the deprivations of the previous years. In short, the political opening meant a new wave of demands for increased consumption at the same time that the economic crisis and international actors were generating pressures to manage the crisis at least in part by containing consumption. The ultimate irony of the failure of the Banzerato was that circumstances were forcing Bolivia to attempt to form a central government capable of imposing strong economic measures on a society that was hoping democracy would lead to a regaining of lost economic ground—this when the state was extremely weak, public institutions in shambles, and civil society fragmented.

The political opening up was introducing an institutional contradiction into public life that was and is challenging the capacity of Bolivian politicians to engage in constitutional engineering. If Bolivia was to shift into a formal democratic mode, a government would have to be generated by means of political parties. Once in place, such a government would have to confront the economic situation with policies that ran counter to the logic of gaining votes and sustaining parliamentary majorities to support an executive-centered government.

In Bolivia, as elsewhere in Latin America, a contradiction was looming between the function of state-centered economic crisis management, which fell increasingly on the executive, and the democratic function of representing civil society to the state through political parties and parliaments. The logics of the two functions ran counter to each other, a reality exacerbated by the substantial demands on state resources generated by the patronage-hungry parties themselves. The situation carried a built-in tendency toward an antagonistic split between the executive and legislative authorities that threatened to diminish the capacities of the government and/or tempt the executive to dispense with the niceties of democratic procedure to avoid immobilism in regard to the economy. This contradiction was to become a more or less permanent problem of constitutional engineering in Bolivia.

An institutionalized relationship between civil society and the state was obviously crucial in sorting out these problems. If one looks at Bolivian civil society in the late 1970s and 1980s, through the confusion three basic lines of ongoing conflict stand out, each with its own institutional expression. The first line of conflict was the long-standing intra-elite struggle to circulate state-based jobs and perks, or what the Bolivians call the politics of *cargos y puestos* (jobs and positions). This dynamic has run through Bolivian politics for decades and is rooted in the dependent nature of the middle class, the fact that hard sources of wealth historically have been few and not readily transferable, and the fact that the state has been the major generator of jobs. The patrimonial nature of the Banzer regime enhanced this tendency, which was also reinforced by the state-centric model introduced by the revolution of 1952. The aggregate social expression of this dynamic is what is often called the "political class," a grouping drawn mainly, but not exclusively, from the middle class and defined by its wealth and status being derived mainly from public positions. The main institutional expression of this grouping was and is the political parties and factions. During the later Banzer years the dynamic of "ins" and "outs" was absorbed by the patrimonial nature of the regime, and the parties were thereby to some extent contained. Once the transition to the democratic regime was set in motion, however, the number of parties and factions within parties multiplied rapidly.

The second line of conflict had to do with class. The major division was between the emergent private sector interests that were beginning to take the form of a national bourgeoisie and the working class, which, led by the miners, had a long history of militancy. The peasantry constituted another potential class, but it was and is still too diverse and divided to act politically as a class or a majority fraction of a class for that matter. Class conflict was fueled by the ongoing battle over capital accumulation and cost allocations, and exacerbated by the looming economic crisis and the pressures to impose austerity programs.

Class-based political action originated in several organizations. Although private sector businesses were organized in trade associations, they were coming increasingly to express themselves politically through their principal association, the Confederación de Empresarios Privados de Bolivia (the Confederation of Bolivian Private Entrepreneurs, CEPB). Similarly, the working class was organized in functional unions, but its main political expression was through the Confederación Obrera Boliviana (COB). The peasantry at the base was organized in a myriad of local *sindicatos,* and at the national level at least three would-be class or racially focused organizations vied for leadership.

At that stage neither of the two main antagonists (CEPB and COB) articulated their political behavior primarily through political parties. Although individuals were affiliated with individual parties, the CEPB and the COB operated independently, and no single party or group of parties could claim to speak for either class. For most of the ensuing period, both acted to press their interests directly on the state by way of the executive. The same tended to hold true *mutatis mutandis* in regard to peasant organizations. The behavior of these associations highlighted the sharp disjuncture between the dynamics of the party system and the dynamics of class and/or interest groups. That, in turn, reinforced the general problematic disjuncture between electoral and parliamentary politics and the executive-centered process of governance.

The third line of conflict was regional. Regionalism, or *patria chica,* is not new to Bolivia, but, the policies followed since 1952, which stimulated the economic and political emergence of Santa Cruz and eastern Bolivia, rekindled regionalism and added some new twists. Regionalism cut along two lines of conflict. The first was that of Camba Bolivia (Santa Cruz and the East) versus Kolla Bolivia (the Andean departments), discussed above. The second, stimulated by the success of Santa Cruz politically, was the more old-fashioned kind of zero-sum rivalry in which all departments vied with one another for resources from the state.

The main vehicle of both types of regionalism was the departmental civic committees that emerged in emulation of the extremely successful civic committee of Santa Cruz. Although ostensibly private, the Santa Cruz committee became the dominant political force in the department, where for all practical purposes, it controlled the government as well as the state-financed regional development corporation. Although the power of the other civic committees varied, it would be hard to overestimate the power of the Santa Cruz committee. The civic committees acted independently of all other political organizations, especially the parties. At most, the committees sought to impose local candidates on the national party lists and tended to treat local elected legislators as instructed regional delegates rather than party-based representatives. The committees likewise acted to press their interests on the state, in the main directly on the executive.

The structural situation confronting Bolivia in the late 1970s and early 1980s was not very propitious. The economy was entering what would be perhaps the worst crisis in the nation's history. The political system was in a state of well-advanced decay. The state, although large and formally powerful, in practical terms was an enfeebled giant lacking stable connections to the civil society it sought to hold together as a national entity. Civil society itself was fragmented into factions, groups, classes, and regions oriented toward the aggressive pursuit of particularistic interests against a state that had virtually no mechanisms to mediate and filter the demands or to temper the interrelationships among the antagonistic fragments.

The Collapse of Control

After Banzer made his announcement on November 9, events moved rapidly. It was obvious that his strategy was based on that followed by

Barrientos in 1966 when he successfully legitimated his hold on power through elections. Banzer requested that the military place him on active reserve so as to clear the legal ground for his run. And, at the same time many of the party fragments associated with his regime sought to form a new political party (Partido de Unidad Nacional, PUN) to support his candidacy.

The military high command, however, balked at his maneuver. In late November Banzer sought to reconstitute the command with men more loyal to him. Within days his inability to bend the military to his will became clear in a surprise announcement that he would not be a candidate for the presidency, ostensibly to "leave room for a younger generation of leaders."

Banzer's formal (and forced) withdrawal all but obliterated his authority and threw the system into confusion as the patrimonial core began to crumble. In an apparent attempt to recoup some degree of governmental and military unity, the high command came up with a formula in which the post of commander in chief, abolished in 1973, was resurrected and given to Banzer, and another general, Juan Pereda Asbún, was to be the presidential candidate, backed by a so-called nationalist movement.

With an apparent solution in hand, the military then sought to manage the process of a democratic opening, and for all intents and purposes to predetermine its outcome. With the announcement of elections, the ban on political parties was lifted. The ban on union activity was left intact, however, a move clearly aimed at containing the fast-reviving mine workers' federation (FSTMB) and the general labor confederation (COB). Like the generals in Peru, the Bolivian high command was trying to create a political opening while controlling social mobilization. Although the Peruvians were largely successful in this tactic, the Bolivians failed dramatically.

As Christmas of 1978 approached, the government announced a partial amnesty for political opponents in jail or exile, but almost all of the most important opposition figures, including Juan Lechín and Hernán Siles, were not among the favored. The opposition immediately charged, with reason, that the military was seeking to stage-manage the elections and permit only approved and unoffending parties and individuals to take part.

On December 28 the wives of six miners excluded from the amnesty entered the offices of the archbishop of La Paz and began a hunger strike. Their demands were unrestricted amnesty, the resumption of trade union activity, the removal of troops from the mines, and the like. The women's action proved to be critical, not so much as a primary cause of the regime's demise but as an event that ratified the regime's loss of control over the political opening. The strike quickly became the rallying point for all the opposition, which grasped that the women had maneuvered the regime into a no-win situation.[3]

The government sought to discredit the strikers by means of all the old canards but to no avail. On January 18, for all practical purposes, it gave in to the demands except that troops remained stationed in the mines. With that the lid was lifted from the Pandora's box of Bolivian politics: all of the pent-up energies, frustrations, demands, and ambitions forcibly held in check during the Banzerato burst out and literally overwhelmed the regime and the state.

The first manifestation of the new reality came from the political class. Over fifty parties made their appearance, and in subsequent years even more were formed. The array evidenced the job-hungry factionalization of the class. The sheer number demonstrated that most were mainly the expression of personal and factional ambitions, for not even the most careful hairsplitters could justify the multiplicity or even classify the parties on ideological or programmatical grounds. Most were little more than tiny cabals that were given the derisive name of taxi parties because as local wags said, they could hold their conventions in a taxi cab.[4]

The two most significant parties continued to be the MNR and FSB, both of which announced their opposition to the official candidacy of Pereda and their intention to pursue their own electoral purposes. Pereda was then forced to put together his own "political front." It was made up of segments of the private sector that had supported Banzer, the remnants of the old Barrientista group led by Tapia Frontanilla, and dissident factions from the MNR, FSB, PRA, and PIR parties. This incongruous collection was given the equally incongruous name of the Nationalist Union of the People (Unión Nacionalista del Pueblo, UNP). With the possible exception of the private sector group, which was pursuing its interests, the UNP was obviously little more than a congeries of political-class types who saw a better route to the power and perks of office with Pereda than with their previous ostensible party formations.

As the political parties tried to sort themselves out, there was a boom in the activity of worker and peasant unions. In labor union elections official government candidates were overwhelmed by the previously repressed leadership voted back into office. As on many past occasions, Juan Lechín Oquendo was reestablished as the top leader of the working class.

The situation in the traditional agrarian sector remained confused and volatile. The most important development was that any semblance of an official campesino confederation tied to the state through a military-peasant pact all but disappeared. By 1978 there were at least three rival, more or less autonomous peasant confederations. The first was the official Confederación Nacional de Campesinos (CNC) led by Oscar Céspedes. The CNC coordinated the pacto militar-campesino. The second was the Movimiento Revolucionario Tupac Katari (MRTK) led by Genaro Flores and linked to a rival union movement. Flores was himself a product of the pacto militar-campesino, but during the Ovando-Torres period he had begun a gradual shift away from the military-controlled peasant union and toward an independent peasant union (Bloque Independiente Campesino) with close ties to the COB. Flores was also part of the new peasant-campesino awareness of the legacy of Julián Apaza, otherwise known as Tupac Katari, the Indian rebel executed by the Spaniards on November 15, 1781. It was Flores who led a large group of regime-affiliated peasants away from the pacto militar-campesino in 1974 after the Masacre de Tolata. The third was the Movimiento *Indio* Tupac Katari (MITKA), led by Luciano Tapia Quisbert and Constantino Lima, a full-fledged political party. Founded in 1975, the MITKA combined the Indian-centered ideology of Fausto Reinaga and the memory of Tupac Katari. During the 1978 elections the CNC supported Pereda, the MRTK joined the UDP, and only the MITKA ran as a political party.

The leaders of the main political parties sought to overcome the fragmentation of the party system by forming broad fronts. The Left was by far the most split and produced two fronts. The most important formed around Hernán Siles Zuazo and his Left offshoot of the MNR, the MNRI, which had been founded in exile in 1971 after Paz led the main wing of the MNR into the alliance with Banzer. Called the Popular Democratic Union (Unión Democrática y Popular, UDP) it was a disparate coalition of both Marxist and non-Marxist Left groups including the Bolivian Communist Party (PCB).

The Left as a whole and the UDP in particular was at a deep level ideologically divided—beyond matters of strategy tactics, factions, and personalities. Since the revolution the Left has evolved around a tense, semiforced alliance between those identified with the populist version of the original MNR state capitalist vision and the many, more Marxist groups oriented toward some variant of state socialism. This basic division was contained when the Left was in opposition confronting a common enemy but always undermined the Left when it approached power, as was shown during the governments of Generals Ovando and Torres.

There were two relatively new groups on the Left that sought to use the elections to project their images. The Revolutionary Movement of the Left (Movimiento de Izquierda Revolucionaria, MIR) was founded in the early 1970s by young Left dissidents from a variety of groups. It had the quality of a new generation, which gave it a fresh vitality. The MIR was active in opposition to Banzer, and during those years built a popular image as a relatively pure Left alternative. Like the rest of the Left, however, the MIR was internally tense because of divisions between the more "social democratic" groups that saw themselves as the embodiment of the true revolutionary spirit of 1952 and more marxist groups oriented toward a more state socialist vision. In the late 1970s the MIR formed an important part of the Siles-led UDP.

The other potentially important new Left group was called Socialist Party No. 1 (Partido Socialista No. 1, PS—I). It was founded and led by the flamboyant maverick Marcelo Quiroga Santa Cruz, who had gained notice as a vocal opponent of Barrientos and then as a visible minister during the two military populist governments. Quiroga, as usual, chose to go it alone in the elections. The fact is that his party was essentially a leftist version of the traditional personalist-type party so common to Bolivia.

To the right the situation was also somewhat confused. In addition to nationalist-front-backed General Pereda, the other old war-horse of 1952, Victor Paz Estenssoro, occupied a main leadership position. Siles had come to stand for the populist version of the MNR, Paz was by then firmly identified with the more antipopulist state capitalist strain of the MNR. Aside from any ideological or strategic differences, the two titans had developed a personal enmity and this fact, along with personal ambition, brought to naught the dreams of some to reconstitute the original broad-spectrum MNR. Paz had succeeded in pulling together most strains of the MNR into a group called the historic MNR or MNRH. For electoral purposes, he overcame another enmity and formed a front with yet another old MNR figure, Walter Guevara Arce, who since the 1960s has led an MNR offshoot group called the Authentic Revolutionary Party, or PRA.

Neither the campaign nor the election of 1978 did much to clarify the situation politically. Perhaps the most significant feature of the campaign was the hapless attempts of the divided military to orchestrate the process. When the polling took place on July 9, Pereda predictably claimed victory, but his claim rang false in the face of the obvious massive fraud that had taken place. Popular revulsion was so intense that Pereda was forced to call on the electoral court to sort out the charges and countercharges by all sides and deal with the fact that there had been recorded some 50,000 more votes than eligible registrants.[5]

Banzer sought to rise above the scandal by declaring that on August 6 he would turn over the government as planned, but unless the mess was cleared up he would give it to a military junta. Pereda and his civilian backers, seeing their chances for power slipping away, sought to mount a coup d'état. The confusion and fragmentation in the military immediately became patent. Although he was far from in control of the military, Pereda did succeed in getting the important garrisons of Cochabamba and Santa Cruz to back the rising he announced on July 20 from the city of Santa Cruz. Banzer attempted to resist the coup but was unable to turn up sufficient backing in the military. His fabled power had all but evaporated.

In the face of Pereda's threats to bomb the presidential palace, Banzer capitulated, and after a tearful farewell speech turned over the presidency to the man who some months before had been seen as his handpicked successor and puppet.

In some ways, the coup of 1978 was an unremarkable event but it did highlight some important features of the evolving political scene. It exposed the advancing disunity of the military, and marked the second time in less than a decade that control of the central government was determined by an action mounted in the provinces. Likewise, for the second time in less than a decade, the civil-military base of the coup was the capital of emergent eastern Bolivia, Santa Cruz.

In retrospect, it is clear that the Pereda government was little more than a footnote in the unfolding political process. Civil resistance to the government was widespread on all fronts especially labor and the patronage-hungry political parties. And, more important, Pereda's hold over the military was tenuous; the generational group was in all but open rebellion.

Following in Banzer's steps, Pereda tried to give his government some cachet by appointing prominent individuals from the private sector to key economic posts. He also recruited individuals from a variety of party groups and factions. However, the appointments again reflected patrimonial links to individuals and not structural links to class, party or regional power groupings. In short, they did not really forge a pact of power to underwrite his or any government. Like Banzer in his later years Pereda was epiphenomenal to the real forces shaping power in Boliva.

One significant characteristic of the new situation began to manifest itself: sharp awareness of the economic crisis. At that point the major outlines of the crisis were declining growth rates, an increasing trade imbalance, a mounting current-account deficit, and a large foreign debt, a notable portion of which was relatively short-term, high-interest notes. Still, the government all but announced that it did not perceive itself as having the political muscle to develop the kinds of austerity policies being called for by international lending agencies such as the World Bank or the IMF. As a result, no steps were taken toward that end, the crisis was for all practical purposes ignored. This nonapproach to economic crisis was to be typical of most subsequent governments in this turbulent period. Not surprisingly, the crisis worsened and became a permanent constraining feature in the policy environment of the governments.

Pereda never got control of the situation, and on November 23-24, 1978, the generational group led a coup and installed General David Padilla in the presidency. Finally, the generational group had arrived at power, and a number of its prominent members who were mainly lieutenant or full colonels, such as Gary Prado, Raúl Lopez Leytón, Ólvis Arias, and

Rolando Saravia held cabinet posts.[6] The new government explicitly defined itself as transitional, announced elections for July 1, 1979, and promised not to run an official candidate. Padilla made no real effort to control the situation politically, instead focusing his attention on designing the upcoming elections.

More important, the Padilla government actually announced that no new economic measures would be taken, let alone any of the austerity measures that the IMF and World Bank had been pushing. Its reasons were the same as Pereda's, namely, its political weakness. At a deeper level Padilla and the generational group were explicitly institutionalists (persons who favored the interests of the military as such over ideological or personal considerations), and it is clear that they feared that such measures would reap further disdain for a military that was already less than popular. Hence, in spite of its prodemocratic and—to some—populist image, the Padilla government, like those of Pereda and Banzer in his last years, was more than willing to leave the hard decisions on how to deal with the crisis, largely produced by the military-backed Banzerato, to some future civilian government. In sum, many in the military were content to seek to cut their losses and duck all responsibility for the economic crisis or its resolution.

The lack of governmental action on either the political or economic fronts had some serious consequences. One was the obvious fear in the private sector that labor was making too much political and therefore de facto economic headway, and that this might be accentuated in an open democratic system. Hence, there were concerns raised by some about re-democratization. More significant was that the top private sector organization, the CEPB, began to organize itself to become the chief political expression of the private sector. Finally, there began an increasingly open and conflictual dialogue between the CEPB and the COB, both of which sought to press their demands and interests directly upon a self-declared lame duck government in nominal charge of a debilitated state.

One of the more important acts of the government was its aggressive support of construction of a large metallurgical plant in the locality of Karachipampa in the Department of Potosí. Karachipampa was backed particularly by the generational group, which came to be called, somewhat less than fondly, "los Karachipampas." The term was pejorative because people pointed out then that Karachipampa would be a large, costly, inefficient white elephant—and it later proved to be just that. In addition, there were public charges of illegal enrichment on the part of some generational officers and others.

Implementation of the Karachipampa project revealed that whatever its disputes with Banzer, the generational group shared his fundamental approach to the role of the state and the public sector in the economy. Indeed it demonstrated that the military as a whole was predisposed toward the state side of the state capitalist approach to development pushed by Banzer. This "statist" bias was not lost on the private sector, especially those parts of it that were pushing for a rollback of the state in favor of the private sector.

One can argue that by at least that point the private sector began to find itself in a kind of dilemma. On the one hand, many in the private sector clearly feared that an open democratic system might lead to the dominance of labor and the Left, which could threaten the interests of the private sector if not its very existence. On the other hand, the military, which in the early 1970s had been the private sector's main line of defense from the Left, was unable to formulate a policy to deal with the increasingly grave economic crisis and, furthermore, had a distinct statist bent that was also at odds with what at least some segments of the private sector saw as their long-term sectorial interests.

If we take a long view of the 1970s we can see it as an important gestation as well as learning period for the private sector and the rising bourgeoisie. There is little doubt that the Banzer rising of 1971 was aimed at, among other things, protecting the capitalist side of the state capitalist model from the perceived revolutionary threat of the Left under Ovando and Torres. Moreover, the antipopulist policies of the Banzer government emphasized capital accumulation over popular consumption, and its consequent allocations of costs and gains favored the private sector. Finally, many components of the private sector clearly were effectively created and nurtured by the state under all state-capitalist-oriented governments from the MNR in the late 1950s through Banzer. Capitalism in Bolivia was produced by the state and the nascent bourgeoisie began as a dependent creature of the state.

By the late 1970s segments of the private sector had begun to realize that there was a down side to the state capitalist model and the policies pursued by governments backed by the statist-oriented military. As we noted, the problems first emerged in the medium mining sector, but later the realization began to surface that once the threat from the Left was under control, there was a built-in contradiction between a state driven by the need to generate surplus to maintain its ever-expanding apparatus and a private sector oriented toward the private appropriation of surplus. Thus, voices calling for a rollback of the state and an opening of the economy to "market forces" began to be heard. At that point, however, the realization was only beginning and the private sector was in fact confused and divided over what attitude to take toward the military, the state, and issues such as democracy versus authoritarianism.[7]

Elections and Instability

The electoral process of 1979 was in many ways similar to that of 1978, but there were also some new developments that began to give a more coherent shape to the political forces that would contend over the next few years. The electoral court tried to diminish the complexity of the process by introducing a simplified ballot. It also tried to reduce the number of contending parties by establishing fines for those that did not receive a minimum of 50,000 votes, a maneuver that failed because of pressure by minority parties like the PS-I. Fifty-seven parties declared their intention to participate.

As in the previous year, the multiplicity of parties forced the leaders of the political class to form broad electoral fronts. In 1979 three fronts, led by three long-prominent personalities, dominated. Siles weighed in with an expanded UDP, the three major components of which were the MNRI; the MIR, which provided the vice-presidential candidate, Jaime Paz Zamora; and the PCB. Victor Paz likewise formed a front called the MNR Alliance, or AMNR; it embraced components of the Christian Democrats, an off-shoot of a major peasant-oriented party, and the Peking-line Communists of the PCML. Hugo Banzer also assembled a front, but the main base of his candidacy was a new party formed in 1979. Called Acción Democrática Nacionalista (ADN) and hoisting the banner "Orden, Paz y Trabajo" (order, peace, and work), the party was to prove significant in the political equation. The rest of the parties, with the exception of the PS-I, were not of much consequence in the election.

In retrospect, the formation of ADN was a major political development. At one level the ADN was a classic personalist party. Banzer and his former retainers created it not only to contest the presidency but also to elect a bloc of deputies and senators who could defend him in Congress from the legal actions *(juicio de responsibilidades)* being brought against him and his government by former opposition groups. The major suit amounted to an attempt at post hoc impeachment and would be a crucial political variable over the next months.

On another level the formation of the ADN reflected the actions of a number of individuals from the middle class and the private sector who were looking for a political vehicle ideologically differentiated from the various factions of the MNR and the Left parties. Men like Eudoro Galindo recognized that dominant personalities or caudillos were still decisive in Bolivian politics and therefore were drawn to Banzer as their best shot at the presidency. As a result, there were many ADN cadres who, although they backed Banzer, were working to turn the party into an institutional force that would outlast the fortunes of Banzer or any other individual. Hence, the party had a significant modern component that sought to go beyond being a classic personalist party. From the outset, then, there was tension in the ADN between those who were trying to create a modern nonpersonalist party and those primarily committed to Banzer the individual leader. The latter were referred to as Banzeristas within the party.

In a bid to disassociate the military from Banzer or any other candidate, the high command in April forced him and five other generals connected to him to resign their commissions and take early retirement. Nonetheless, various groups including the ADN assailed the Padilla government and by extension the military for supposedly supporting one or another presidential candidate. For the military, the Padilla government did institute a study of the process, which concluded not surprisingly that no single candidate, party, or front could post a clear majority. The military also had Padilla call in the principal candidates, like Paz and Siles, and demand promises from them that they would not seek reprisals against the military should they win. The reality, however, was that the military as a whole was deeply divided on all matters political and it had no singular or dominant position on the elections.

Although the campaign was tense and punctuated by some violence, most agree that the elections were relatively honest. As was expected, no party won a clear majority in the presidential contest and therefore the task of choosing a chief executive from among the top three candidates constitutionally shifted to the legislature.

One problem that surfaced immediately was that, owing to a complex proportional representation scheme, the proportions won in the total popular vote were not reflected in the makeup of the new bicameral legislature. For example, Siles and the UDP polled 528,696 votes, or 35.9 percent, but were awarded only 8 Senate seats and 38 in the House of Deputies. The Paz AMNR on the other hand polled 527,184 votes, or 35.8 percent, but seated 16 senators and 48 deputies, making it the dominant power in the legislature. Banzer came in a relatively distant third: 225,205 votes, which translated into a substantial block of 3 senators and 19 deputies. Quiroga Santa Cruz caused a mild surprise when his PS-I polled 75,527 votes and received 5 deputy seats.

We do not as yet have any good in-depth analysis of recent Bolivian elections. The gross data, however, show that by 1979 the Bolivian electorate was polarized in ideological or programmatic terms. If one takes Paz and Banzer as representing the center Right, the electorate was clearly tilting right even if the center Left UDP received a plurality. Finally, if one assumes that Siles mainly represented the populist side of the MNR and that the MIR was largely social democratic, the Marxist state socialist Left clearly fared poorly and represented a declining position in the electorate as a whole.

Weak Interim Governments

But ideology and program were only one component of the process. In the newly installed Congress (the first since 1969) personal and party ambitions quickly came to the fore. The result was deadlock. No single candidate or front had sufficient votes to elect a president and none was willing to forgo its own goals to form an alliance. After seven ballots, a president was still not chosen. A way out was found when the bulk of the members agreed to appoint the president of the Senate, Walter Guevara Arce, as an interim president with a one-year mandate and a charge to call yet another round of elections in May of 1980. As one of the original major figures of the MNR in 1952, Guevara had the necessary stature (*figura*) to command credibility. His interim designation demonstrated that the major political parameters set by the MNR, although badly frayed, still held.

Guevara's brief term was significant in that it highlighted most of the major political problems bedeviling Bolivia's attempt to shift toward civil rule within an open democratic framework, especially the relationship between the executive and legislative powers and the role of political parties.[8] Almost immediately Congress cut Guevara adrift without support. He tried to form a broad-based government around some kind of alliance of the parties, particularly the offshoots of the MNR, but they saw him as little more than a bridge to the next kind of governmental set-up, be it produced by election or some other means. Both the Paz and Siles groups made it clear that they would enter the new government only if they could dominate it and use it to prepare for the future. Thus, when Guevara refused to rely exclusively on one group, they all turned on him and entered into open opposition. At the same time the parties were arrayed against one another in Congress, weakening as well that body's ability to perform.

The upshot was that neither the executive nor Congress was in a position to govern, in the sense of formulating policies to manage the accumulating political and social problems. The key questions throughout the interim were mainly those of constructing a viable system of power and rule, and sorting out the apportionment of power and perks among parties, rather than managing the society. Needless to say, Guevara, like Pereda and Padilla, could not come up with a viable approach to the economic crisis.

Given the growing disjuncture between Congress and the executive, the military—however fragmented—remained a key actor in resolving the fundamental questions of power and constitutional engineering. While many in the military, especially the institutionalists, sincerely wanted to withdraw from open exercise of power, the inability of the civil political class to generate a base of support for a government created a situation that continued to draw the military into the central political drama.

The military's concern with the political process was heightened when Left opposition parties led by Marcelo Quiroga introduced a motion for Congress to try (*juicio de responsabilidades*) Hugo Banzer openly for his actions while president, especially repression of the opposition. Whatever else it was, this ploy opened the way to use Congress as an arena within which ambitious individuals and parties could vie for media attention and public support. Individuals and factions across the board jumped onto the bandwagon by adding more particulars to the growing list of indictments against Banzer. Congress's energies were directed more toward this public, post hoc judicial function than either the functions of legislating or supporting a government. And, the juicio against Banzer quickly escalated into a drama in which the Left opposition was maneuvering to convert Congress into a forum legally to judge the role of the entire armed forces. This fact forced the military to rally itself to defend the institution. Soon threats were rumbling from the military toward Congress and the government.

The elections of 1979 did not solve any of the really fundamental political issues of power. None of the principal civil or political actors was oriented toward playing the game of government strictly by constitutional rules. Rather, all were focused on the fundamental power questions, which they tried to solve in their own favor and by any and all means available, including extraconstitutional means. When push came to shove, the issue was power and perks, not democracy. In short, the prime commitment of the panoply of civil and military political elites was to attaining and keeping power, not to democracy as either a way to gain power or a framework to exercise power.

Hence, while the open "democratic" maneuvering took place, there was other maneuvering behind the scenes. Factions of both civil and military elites were fabricating diverse plots and schemes. As in the past, although the military had a range of motives peculiar to itself to pursue intervention, civil political elites also sought out military allies to mount coups; potential military intervention still was as much a product of civilian inducement as it was military motives. This time various civil factions used the threat of a congressional juicio to persuade military officers to back their extralegal plans for achieving power.

Although the ins and outs of the plotting of this period are far from fully known yet, there is evidence that a broad civil-military coup coalition began to form. The military factions came to center on Colonel Alberto

Natusch Busch, who had exercised considerable power as minister of agriculture under Banzer. The civil wing centered on a cabal of MNRH leaders associated with Victor Paz but embraced other groups, including some leftists, as well.

Apparently, a grandiose scheme began to take shape around a new and fascinating concept of a "constitutional coup d'état." The operative idea was that because Congress created Guevara's mandate, Congress could also revoke it. The opposition, centered on the MNRH, would grind the government to a halt through constant interpellations. These would be followed by a motion of censure of Guevara's cabinet and a demand for its resignation. The resulting immobilism would precipitate a coup by Natusch to constitute a temporary military government sanctioned by Congress, which would then transform itself into a constituent assembly with the task of drafting a new constitution and specifically new electoral and party laws. Clearly, the MNRH and other civil elites saw this as an opportunity to design an electoral system more in their favor. Other schemes also floated about.

Needless to say, Guevara was forced to spend time wondering which scheme would be hatched, when the military might strike, and how civil elites might use the Congress to shake his government. Things were moving quickly. On October 11 the 6th Division in Trinidad declared itself in rebellion and called for the ousting of both Guevara and Congress because of congressional "provocations" toward the military. That coup did not prosper, but it did indicate to the civil elites that if they did not form an effective coup alliance with the military, then Congress and the parties could well go down with Guevara at the hands of other military factions. Coup rumors abounded and brought expressions of concern from the United States and the international community at large. The civil plotters from the MNRH were betting, however, that the international community would accept a coup if Congress was involved and remained functioning after Guevara was ousted.

Guevara, a wily old politician himself, was not about simply to lie down and wait to be ousted. He publicly attacked Congress for undercutting the capacity of his government to deal with the economic crisis. Indeed, he argued that if Congress could not get its act together his mandate should be extended for a year to empower him to put together an economic package. The validity of Guevara's appeal was made obvious when some minor decrees designed to curb the importation of luxury goods were criticized in Congress and led to a move to censure two government ministers. The general plot thickened when rumors began to circulate that Guevara was pursuing his own talks with military factions to mount a coup on his behalf against Congress. It was no secret that the parties and especially the

MNRH were then dedicated to the strategy of ousting Guevara through a deal that would permit them to position themselves for the next shot at power.

The incredible Byzantine fluidity of Bolivia politics was laid bare by subsequent events. On November 1, 1979, military units in La Paz, acting in response to Guevara's ousting of their commander, Colonel Alberto Gribowsky, precipitated things by launching a coup prior to the finalization of plans between the civil and military groups. Although dismayed that the units acted before the planned congressional action, Natusch was compelled to put himself at their head and seize the presidential palace. Caught off guard, the plotters in Congress lost control of events, and contrary to plan, Congress reacted by condemning the coup and backing Guevara. Natusch found himself sitting in the presidential palace confronted by a recalcitrant Congress.

From the outset it was clear that Natusch had no concept of government other than to seize and hold power. He ordered the balky Congress closed on November 2. Then, in a bid for some mode of legitimacy, he termed himself a national revolutionary and called on the Left and particularly labor to back his regime. Specifically, he tried to portray himself as a military leader in the mold of his uncle Germán Busch, a war hero who mounted a military populist government in 1930s, to which all succeeding populist groups, both civil and military, always harked back. In a dramatic gesture Natusch offered the COB a co-government with the armed forces. The COB vacillated, but went so far as to limit the duration of a general strike it had called.

The wavering of the COB was not unique; few if any political forces were committed to Guevara or to the formula that brought him to the presidency. Moreover, all were aware that the coup was a premature expression of civil-military plots and not a purely military affair. And the behavior of all relevant groups showed that the commitment to democracy was not the expression of a primary value but a tactical maneuver to reorganize power holders; all were still open to nondemocratic formulas if they offered a route to power.

Aware of the political fluidity of the situation, Natusch and his military backers looked for some political formula to overcome the popular resistance building in the streets of the capital and to hang onto some shred of power and authority. Natusch promised to call elections again for May 9, 1980 (the date Guevara was committed to), and on November 7 allowed Congress to resume its sessions.[9]

Even as they maneuvered politically, Natusch and his backers in the high command violently repressed resistance. Especially during the week of November 2 troops all but ran amok in La Paz in an increasingly desperate attempt to crush resistance. Those were bloody days for Bolivia. Most estimates put the death toll at well over 200, and many more were wounded. After more than ten days of slaughter, the officers told Natusch that they had not broken the resistance and that submission could not be brought about short of imposing a draconian military dictatorship—which at that point they were not willing to do. The pressure to find a political solution increased.[10]

Natusch offered to form a tripartite government based on the armed forces, representatives of Congress, and the COB. Some groups in Congress, like the ADN and PCB (demonstrating that ideology was all but irrelevant), reacted favorably, but other parties resisted not out of rejection of an authoritarian regime but out of concern for tactical damage to their particularistic aims. Some of the COB leadership also showed some interest in negotiations, but pressure from the rank and file, especially the miners, against such a move was fierce. The scheme fell apart, and politically the situation lapsed into a standoff. Neither the military nor Congress could at that point work its will against the other, in part because neither was able to define a clear will.

With no formula to transcend the governmental crisis, it became evident to all that the only way out was to return to some version of the status quo ante. A deal was struck by which the military agreed to give up Natusch and formal power and Congress agreed to dump Guevara. Congress then constituted a new interim civil regime charged with calling presidential elections in May 1980. The interim president was the president of the Chamber of Deputies, Lydia Gueiler Tejada, a longtime politician with roots in the MNR.

The Natusch adventure had sprung from two crucial factors in the Bolivian political situation that starkly revealed that all relevant political elites were more than resistant to committing their fates to a real democratic opening. The military obviously feared losing control of the situation, and feared as well an investigation and legal reprisals by a democratic regime. An uncontrolled democratic opening was fraught with danger both for the institution and for scores of officers who had been in and around power for over a decade and a half. The main civil parties arrayed in Congress, like the MNR, MNRI, ADN, PCB, and others, were obviously no more sanguine about a democratic opening. Each had demonstrated by its behavior that it preferred a quicker and surer way to power, and all feared that once one party or another was in power, it would act to suppress and marginalize its rivals. The latter belief was founded on an appraisal of past behaviors and a projection of the parties' own tactical intentions onto others. In such circumstances the only rational course was to assume the negative intentions of other groups and act accordingly.

The chief party group behind the Natusch ouster was the Paz wing of the

MNR. Since its earliest days in power the MNR had shown that its model of governance was the Partido Revolucionario Institucional (PRI) of Mexico, which had successfully constructed a single-party authoritarian state operating behind a formal democratic facade. Thus, the MNR had always been looking for some formula to give a mode of democratic legality to its would-be political dominance. The latest version was the constitutional coup, conceived in the fertile mind of MNR stalwart Guillermo Bedregal, who was the party's principal liaison with Natusch. The constitutional coup was conceived as a first step in an unfolding grand alliance between the MNR and the military on the way toward some variant of the Mexican model.

The Natusch ouster showed that no party, group, or faction could orchestrate the political situation to its taste. The interim government of Gueiler was a way out of the Natusch fiasco—that is all it was. The underlying disarray continued, and if anything was exacerbated. The central problem confronting Bolivia was still that of constitutional engineering: to find a scheme that would enable reorganization of an effective decision-making capacity at the center. Until that was achieved, none of the other severe problems of the nation could be addressed.

The Gueiler government was the product of a compromise among the political parties, most of which were now pointed to a strategy of holding the military at bay while they tried to cobble together an electoral solution to the political impasse. As a result, the government tried to give itself a broad coalitional cast. However, it was generally agreed that Paz and the MNRH were the strongest force in it, and Gueiler's policies, especially economic policy, were viewed as in effect the policies of Paz and the MNRH. If this perception is accurate, Paz and the MNRH ended up trading off long-term potential electoral popularity for short-term power and influence in a very weak government.

From the outset Gueiler's government was battered from all sides as the multiple lines of conflict ripping at Bolivian society began to manifest themselves with a vengeance. By the time Gueiler was hustled from office in July of 1980, she had done battle with the military, the parties, class organizations, and regional civic committees. Gueiler had been pushed into incessant open conflict with the military. The first, and in a sense continuing, crucial issue had to do with her attempt to appoint a high command at least nominally loyal to her and to the process of a democratic electoral opening. The military, led by the army, rejected the authority of a civilian president to determine its personnel makeup, especially at the highest ranks. The military obviously viewed any civilian government produced by the mainstream parties with deep suspicion and openly decided to function autonomously from any government oversight and control.

The chief spokesman for the military was General Luis García Meza, who had served as army chief under Natusch and after being shifted out regained the post midway into the term of the Gueiler government. García Meza, who was Gueiler's cousin, publicly defied the new president over the issue of military autonomy. He patently tried to become the dominant force in the military by articulating the fears of the officer corps in regard to reprisals by civilian political parties. García Meza's line became that democracy in Bolivia was premature and apt to lead to a chaotic political process that could endanger national institutions, especially the military.

García Meza's bid for supremacy in the military was backed by Colonel Luis Arce Gomez, who had had a somewhat sinister military career. Arce Gomez, who was an expert in intelligence and demolitions, was made chief of military intelligence under Natusch, a position he held onto with the ascension of Gueiler. He in effect put military intelligence at the service of García Meza's ambitions. Together the two worked to bring themselves and the military to power through a two-pronged strategy of wresting control over the army while simultaneously disrupting and discrediting the Gueiler government and the electoral process.

The duo had to maneuver on two fronts because there was obvious resistance to them in the military. In the first instance, the factional problems continued and García Meza's open ambitions were most directly resisted by the institutionalists of the so-called generational group. In addition, there was resistance by other powerful officers with their own personal ambitions, like General Hugo Echevarría. Echevarría had converted his command into almost a personal fiefdom and he began to use it to play on the regional feelings of Santa Cruz and its suspicions of all central governments and institutions.

The Echevarría development was most significant and showed that in consequence of its considerable internal strife, the high command was beginning to deteriorate into a quasi-feudal barony that was beginning to privatize components of the military. This fact underscored a long-standing and accelerating trend in Bolivia toward the dispersal and privatization of the capacity to exercise force.

A manifestation of the trend was the proliferation of militias nominally connected to the MNR that sprang up in the wake of the revolution of 1952. The process continued in the 1960s with the appearance of armed guerrilla groups on the left and moves like that of Barrientos's to establish an armed paramilitary force (FURMOD) directly loyal to the leader, as well as the appearance of regionally identified armed groupings. The trend took a new and dangerous twist with the development of paramilitary squads under the personal control of military officers. Arce Gomez, for example, began to develop an ill-concealed paramilitary unit under his personal control. Moreover, rumors circulated that the unit overlapped

with other private armed units that were developing around powerful figures in the growing international commercialization of cocaine. Whatever
else it signified, the trend highlighted and reinforced the decomposition of
the key institutions of the central state, which had become a very weak and
incohesive entity alienated from and set off against Bolivian society.

Even as she pondered her problems with the military, Gueiler was also
faced with an economic crisis that could no longer be ignored. The national debt had passed the $3 billion mark, production in key areas was
dropping, GNP rates were negative, and the government's deficit was growing. For years all players had realized that unless someone had the power
and inclination to impose a radically new developmental model, policymakers would have to come to grips with the internal logic of the state
capitalist economic model and the demands of critical international fund-
ing agencies like the IMF. As the stabilization of 1956 and the program of
Banzer in 1972 showed, the situation forced policymakers toward the imposition of austerity programs that carried cost allocations that fell most
heavily on the urban and rural popular sectors.

Crisis and Structural Impasse

The problematic and almost structurally rooted contradiction involved
in trying to carry out a process of democratic opening in a context of
economic crisis had both a national and international dimension. As we
noted, the democratic opening was generating heightened bread-and-butter demands while the logic of state capitalism and the IMF pushed for
austerity policies directly counter to those demands. The contradiction
exposed a built-in institutional rift in any democratic constitutional regime
between the legislature, which as the base of power of the parties was linked
to the articulation of demands from civil society, and the executive, which
was being forced into the role of managing the economic crisis. Hence, the
salience of the "politics of economic packages."

The previous post-Banzer governments had ducked the economic-politi-
cal crisis, although Guevara was trying to put together an austerity package
when he was politically done in. Gueiler had no real choice and simply had
to act. On November 29 she decreed measures that included a 25 percent
devaluation, the end of numerous government subsidies, and price increases on, among other things, fuel. In addition, her government revised
the tax code on private mining to alleviate much of the negative pressure
on profits imposed under Banzer. The IMF, although not totally pleased
with the measures, especially the percentage of devaluation, responded
favorably with a U.S. $111 million standby loan.

It is by no means insignificant that Gueiler's package was imposed by executive decree. In fact, throughout the postrevolutionary period all such austerity or stabilization programs were put in place by executive decree. In most cases Congress, if it was in session, which obviously it not often was, resisted them. This trend in policymaking was to continue and be reinforced throughout the subsequent transition period.

The growing disjunction between the executive and legislative powers stands out most clearly in economic policy. The fact is that Congress has played little to no role in its formulation. The process has been monopolized by the executive branch, and usually by a small group of appointed technocrats around the president. This mode has been forced on the policy-making process in recent years by the increasingly severe nature of the economic crisis and by international actors like the IMF; often IMF technocrats play a direct role through consultation with cadres of national technocrats serving at the pleasure of the president.

The trend to executive economic policymaking by decree has been further reinforced by the fact that particularly in times of "open democratic politics" various groups and classes of civil society try to use representative institutions to resist or blunt such austerity initiatives. Hence, there is a growing disjuncture between the representative function of government expressed in the political parties and Congress and the increasingly significant "managerial" function of government, which is lodged mainly in the executive branch and its appointed technocrats.

Gueiler's package provoked widespread protest, particularly among workers and peasants; the latter were particularly hard hit by the rise in transportation costs. The COB and the newly founded (June 1979) Confederation of Bolivian Peasant Workers (Confederación Sindical de Trabajadores Campesinos de Bolivia, CSUTCB) carried out strikes, stoppages, and roadblocks to bring pressure on the government. Popular protest was reflected in Congress, where economic ministers were subjected to interpellations and moves were afoot to censure the entire cabinet.

Again, the scenario around the Gueiler austerity package was a harbinger of a general policy-making style that has prevailed since and is connected to the profound difficulties involved in trying to establish a democratic political regime in a context of chronic economic crisis. To the extent that economic policy initiative exists, it has fallen to the executive branch, from which, after largely *in camera* discussions, a package emerges and is decreed. Civil society has been largely reactive to the process in the form of protests aimed at stopping or modifying the package. Protests have been staged by the myriad organizations of civil society such as unions, civic groups, and professional associations. By and large these collectivities have bypassed the parties and Congress and pressured the executive directly in the form of actions designed to bring all or parts of the productive activities of society to a halt. The parties and factions in Congress usually try to catch up to the autonomous forces of civil society and line up to block the executive's economic packages. In this sense, the groups of civil society use Congress as a blocking instrument, but that use has always been secondary to their direct actions aimed at the executive. The reasons for the emergence of this strategic political game are many, but a principal one is that executives have been forced to ignore Congress and manage the economy by decree. Hence, the capacity to bloc legislation in the Congress is clearly secondary to the capacity to pressure the executive.

As we will see, the COB became as the single most significant voice of the popular sectors against the austerity packages of the Gueiler government and its successors. In 1979 and 1980, however, the COB showed real restraint in not pushing protest to the point of placing the government in jeopardy. Behind that restraint was the obvious decision by most of the COB leadership to back an electoral way out of a political dilemma. The decision was based on a perception that a military-backed authoritarian regime would be significantly more deleterious for the Left and the popular classes, and that the scheduled elections for June 1980 would in all likelihood produce a UDP government over which the COB would have significant influence. Whatever the reasons, the behavior of the COB evinced a shift to at least a short-term tactical commitment to the formal democratic electoral process.

The perception of the COB that the most acute danger came from the military was well placed. By April, García Meza succeeded in regaining his position as army commander, from which he began publicly to assail Gueiler and most of the prominent center Left politicians. He also began to attack the very viability of the fledgling democratic process. Simultaneously, there was mounted a campaign of violence designed to intimidate the civil political groups and in general disrupt the electoral process by creating a climate of insecurity. At the time supporters of a democratic opening charged that Arce Gomez was the coordinator of the campaign.

Actually the campaign had begun some weeks prior and started to turn ugly in February and March in terrorist incidents directed at center Left civilian targets and especially progressive Catholic clergy and organizations supported by them. A particular target was the Catholic weekly *Aquí* and its director Luis Espinal, S.J. Many held that the attacks were obviously coming from the military, and a broad spectrum of political and civic groups, among which progressive clerics were prominent, banded together to form the National Committee for the Defense of Democracy (Comité Nacional de Defensa de la Democracia, CONADE). It was an important organization in the coming months.

CONADE and others proved incapable of defending Espinal. On the morning of March 12 his battered body was discovered near a municipal slaughterhouse. Father Espinal's supporters were and are firmly convinced that his death was connected to stories he had run in *Aquí* regarding the development of paramilitary forces under the direction of Arce Gomez and other less-than-flattering revelations about doings in the military, like cocaine trafficking. One particularly disturbing revelation was of a growing connection between Bolivian military intelligence and counterparts from the by then highly skilled Argentine military's repressive apparatus—this in particular was a fateful development.

The campaign against the elections and the Left mounted in intensity over late April and May. Indeed, it reached the point where García Meza did not make much of an effort to disguise his intentions. So patent were the coup preparations, that the new U.S. ambassador, Marvin Weissman publicly warned García Meza and the military not to make a coup lest Bolivia suffer diplomatic and economic reprisals from the Carter administration. The García Meza clique responded by declaring Weissman persona non grata, threatening his life, and launching a violent anti-American campaign.

From a political point of view one of the more interesting occurrences of the period took place on April 29 when the military high command and seven officers of the COB with President Gueiler's concurrence signed a formal agreement to respect each other's institutions and to sustain the electoral process. The significance of the event lay not in the content of the agreement, which was to prove useless, but in the fact that under the government's good offices such an agreement was reached between an ostensible arm of the state and an interest group of civil society.

The agreement reflected the essentially corporatist structure of the Bolivian state and ratified that the internal coherence of the state had all but come undone. The civilian government was so weak that it had to carry on a species of intergovernmental negotiations with a supposedly subordinate institution of the state, the military, and a nongovernmental agency, the COB, that was being recognized as a quasi-sovereign entity within the state. Indeed, the COB was to assert its semisovereign status within subsequent civil democratic regimes, a status it had consistently claimed since the early days of 1952 when the MNR recognized the COB concepts of *co-gobierno* and the *fuero sindical*. The military, in turn had clearly come to see itself as a source of governmental authority with primacy over any civil political process. One might add here that in prior years civil political groups had in effect encouraged the military to assume such de facto authority. In the aftermath of the Natusch affair the vast majority of civil political groups finally began to swing firmly behind a democratic opening. It was a bit late in the day.

In spite of the continuing violence and intimidation, the elections came off as planned on June 29, 1980. The polling went relatively smoothly, and most people consider it to have been fundamentally honest. As in past elections the party spectrum was wide and fragmented; some twelve electoral groupings embracing at least twenty-eight parties contested the elections, but the major contenders were again the UDP, headed by Siles, the AMNR, headed by Paz, and the ADN, headed by Banzer. Again Quiroga Santa Cruz ran a vigorous campaign at the head of his PS-I and could not be discounted as a force. Proving the maxim that the major characteristic of political parties in Bolivia is fissure along personalistic lines, Guillermo Bedregal, a long-standing Paz lieutenant who was the main MNR figure in the Natusch affair, broke from the party and ran for the presidency at the head of a new MNR offshoot called, somewhat ironically, the united MNR. Bedregal's group and the rest of the field were minor contenders of the taxi party type.

To some extent the election was a replay of 1979. The major change was a sharp drop in votes for Paz and the AMNR group to 263,706, with ten senators and thirty-six deputies. One of the main reasons for the drop-off was the association of Paz's name with the Natusch coup (vehemently denied), but more significant was the general perception that Gueiler and her austerity program were really creatures of Paz and the mainline MNR. Siles and the UDP polled a bit less than 1979, 507,173 votes, but the UDP fared better in the proportional-ballot congressional test, with ten senators and forty-seven deputies. Banzer did about the same as 1979 in the presidential contest and a bit better in the congressional test, with six senators and twenty-four deputies. Quiroga Santa Cruz pulled a strong 113,959, with one senator and ten deputies. As in 1979, the electorate was polarized in terms of the manifest ideologies of the candidates and parties, this time a slight tilt toward the left. Most significantly, the combined forces of the center Right gave it the capacity to dominate Congress, especially the lower house.

Government by Kleptocracy

There was no immediate reaction by the military to the election. Siles began preparations to assume the presidency including meeting with García Meza and the high command. However, García Meza and his clique had other plans. On the morning of July 17 the 6th Division, headquartered in the interior town of Trinidad, capital of the department of Beni, declared itself in rebellion. By the end of the day García Meza, who was "visiting" Trinidad, emerged as the strong man of a military junta.

Violent coups d'état are hardly new to Bolivia but the action of July 17,

1980, had a number of new dimensions to it that were also a sinister harbinger of things to come under the new military government. In the first instance, owing to Argentine "technical assistance," the coup was extremely well planned and executed. As it turned out, the pronouncement from Trinidad was part of a trap into which the civil democratic forces and a substantial portion of the labor Left fell.

When word of the action in Trinidad reached La Paz, the Gueiler cabinet went into emergency session and the groups in CONADE met at the downtown headquarters of the COB; almost the entire civil leadership especially of the labor Left, conveniently gathered in two central sites. The two sites were shortly surrounded and their occupants violently taken into custody. Most notably, the actions were undertaken not by regular military units but by paramilitary groups under the command of Arce Gomez, who assumed the position of minister of interior in the new military government. When the paramilitaries took the COB headquarters, they singled out Quiroga Santa Cruz and shot him dead on the spot.[11]

To forestall the kind of mass resistance that undid Natusch in 1979, the paramilitary units then fanned out through the city, attacking preselected targets of potential civilian opposition. In a particularly cynical ploy, paramilitary groups led by convicted killers like Fernando "Mosca" (the fly) Monroy used ambulances of the social security institute to slip behind civilian barricades and then attack those manning them from the rear. Once the capital was secure, regular military units moved into the mines and crushed civil resistance. The repression was especially brutal and bloody in the Corocoro mine.[12] Paramilitary and regular units also moved throughout the countryside, especially in the Department of La Paz to preempt or crush resistance from the peasantry. It was a ruthless and extremely effective coup.

García Meza quickly emerged as the strongman of the military-based government. At the beginning the new government did receive some cautious civil support from individuals in the private sector, Banzer and the ADN, and other members of the political class who were angling for governmental positions. The justification for the coup was the charge that civil and democratic institutions were in disarray; more important perhaps was the ability of García Meza and others to play on the fear in the military of civilian legal reprisals against the institution.

García Meza announced his intention to launch a government of "national reconstruction" aimed at the overhaul of Bolivia's political and economic institutions. To this end, some moves were made to formulate needed economic policies and to form commissions charged with drafting new institutional schemes. Still, little came forth in the area of economic policy, owing in large part to the rejection of the García Meza government by the international financial and governmental community. Likewise, the civilian reform commissions came to naught as civil political leaders abandoned the government.

The fact is that the García Meza government was the most brutal, corrupt and destructive in recent Bolivian history. With Arce Gomez installed in the Ministry of Interior, the government set out not only to crush opposition, especially among workers, peasants, the progressive church, and Left parties, but also to intimidate the entire society. During its first months the government was remarkably effective in imposing a terrified apathy upon Bolivian society.

Once the initial fighting was over, the main instruments of repression were Arce's paramilitary squads, some of which had been converted into a special police force (Servicio Especial de Seguridad, SES) operating out of the Ministry of Interior with the technical assistance of Argentine "security" specialists. Taking a leaf from the book being written by the military regime in Argentina, García Meza and Arce Gomez used arbitrary arrest, torture, and the disappearance of suspects as their main methods of social control. Almost immediately the will and capacity of the Left and the popular forces to resist was broken. In one bizarre drama a badly shaken Lechín, who had been captured at the COB on the seventeen, was dragged before television cameras to plead with his followers not to oppose the government. Other would-be resistors were simply brutalized into submission.

The malevolence of the new García Meza government repelled Bolivia's civil society, including the middle class and the emergent national bourgeoisie. It had a sustained, systematic nature that was new to public life. In the past repression tended to be episodic, and violence was mainly a characteristic of the heat of the moment. Above all, familial and friendship ties among the relatively small elite in Bolivia tended to blunt and soften the violence and repression felt by the middle and upper classes. However, Arce Gomez and his Argentine-trained paramilitary groups drawn from the youth of Bolivia's lumpen proletariat were not inhibited by the traditional constraints of political conflict among Bolivia's political class.

Aside from day-to-day circumstances an incident on January 15, 1981, brought home to the middle classes the savagely alien nature of the García Meza government. On that day SES agents led by Arce Gomez burst into a house in the middle-class Sopacachi district of La Paz where nine leaders of the MIR were meeting. According to the one survivor, Gloria Ardaya who had hidden under a bed, the SES agents proceeded pitilessly to brutalize and murder the eight other MIR leaders. Because the bulk of the MIR leadership was drawn from the middle class, the event sent a cold chill through middle-class families.

Although some in the private sector and on the right had assumed that this government would mean a return to authoritarian, imposed state capitalism à la Barrientos and Banzer, they soon learned otherwise. The government demonstrated that it had no coherent plan of rule, or even a set of goals, and that it had no intention of drawing in any meaningful way on any civil group for expertise in regard to either. It quickly degenerated into a cabal of officers without stable ties to any class, sector, or region of civil society. Although some civilian individuals continued to hold positions in the government, civil society as a whole, from left to right, shrank in revulsion from the government.

The barbarousness of the government and its ineptness in formulating economic policy were not the only reasons for the revulsion and disaffection of civil society. Bolivia and the entire world shortly realized that the Garcia Meza government was deeply involved in the international traffic of cocaine. Indeed, the U.S. Drug Enforcement Agency and other agencies openly accused high-ranking officers and government ministers, including Arce Gomez, of direct personal ties to the trade, which in Bolivia is referred to as "narcotráfico."

The revelation of the government's involvement in narcotráfico also brought to light other sinister connections, those to the murky world of international neofascism. Specifically, it was learned that individuals like García Meza and Arce Gomez had direct personal links to the Italian neofascist terrorist Pier Luigi Pagliai and to the notorious former Nazi SS officer Klaus Barbie. The latter, who was known during World War II as the butcher of Lyon, had been living none too secretly in Bolivia for years under the name of Klaus Altman. Other Bolivian governments had for whatever reasons protected Barbie, but the García Meza regime brought him and Italian terrorists directly into the political process as security advisers and trainers of its paramilitary squads.

The connections to cocaine and neofascist terrorism made the García Meza regime increasingly an outlaw government internationally. Indeed, contrary to Bolivian expectations, the new Reagan administration in the United States wanted nothing to do with García Meza and company, and eventually put itself at the head of what amounted to an international financial quarantine of the regime that in some senses was to prove its undoing.

The corruption of the government did not stop with the cocaine connection but spread across all of the traditional modes of corruption known historically in Bolivia. The difference now was that all former constraints were put aside, and the clique in power was all but openly looting the country. One particularly revealing story surfaced in May of 1981: García Meza and two other commanders, Waldo Bernal and Ramiro Terrazas, had entered into a private agreement with a Brazilian firm for the mining and commercialization of semiprecious stones from publicly owned lands at La Gaiba that were technically under the control of the military production corporation COFADENA. The action highlighted that fact that, as in the Philippines under Ferdinand Marcos, the distinction between the public patrimony and the private property of government officials had all but vanished. The private appropriation of the national patrimony that occurred under García Meza reflected the further degeneration of the neo-patrimonial logic of rule that developed during the late 1960s and 1970s. Indeed, the seizure of formal state power had become a license to steal.

In 1980-81 Bolivia lacked a single patrimonial personality at the center capable of holding the system together as Banzer had done in the 1970s. García Meza never had the same control over the state apparatus. His hold on the military was particularly tenuous, and reputedly was based largely on cutting certain officers in on the corruption while paying others off. Nonetheless, coup rumors were ripe.

The reality was that the military was no longer a coherent institution that could be controlled through a hierarchical structure descending from the high command. The previous trend of internal decomposition had been reinforced and the officer corps had become more a congeries of individuals with variable bases of power as military units, like the rest of the public sector, began to be used as quasi-private armies.

To the extent that armed force was still the chief arbiter of politics (the extent was considerable), the decomposition of the military meant that Bolivia was regressing even from a patrimonial system into the more patriarchal forms of power characteristic of feudalism, if not warlordism. At best, the officer corps had become a set of armed feudal barons; at worst, parts of the corps had become little more than predatory war-lords. What little system of governance that existed under this version of military rule was not much more than a kleptocracy.

The decomposition of Bolivia's political institutions had proceeded to a point where the urgent agenda of issues revolving around models of development, distribution of gains and losses, and management of the economic crisis took a back seat temporarily to the naked power struggles of the armed kleptocrats and their venal allies in the political class. As a government, the García Meza group was increasingly isolated both nationally and internationally. Hence, although the government could cow the citizenry and loot the nation, it was in fact extremely weak when it came to governing in the sense of defining and enforcing policy.

Like the governments immediately before it, the García Meza regime was unable to take the tough economic decisions, and the few sallies it made in this area provoked protest that induced it to back off. As a result, the economic crisis worsened and popular revulsion against the government spread throughout all groups, classes, and regions. Under García Meza, Bolivia became a society in which the military and the state were set off against the entire civil society. The government had no class or ideological content and did not articulate the interests or values of any sector.

By early 1981 the inherent weakness of the government began to manifest itself. More and more sectors of civil society began to protest against it in the forms of strikes and other civic actions. Resistance was particularly strong in Santa Cruz. Actually, García Meza got caught in the middle of an interregional battle that had been raging since the late 1970s. In brief, the battle was driven by the bitter stand of Santa Cruz against the attempt by the Department of La Paz to establish a development zone in the northern part of the department based on the production of sugar. This was perceived as a direct threat to the sugar industry of Santa Cruz, which was one of the pillars of the Santa Cruz prosperity. The San Buenaventura project pitted the civic committees and development corporations of both departments against each other in an increasingly acrimonious debate and bedeviled every government of the period. During the Gueiler interlude, La Paz was able to work its will through Congress, but the president waffled on actually putting the project into practice.

By July of 1981 García Meza was in difficult straits politically. In a blatant attempt to win the support of La Paz, the dictator threw his weight behind the San Buenaventura project and decreed it into existence. This action produced some demonstrations of support in La Paz but earned García Meza the unyielding enmity of Santa Cruz. In a matter of weeks the resentment would take concrete shape in a series of events that would shake the government to its core.

García Meza also had to fight off numerous coup attempts from within the military, including those from officers loyal to Banzer, to Natusch or to the institutionalist group. Some of the attempts were in the service of rivals' ambitions; others were aimed at saving the military from being overwhelmed by the corruption and venality. García Meza survived these early moves by rather openly buying the support of colonels in charge of key regiments.

In some senses the major weakness of the regime was on the international front. Because of its conspicuous connections to the drug trade and to neo-Nazis the Bolivian ruling group was excluded from the "Kirkpatrick doctrine" of support for "conservative authoritarian" regimes as an offset to "left totalitarian" regimes à la Cuba. The United States pressured the IMF, and the World Bank to cut Bolivia off from any financial support. Because some accommodation with the United States and the standard international financial agencies was perceived by all as crucial to Bolivia's economic future (barring some socialist revolution), the García Meza group was increasingly depicted as the major roadblock to such an accommodation.

Realizing his extreme weakness, García Meza moved in early 1981 to improve the government's image. He dropped Arce Gomez and officers openly connected to the drug groups from his cabinet. At the same time he announced the government's intention to clean up its act and to crack down on the drug trade. These moves convinced no one, and increasingly opposition focused on García Meza himself.

In the end it was a combination of internal military politics and regionalism that brought García Meza down. The situation was brought to a head when García Meza approved the San Buenaventura project. His opponents within the military moved to take advantage of the conflict with Santa Cruz. On August 3 supporters of Natusch and the institutionalists joined forces to launch a coup from Santa Cruz, an action backed enthusiastically by the citizens of Santa Cruz. The situation immediately became a standoff between García Meza's supporters centered in La Paz and the rebels in Santa Cruz. Fearful of a civil war, the military looked within itself for a solution. In negotiations publicly facilitated by the church, a deal was struck in which García Meza would relinquish the presidency and Natusch would leave political affairs for good. On August 4 García Meza was out and a bloody confrontation avoided.

It is important to stress that the ousting of García Meza was the result of a negotiated settlement among the baronial officer corps. It meant the departure of an individual but not the end of the de facto system that had developed around him—especially the dominance of the officer corps as a collegial body of warlords rather than a hierarchical institution. García Meza's fall, however, did embolden various segments of civil society to press the central government and the military to come to terms with the two central issues of the day: the economic crisis, and the need to define a system of central governance that could gain some degree of legitimacy both at home and abroad.

Looking for a Way Out

After an attempt at a junta of service commanders that failed because of internal wrangling, the officer corps put forward General Celso Torrelio as the new president. In the eyes of most, Torrelio was perceived to have achieved his post because of his relatively clean public image and because he was relatively weak compared to other top-ranking officers. The main fear was that he would be little more than a *tonto útil* (useful fool) of the kleptocrats who remained firmly in control of numerous important units.

A major goal of the new Torrelio government was to end Bolivia's international isolation. The key to that goal was to win the recognition and support of the United States. In September and October the government announced its intention to combat the cocaine trade, and to back up this assertion it turned over to U.S. authorities a widely known dealer, Alfredo "Cutuchi" Gutierrez, who was wanted in the United States for skipping bail. The Reagan administration responded favorably and dispatched a new ambassador, Edwin Corr, in November.

Corr was a career officer just coming off a successful period as ambassador to Peru, and an expert in narcotics matters. Under his energetic leadership the U.S. embassy became an active player in the unfolding political game, and particularly in what turned out to be an important transition from authoritarian to formal democratic rule. The United States vigorously pushed four major goals: control of cocaine production and trade; a changeover to formal democracy; a rollback of the role of the state in the economy; and the development of an organized and politically active private sector.

Responding to U.S. as well as internal pressure, Torrelio announced a plan to redemocratize Bolivia over a period of three years. To the surprise of many, the confederation of Bolivian Private Entrepeneurs (CEPB) called for more speed and began a campaign to force the military out of politics. Unless the military withdrew, the confederation argued, Bolivia risked a mass uprising that would have unpredictable results. Torrelio angrily dismissed the call of the private sector to constitute a civilian government of "national reconciliation" to preside over elections, and launched a bitter tirade against the private sector and the political parties. He exculpated the military and laid responsibility for Bolivia's problems at the feet of the civilians. The exchange marked the first open, public breach between the chief organization of the private sector and the military, which since at least Barrientos was perceived by many, especially on the left, as the instrument of private sector interests.

From that point on the CEPB became a leading force pushing for a return to formal democracy. At the same time it called for programs to end the financial crisis and to reinvigorate growth by way of a return to a more open and market-centered economic model. The vigorous position taken by the CEPB marked a significant development on the political scene.[13]

The bulk of the private sector in Bolivia was a creation of the revolution nurtured over time by governments pushing the state capitalist development model. During the Banzer years the private sector began to consolidate itself as a political force but in the main was divided between those content with patrimonial paternalistic ties to Banzer and those pushing for an independent, more class-based position. During the 1970s and early

1980s the sector was split and confused over issues like authoritarianism versus democracy and the role of the state in the economy. Many felt safer under military-based authoritarian rule and had become dependent on a nurturing state. Others, as we saw, questioned this position and considered that a military-imposed state capitalist system was no longer in their favor, and that the sector would fare better as a coherent and autonomous force actively participating in a pluralist system. Events after 1978 began to push the bulk of the sector toward the latter position, a trend reinforced by experiencing the García Meza government. Although some individuals in the sector participated in that government, the majority of the key individuals in the sector ended by being disillusioned with military-backed authoritarian rule.

Thus, the CEPB-Torrelio exchange reflected a number of important developments in the political role of the private sector. It signaled that for perhaps the first time since 1952 there existed a national bourgeoisie willing and capable of acting as a class with a broad political and economic strategy to advance its interests. The leadership of the CEPB in pushing that strategy by way of public statements and publications confirmed that it had become the chief organizational spokesman of the private sector. Indeed, as we will see, the CEPB was to become the organizational equivalent to the private sector that the COB was to the working class. Bolivia now had two vigorous and potentially antagonistic class-based organizations qua interest groups. In the weeks and months to come the CEPB and the COB became the focal points of the class fissure in Bolivia and assumed the role of political actors often much more significant in shaping events than the political parties.

Although the CEPB was a forceful partisan of a democratic solution to the political impasse, the private sector as a whole backed into its commitment to democracy, in a sense. It came to its position not out of a primary commitment to democratic values but because of its experience and disillusionment with the authoritarian alternatives. Particularly important was the fact that many leaders in the sector became convinced that the military was no longer, from their point of view, a viable base for a stable political regime. The shift from a position of reliance on the military to one of serious questioning occurred over time and involved a number of complex and subtle factors.

As we saw, this shift in attitude and perception really began during the Banzer regime. Important components of the private sector, especially mining began to see that a heavy state presence in the economy was no longer in their interests. From their point of view, the state, by competing with the private sector for surplus, had changed from an entity that protected the sector to one that was parasitic on it. Likewise, they were grasping that the military had become an integral part of the state-centric capitalist model and that the institution as a political actor had a definitive orientation toward a patrimonial and neomercantilist state structure. Whether as a backer of a left populist model or a right antipopulist model, the military in Bolivia was, in their view, fundamentally statist and therefore any long-term, military-based rule would inevitably run counter to the interests of the private sector as a whole, as opposed to any specific individuals who might benefit. Indeed, during the 1970s the sector was divided between those who pushed this view and those who directly participated as individuals in the Banzer regime. The statist bent of the military was confirmed to many by the Karachipampa project pushed by the avowedly reformist Padilla government.

At a deeper level the García Meza regime was as traumatizing for the private sector as it was for all other sectors of Bolivian civil society. In one sense it showed that the decomposing military institution was simply too unpredictable as a political force and could no longer be trusted to serve interests any wider than those of some clique of kleptocrats. Under García Meza the state had become definitively parasitic on if not predatorily hostile to civil society. More fundamentally, many feared that García Meza and his associates had through the blatancy of their behavior called into question the very viability of the traditional military and thereby jeopardized the ability of the military in the long run to protect the private sector and some mode of capitalism from a potential threat from the revolutionary Left.

Thus, the private sector was becoming aware that if the military was to survive as a coherent institutional force capable of defending the system, it would have to withdraw from direct control of the state and see to the repair and reorganization of its organizational structure and integrity. The only way this could be accomplished was through creation of an open, pluralistic process of formal democracy. In short, commitment to redemocratization in the private sector developed as a "second-best option." In this the private sector was not unique. By our reading of the record, all the major group, class, and regional elites in Bolivia came to back democracy as a second-best option. Over the years all had shown a clear disposition to use extraconstitutional shortcuts to power in league with factions of the military. By 1981-82 none of the key elites in civil society from left to right any longer trusted their ability to control and use the fractious military.

The Torrelio government was showing no rush to leave power. As a result, all components of civil society began to push for a return to democratic rule. At this level at least, actors as diverse as the CEPB, the COB, the church, and the U.S. embassy began to act in something resembling concert. Any consensus, however, was restricted to the level of a formal, political way out. On the crucial issue of managing the economy, divergence was still the order of the day. Owing to Torrelio's bids toward the U.S. embassy, the financial barriers around Bolivia began to be lowered. In January 1982 the International Development Bank released a loan of $97 million to construct a gas pipeline. The government then moved to build on this by tailoring economic measures to conform to IMF guidelines. In February and March the government decreed two austerity packages that involved a currency devaluation, the lifting of price subsidies, and the raising of prices and taxes.

As it had before, the COB led the opposition to these measures. In fact, the COB definitively adopted a rejectionist position on all IMF-inspired or -designed austerity programs. Aside from issues of formal constitutional engineering, the main substantive issue remained, and became even more, "the politics of economic packages." On this the lines of divergence between the COB and the CEPB became clear, with the latter pushing for an IMF-style stabilization to be followed by a sharp withdrawal of the state from the economy. This battle was to loom large in the months ahead. At that moment the mild Torrelio package went through, but all agreed that a fundamental resolution of the economic crisis was still to be found.

In subsequent weeks the Torrelio government steadily lost control of the situation, both in relationship to a resurgent civil society and to its own military household. Even as the CEPB emerged as the spokesman of the private sector, labor unions reemerged and regrouped behind the COB, the regional civic committees pushed their interests, and the political parties jockeyed for position in the hoped-for democratic opening. Within the military the García Meza group continued to vie with the institutionalists to control command positions.

Fearing the drift to civil rule, the cohort of colonels that had backed García Meza made its bid for power in July of 1982. The most powerful colonel of the group, Faustino Rico Toro, declared that Torrelio no longer had the confidence of the major regimental commanders and therefore the presidency should pass to him. The high command realized Torrelio's position was no longer viable and removed him, but other factions were in no way willing to accept Rico Toro. Instead, the high command, in conclave passed the presidency on July 21 to General Guido Vildoso. The new president signaled his tilt toward those who wished to save the military by removing it from politics; he indicated his intention to lead the military in a hasty but orderly retreat back to the barracks. The big issue immediately became how to manage the retreat and turn power over to civilians.

By that point the military had lost any real ability to control the process, and even less to dictate outcomes. It fell to civil society to define not a solution to the crisis but what was referred to as *una salida* (a way out). The Left lined up behind Siles, and the UDP wanted new elections mainly because all signs were that it could be a big winner. For the same reason, the MNRH, ADN, and the private sector were less than enthusiastic about new elections. Key figures in the private sector then came up with the salida of convoking the Congress elected in 1980. The MNR and ADN responded positively to that notion because they would have control of both houses in that Congress. For complex strategic reasons, the MIR also backed the salida.

After much jockeying back and forth, a church-sponsored meeting of all the key sectors of civil society came up with the tentative compromise of convoking the Congress of 1980 but with the provision that it would elect Siles to the presidency. On September 17, 1980, the military high command accepted the civilian-engineered salida and agreed to turn over power to Siles and the 1980 Congress in October. Thus ended one of the darkest chapters in Bolivian political history.

Notes

1. For analysis of the broad regional trend back to democracy, see James M. Malloy and Mitchell A. Seligson, eds., *Authoritarians and Democrats: Regime Transition in Latin American* (Pittsburgh: University of Pittsburgh Press, 1987).
2. The tendency to back into democracy as a second-best option was not unique to Bolivia's elites. Dankwort A. Rustow, "Transitions to Democracy: Towards a Dynamic Model," *Comparative Politics* 2 (1970): 337.
3. A favorable account of the strike is provided in Asamblea Permanente de Derechos Humanos de Bolivia, *La huelga de hambre* (La Paz, 1978).
4. The proliferation of parties is treated at length in Raul Rivadeneira Prada, *Laberinto político de Bolivia* (La Paz, Centro de Investigación y Consultoría, 1984).
5. Discussion and documentation of alleged fraud is provided in Carmen Alcoreza and Javier Albó, 1978: *El nuevo campesinado ante el fraude* (La Paz, 1979), and Asamblea Permanente de los Derechos Humanos de Bolivia, *El fraude electoral* (La Paz, 1978).
6. Padilla reflected on the coup and his government in David Padilla Arancibia, *Decisiones y recuerdos de un general* (La Paz, 1980). The coup is also discussed in Gary Prado, *Poder de Las Fuerzas Armadas, 1949-1982* (La Paz: Los Amigos del Libro, 1984), pp. 333-52.
7. See Confederación de Empresarios Privados de Bolivia, *Pensamiento de la empresa privada Boliviana* (La Paz, 1981).
8. The role of the legislature in Bolivia is treated at length in Eduardo Gamarra, "Political Stability, Democratization and the Bolivian National Congress," (Ph.D. dissertation, University of Pittsburgh, 1987).
9. A detailed account of the plotting and scheming behind these events is contained in Irving Alcaraz, *El prisionero de palacio* (La Paz, Editorial Amerindia, 1983).

10. One account of the violence is Asamblea Permanente de Derechos Humanos de Bolivia, *La masacre de Todos Santos* (La Paz, 1980).
11. General treatment of the coup and its aftermath is contained in *Bolivia: Cronología de Una Dictadura* (La Paz, 1982); *Los cien primeros días de una larga noche* (Quito, Ecuador, 1981); and Pablo Ramos Sánchez, *Radiografía de un golpe de estado* (La Paz: Editorial Puerta del Sol, 1983).
12. An account of repression in the mines is Asamblea Permanente de Los Derechos Humanos de Bolivia. *La heróica resistencia de los mineros de Bolivia* (Lima, Perú, circa 1981).
13. CEPB documents of the period are contained in its previously cited volume, *Pensamiento de la empresa privada boliviana.*

5

Economic Crisis, Antipopulism, and Democracy

On October 5, 1982, the Congress first elected in 1980 met and by a vote of 113 to 29 elected Hernán Siles Suazo to be president of Bolivia. On October 10 Siles was sworn in as president and Jaimc Paz Zamora took the oath of vice-president. The two then set about to construct what in effect was a coalition government built around Siles's MNRI, the MIR of Paz Zamora, and the Bolivian Communist party (PCB).

It was an auspicious time. The military was at least temporarily neutralized as a political factor. All of the major sectors of the political class had become disillusioned with military-based authoritarian regimes and supported some mode of democracy, at least as a second-best option. The broad populace had demonstrated over and over that it wished some kind of civil democratic mode of governance. Furthermore, the clear electoral trend was toward Siles and the UDP, and all agreed that had new elections been held they would have moved toward a majority. In sum, there was a reservoir that the new president could tap as a source of authority and political power.

There was also a down side. The election of Siles had been the result of a compromise or pact among the major political parties. This was a positive sign, but still it was not a pact to govern, nor was it in any way a basic solution to the problem of political power. Indeed, the non-UDP parties, backed by the private sector and the military, used their power to avoid an election that might well have produced an electoral resolution of the power issue. In spite of the symbolic establishment of democracy, the pact was little more than another salida or temporary way out of an acute political crisis by postponing any joining of forces around the deeper power issues. Such a salida allowed the political contenders to avoid direct and potentially violent confrontation and bought time, but in so doing, they set up a government that was weak and incapable of governing.

157

From the outset the Siles government was constitutionally weak because of the fact that the main opposition parties had the capacity to form a blocking majority in both houses of Congress. Moreover, given the implicit affinity between the MNR and the ADN on broad economic issues, and the structural tendency of the Bolivian political process toward a game of "ins" and "outs," it was all but guaranteed that they would join forces to oppose and undercut the new government.

The structural or constitutional weakness of the new government was reinforced by another significant factor, the economic crisis. The central policy problem confronting the Siles government was to manage the economy through the accumulated problems that had ballooned into what all described as the worst economic crisis in Bolivian history. There was little question that Bolivia could not solve the crisis on its own and really needed international help, especially with its $3.5 billion foreign debt. International isolation had been one of the things that brought down García Meza and the military.[1] The question now: Where was the help with the foreign debt to come from, and at what price?

The reality of the situation was starkly clear. Bolivia is an overwhelmingly dependent country, and that palpable fact has limited the options and shaped the policies of all its governments since 1952. The issue of what model of development could or would be implemented had always hinged, at least in part, on Bolivia's international options and constraints. Specifically, the state socialist option depended on the willingness and the ability of elites in control of the state to break out of the orbit of the United States and persuade the socialist bloc to assume substantial economic, political, and military responsibility for Bolivia. Such a move was the basis of the successful consolidation of a state socialist model in Cuba.

In Bolivia elites committed to that route were never powerful enough domestically to infuse the state with such a will, and the international constellation was always such that there is overwhelming reason to believe that the Soviet Union would not have been willing or able to assume the role of Bolivia's protector and benefactor. Left politics in Bolivia had always been shaped by these realities, with the result that a substantial portion of the labor Left had always ended by buying into a populist version of the state capitalist model. Hence, from at least the late 1950s the dominant thrust was toward some version of the state capitalist model, which— whatever the rhetoric of the day—always locked Bolivia into the Western capitalist system and to substantial reliance on the United States and international organizations largely influenced by the United States.

Given this backdrop, there was deep irony in the election of Hernán Siles to the presidency in 1982. It was during his first presidency (1956-60), that the thrust toward a state capitalist model over a socialist alternative was defined in Bolivia. Moreover, articulation of political will in the international context of the day forced Siles to accept a strong IMF stabilization program, which he then had to spend most of his presidency imposing on the recalcitrant Left. A further irony lay in the fact that to bolster the capacity of the MNR-controlled state to impose the model, it was Siles who, with renewed U.S. military aid, began the resurrection of the military as an arm of the state to offset worker and peasant militas.

Here in 1982 Siles was back in the presidency in circumstances of almost complete déjà vu. Again the nation faced a severe economic crisis. Again a Bolivian government had to look to international actors, especially the IMF, in attempts to cope with the crisis. Again Hernán Siles Suazo had to find a way through this political and economic thicket. As it turned out, the situation of the 1980s was economically more complex and politically more problematic than 1956.

In the first instance there was a basic underlying tension between the pressing economic need to stabilize the economy, which in that context meant some kind of austerity program, and the political reality of the popular expectations awakened by the process of the political opening. This tension was enhanced by the nature of the UDP coalition, which over three elections had garnered broad popular support by articulating the aspirations of those who had borne the brunt of previous antipopulist regimes.

Siles himself had shifted left over the years since his last presidency. However, the old MNR stalwart had not acquired a state socialist orientation but had remained within the parameters of the original populist vision of the MNR. Siles and a large part of the MNRI were essentially populists, and therefore their relations with more Marxist-oriented Left groups were always strained. Indeed, the tension between a populist MNR vision and more radical Marxian socialist positions continued to undermine unity on the left and undercut the Left's ability to mount a joint front. This reality came to the surface during the Ovando and Torres interludes. Both of those governments were as much weakened and destabilized by their erstwhile supporters on the left as they were by their avowed enemies to the right. Siles was about to face the same political reality.

Basically, Siles confronted two interrelated dilemmas. The first was the division on the left between populists and Marxist socialists (by the way, in present contexts populists are often also referred to as social democrats). The second was the underlying tension between the political logic of populism and the imperatives of the economic reality that had been driving the process of political economy in Bolivia since 1952. Again, Siles found himself in a situation in which his own inclinations and that of his coalition pushed in a populist direction, while the domestic and international economic realities created an equal and opposite pull toward antipopulist stabilization policies.

The immediate, centrally relevant political actor for the new Siles government was still the COB. The COB was still the major voice of the working class, and whatever the votes of the workers, the COB would still be the major factor mediating the relationship between the working class and the new government. Siles made a number of bids to integrate the COB into his government, but the COB either rejected his overtures outright or demanded such a high political price as to make its formal incorporation impossible.

The COB from the beginning assumed an independent and autonomous position vis-à-vis the government. However, it did press for the government to recognize its "corporate," or *fuero*, rights to be dealt with as the quasi-sovereign voice of the working class unmediated by political parties or the legislature in its dealings with the government. Specifically, the COB assumed the de facto position of being a primary scrutinizer of government economic policy; indeed, it was able to assert all but de facto veto authority over economic policy.

From the first the COB took the position that although it supported the process of democratization and backed the government in general terms, it intended to push its own views on economic policy vigorously even if doing so put it in conflict with the government. As it had demonstrated in previous years, the COB intended to expose any attempts to assign the "social costs" of stabilization to the popular sectors, and in particular it was on record as being implacably opposed to any IMF-style stabilization programs based on monetarist economic logic. Finally, the COB made clear its intention to push three major lines of policy on the government. First, it demanded at a minimum populist-style redistributionist policies favoring the popular sectors. Second, it intended to press for structural and legal changes that would increase the autonomous corporate power of the COB within the state. Third, the COB telegraphed its intention to push for structural changes that would at least increase the role of the state in the economy and eventually shift the economy into a more state socialist mode. Tension, if not outright confrontation, with the COB was guaranteed for the new Siles government.

At this point it would be good to stress that although the COB acted as an entity, its leadership was far from monolithic or uniform on ideological or policy questions. On the contrary, the COB tended to be the main arena in which the myriad of leftist parties and factions vied with one another for the support of the politically crucial working class. Ideological, strategic, and personal differences always ran high in the COB. In that time and context, however, the logic of the internal politics of the COB only served to heighten its differences with the government and push it along a more adversarial path. This was particularly true in the case of Lechín, who at core was probably a populist but who often was forced into more radical positions by rivals in the COB who threatened his longtime popular standing with the workers.

There were a number of factors that helped guarantee that a Lechín-led COB would be confrontational with the Siles government. First Lechín perceived all of the parties of the UDP, and especially the PCB, as his longstanding and often bitter rivals for control in the COB. Internal COB politics demanded that Lechín not be predisposed to help such parties succeed in the eyes of the working class unless they were seen to be doing so under the prodding and pressure of Lechín and the COB. In short, the structural realities of Left politics helped undermine the Siles regime. Then there was the nebulous but nonetheless real factor of personalities. The vicissitudes of politics over the years had engendered some legendary hatreds among the original four major leaders of the revolution of 1952: Victor Paz Estenssoro, Hernán Siles Suazo, Juan Lechín Oquendo, and Walter Guevara Arce. There was particularly bad blood between Lechín and Siles, which among other things was traceable to the split between Siles, and Lechín and the Left of the MNR as a result of the stabilization program that had been imposed by Siles in the late 1950s. The general belief among the cognoscente was that Lechín both hated and distrusted Siles, and that he had no intention to see him succeed in the presidency.

There were plenty of other reasons to expect less than smooth relations between Siles and the COB. Owing to his own strategic decisions, Siles was particularly dependent on and therefore vulnerable to the COB. Throughout three campaigns Siles had stressed the left populist nature of his would-be government such that this had become a central component of his own and the UDP's political identity. As a result, even when he pondered what were in effect antipopulist policies, he was not inclined to reorganize his government and seek support from the center Right to offset the COB and the Left. Failing a credible political strategy from which to threaten the COB and the Left, Siles was to begin and end his presidency as essentially the political prisoner of both. He was never able to turn the relationship into one that generated positive support for his government and thereby increase his ability to seize the political high ground and define a coherent approach to the economic crisis.

During the first days of his presidency Siles acted vigorously against the remnants of the García Meza clique, giving his government an air of decisiveness and courage. Specifically, he moved to reorganize the upper reaches of the officer corps and purge it of men implicated in the García Meza regime and/or the drug trade. At the same time his government with the aid and collaboration of foreign governments captured and/or killed a number of the prominent neofacists associated with the paramilitary squads. Then, most dramatically, the government arrested Klaus Barbie in February 1983 on a legal technicality and shipped him to France—where he still awaits trial as a war criminal.

Although these actions gave the government some forward movement, they did not solve many other real problems. Chastened and weakened, the paramilitary groups and the García Meza clique of so-called Golpistas (persons prone to make coups) nevertheless did not disappear. Siles did assert formal control of the military and appointed new commanders known to be well disposed to a national populist type approach to policy. This fact plus the trauma of the García Meza period served to neutralize the military as a political force, which was obviously to the good. However, the best Siles could get from the military was a generalized support for the democratic process as such and a measure of cautious neutrality toward his government. He was not able to mobilize the military as an active force to support any particular approach to Bolivia's many problems.

Siles was not able to make any substantial progress against the by now well entrenched organizations involved in the drug trade. We still have very little knowledge of the trade and its multifaceted effects on Bolivian social, economic, and political life. For this and other reasons a discussion of the cocaine business in Bolivia is beyond the brief of this work; however, it is obviously a serious factor that, aside from any moral or legal questions is clearly distorting many dimensions of Bolivia society.[2]

The groups managing the trade have developed into extremely powerful armed organizations that assert de facto control over larger and larger portions of Bolivia and Bolivians. In some sections of the interior like the Chapáre region, the organizations had by 1982 developed into quasi-sovereign entities challenging the central state for practical control. Currently, the cocaine trade is pumping hundreds of millions of dollars through these organizations, which allows them to become more powerful and to penetrate other dimensions of Bolivian society.

The drug organizations are another factor undermining the institutional coherence of the state and corrupting public life in Bolivia. The Siles government, and other governments before, found it extremely difficult to bring the organizations to heel. Indeed, there were charges that the drug rings had penetrated his government, particularly the Ministry of Interior. The difficulty Siles had in dealing with this issue demonstrated not only the weakness of his government but, more seriously, the practical weakness of the central state as a sovereign. Additionally, the problem added a discordant note to Bolivian-U.S. relations. The United States pressured the Siles regime into adopting a coca eradication program similar to Peru's. In 1983 an agreement was finally reached between the regime and the United States whereby the United States promised an aid package of $14.7 million if Bolivia eradicated 10,000 hectares of coca production by 1986. The eradication program was to face stiff resistance from campesino groups, especially those tied to the COB; crop-substitution programs have never been well received by the campesinos. In reality, the dimensions of the drug trade go far beyond simple eradication and the destruction of cocaine-processing plants.

The fact is that the drug trade is not going to disappear any time soon and that drug organizations will continue to be a powerful force within Bolivia. Paradoxically, the ongoing economic crisis has served to strengthen the organizations, which have become an important source of income for wider and wider segments of the society, especially poor peasants and workers who when laid off from other jobs head for cocaine growing and processing areas. In some ways cocaine may have become crucial to the nation's economic survival, at least in the short run. Throughout the eighties Bolivia's capacity to legitimately earn foreign exchange has steadily diminished, and this has led to a growing disparity between legitimate exchange earnings and the import bill.

It is now generally agreed that the shortfall in dollars is being plugged by the illegal drug trade, which in some respects is Bolivia's major export industry. The point for the moment is that the drug organizations are deeply entrenched in Bolivia, and that they have become extremely powerful politically and economically. For these reasons, the Siles government was never able to get control of the situation, and itself probably suffered some penetration and subversion by the drug groups.

The Politics of Economic Packages

It was in the area of managing the economy through economic policy that the Siles government was to meet its greatest ongoing challenge. The government constituted on October 10, 1982, was a coalition of three parties: the MNRI held seven cabinet posts; the MIR, six ministries, and the PCB, two. As we noted above, it was structurally isolated and as a result potentially weak. Congress was dominated by the opposition, which was able to turn that into control of the judiciary as well. Moreover, Siles was forced to name to the potentially important post of comptroller a prominent businessman who was not a member of the UDP nor particularly sympathetic to it. The Senate had presented him with a list of three potential comptrollers, of whom Antonio Sanchez de Lozada was the only one not officially affiliated with a political party. As expected, Siles chose Sanchez de Lozada, who had served previously as minister of planning during the regime of General Ovando. Thus, Siles and the UDP controlled the executive but precious little else as far as key institutions went.

For the reasons catalogued here, the Siles government was rather weak relative to the formidable task it confronted in the area of economic policy. And, because the government was for all practical purposes ideologically divided, it was not in a position to define a positive substantive thrust economically. Hence, the government's orientation in regard to the crisis was mainly one of damage control in the form of stabilization programs.

In retrospect, it seems clear that Siles himself did not have a clear economic program in mind when he took office; rather, he looked to those around him to devise economic solutions. However, at the same time his approach to policy was directed firmly toward consensus among the diverse strands of his government. He always acted with one eye on the COB, which refused to accept any responsibility for policy formulation (unless it was ceded a majority of cabinet posts) but maintained a critical stance. From the first Siles was in the unenviable situation that his own erstwhile supporters were simultaneously his major potential opponents in the area of economic policy.

The central politics of the Siles government was the "politics of economic packages" *(paquetes económicos)*; the five or six packages proposed by the government were basically relatively coordinated sets of measures designed to stabilize the economy and contain the crises. From the outset the government suffered from the internal contradiction that the packages were in fact programs of severe cost allocations (austerity) that ran counter to the ideologies and values of all components of the government, not to mention the concrete interests of its bases of would-be popular support headed up by the COB. At best Siles and his cabinet saw the packages as necessary evils to be implemented with distaste, mainly because of the political realities of the domestic crisis and the demands of the needed international agencies like the IMF.[3] Moreover, the ideological inclinations of the regime as well as the pressure of its supporters predisposed it to seek to alleviate the popular costs of the packages, which violated the spirit or logic of those kinds of austerity programs.

Over the next three years a drama with minor variations was played out repeatedly. A designated economic team within the government would devise an austerity package, usually guided mainly by how the package would sit with the IMF and other interested international actors. In pursuit of consensus Siles would submit the package to the cabinet, which usually transformed it into a much watered down version that was then issued by decree. The COB immediately attacked the package as being antipopular and restated its own growing set of demands. The packages as well as the COB's reactions set off further negative reactions from all other groups and segments, which immediately mounted their own defensive positions. The government, battered from all sides, usually gave concessions to the COB and other naysayers, which not only weakened the policy even more but also provoked negative reactions from yet other groups like the CEPB and the regional *comités cívicos*. The upshot usually was that the crisis was unaffected, all key groups of civil society were more unhappy, and the government appeared to be increasingly weak and vacillating. From both the political and economic point of view the policy process was pretty much a downward spiral.

The first sally into the politics of paquetes económicos occurred on November 6 when the Siles government decreed its first stabilization program. Designed largely by a MIR economic team working out of the Ministry of Finance, it by and large represented an attempt at a "populist" program that would have a reduced negative impact on the popular sectors. As a result, it was not a program tailored for IMF approval or to respond to the open concerns of the private sector. It decreed a devaluation of the peso boliviano from $b.44.50 to $b.200 to the dollar. It also raised price ceilings on some items while increasing the minum monthly wage from $b.5,990 to $b.8,490. In addition, the government eliminated private banks from the exchange markets and proposed the nationalization of the electric corporation jointly owned by Canada and the United States. Most significant from a political point of view was the reintroduction of the concept of worker representation in state companies, which was implemented only in COMIBOL, the mining corporation in July 1983—this was an important move toward the concept of co-management that had existed in the early days of the revolution and was again a major demand of the COB.

The major attack against the program came almost immediately from the COB. Its principal complaints were that the minimum wage adjustment was too low and that the program did not combat "imperialism." At that point the opposition from the Left was not as strident as it was to become. Perhaps the tone was muted because Siles had previously requested and theoretically received a 100-day grace period to attack Bolivia's problems. In the end he did not really get the period free of debate and opposition, or from social pressure in the form of strikes of which there were some 204 during the government's first three months.

The dynamics of the process are fascinating and reveal much about the decomposition of Bolivia's formal political institutions. Owing in part to the political split between Siles and Congress, the paquete was issued by decree. Nonetheless, Siles did not want to threaten or challenge the congressional opposition. Thus, the November 6 package was read to a special meeting of Congress convoked by Siles. This was to be the last time Siles would even go through the motions of appeasing the congressional opposition.

All previous attempts to grapple with the economy had also been by decree however, and, of course, during the Banzerato policy flowed along by executive decree. The process of economic management, in fact, for some time had been executive centered. Moreover, in the context of formal democracy executives recognized the near-impossibility of maneuvering economic policy, especially austerity programs, through the legislative assembly and hence they all, Siles included, resorted to decree power.

Circumstances were reinforcing a trend toward an antagonistic split between the function of representing societal interests housed in the legislature and that of the management of the economy lodged in the executive. The process revealed a growing divergence also between a kind of logic of collective good pushed by the executive in the concept of national interest and a set of particularized logics articulated in the legislature in the form of group, class, regional, and factional interests. More often than not the accumulated weight of the latter amounted to a roadblock to the former. To avoid policy paralysis in the legislature executives then turned to government by decree, which often stretched the boundaries of constitutional law. There was, in brief, a built-in tendency for executives to act in a de facto authoritarian manner. That was a fact not lost on the legislature which aside from questioning the substance of the policy, began to attack Siles on constitutional grounds. The attacks later became the basis for attempts to unseat him. In the short term, however, Siles simply ignored Congress and moved to govern without it and around it. Congress, in turn, raised a steady drumbeat of criticism of all aspects of governmental policy.[4]

If Siles could govern de facto without Congress, he could not do so without the COB. Indeed, in the area of economic policy the arena of debate in a sense shifted to the assemblies of the COB. The COB to some degree became a substitute legislature with the de facto capacity to blunt, modify, and some times block government economic policy. It became the most important interlocutor with the Siles government, economically speaking.

The package of November 6 had one more feature that was to have many and mostly negative political and economic affects. The MIR economic team designed a so-called dedollarization program under which all dollar accounts were to be converted into pesos at the official exchange rate. The move was to some extent probably emulating recent policy moves in Mexico. The Bolivian context was quite different. The aim of the policy theoretically may have been to give the government more control over dollars in the economy and perhaps to assess costs on the private sector. The practical results were otherwise. Owing to the rapid rise in the value of the dollar on the illegal parallel market, the decree ended up as a boon to wealthy individuals and companies in the private sector who were able to retire their dollar debts by way of the central bank at a fraction of their value. Some persons in the private sector have estimated that it amounted to a government subsidy of the sector of at least $500 million. Hence, by feeding inflation and debasing the local currency, the decree actually shifted costs from the private sector to the population at large. Among the most negatively affected were those with small dollar savings accounts who saw the value of their deposits reduced drastically.

As 1982 came to an end, the Siles government was in a curious situation. Internationally, the outlook was good. Following the lead of the United States, foreign governments and international financial institutions indicated a willingness to give the Siles government the benefit of the doubt. Economic aid began to flow again. Siles had great prestige internationally and was afforded statesman status when he visited the UN. However, although the international community seemed to wish him well in global political terms (i.e. restoring democracy), below the surface caution and concern were the order of the day regarding the economy and especially Bolivia's foreign debt.

In Bolivia itself, the economic situation was grim; in the opinion of most, the grimmest since the early days of the great revolution. In 1982 GNP fell by 9.2 percent as almost all sectors registered a decline. The drop was particularly sharp in construction (a big beneficiary in the Banzer years), which was off by as much as 40 percent. Inflation was heating up, evidenced in the steady rise of the dollar on the parallel market. One human manifestation of the inflationary situation was the proliferation of small-time money changers who congregated in the centrally located Avenida Camacho in La Paz, which was dubbed "little Wall Street."

The national debt was most alarming: edging toward $4 billion, and among the highest per capita ratios in the region. Service on the debt was around 32 percent of the value of exports. Much of the debt was in short-term loans, many of which had been contracted by García Meza with Brazil and Argentina to help service earlier debts. Foreign exchange flows could not sustain the burden, and Bolivia was in arrears by some $182 million even as obligations due in 1983 and 1984 were looming large.

Disarray in the UDP

The stresses and strains of the situation showed up quickly in the UDP coalition. In early January 1983 a split opened between the MIR and the MNRI. The MIR accused the MNRI of refusing to cooperate in the cabinet and declared that Siles lacked a coherent approach to economic policy. As charges and countercharges flew back and forth, the six MIR ministers on January 7 collectively resigned from the cabinet, effectively ending the MIR's participation in the UDP. The leavetakers continued their attacks and in addition faulted Siles and the MNRI for being weak and ineffective against the Right paramilitary groups and the cocaine organizations. Particularly severe charges of links to the drug trade were leveled at the MNRI minister of the interior.

The MIR was also reacting to Siles's continued reliance on the so-called international technocrats who had returned to Bolivia to work for the regime. The MIR, especially the Aranibar brothers, believed that these "independent technocrats" were undermining the economic recovery program by pushing for IMF-style correctives.

As a result of the MIR withdrawal, another interesting constitutional situation developed. Although the party left, its titular leader Jaime Paz Zamora remained as vice-president; over the succeeding weeks he increasingly moved into overt opposition to Siles and developed open connections with the opposition in Congress. He became, for all practical purposes, a congressional fifth columnist planted in the government. Again, talk of constitutional coups began to fill the air, with one scenario having Congress ousting Siles in favor of Paz Zamora.

Siles's political problems did not end with the disaffection of the MIR. His own MNRI also fell ill to that endemic disease of Bolivia's parties: factional splits. The first open split was between a faction headed by Felix Rospigliossi known as the *palaciegos* (roughly meaning those embedded in the presidential palace close to Siles) and the so-called legalist branch of the party, or MNRI *legalista*. The latter were mainly old-time political stalwarts with roots in the main branch of the MNR. The palaciegos, newcomers who had developed close personal ties to Siles during his exile under Banzer, were perceived and painted as somewhat sinister (particularly Rospigliossi) radicals manipulating the septuagenarian Siles who was portrayed as weakened in his judgment by age.

The legalistas split with Siles's palaciegos over the latter's refusal to recognize the leadership of Federico Alvarez Plata. Alvarez Plata, now a senator, had been elected at the MNRI's national convention in 1979, but the palaciegos did not accept the results of that convention. The palaciegos were supported by a third faction, which called itself Siglo XX and was led by Deputy Mario Velarde Dorado. During the three-year rule of Siles, Velarde would fall in and out of favor with the MNRI and would end up splitting from the party.

Even as the battle between the legalistas and the palaciegos was being played out, the legalistas split again, with one faction of MNRI legislators going over to the opposition in Congress. One of the dissident MNRI leaders, Samuel Gallardo, was elected president of the Chamber of Deputies. On top of these developments the PCB was accused of playing a Machiavellian game of pushing for power in the COB by undermining the economic program of the government. By early 1983 the UDP and the executive branch of government were in all but total disarray.

It took Siles some three weeks to put a new government together, during which time the nation functioned without central direction. This became a pattern during the Siles period and occurred during subsequent cabinet crises. The fact is that Siles had to devote increasing amounts of his time and energy to putting out political fires among his erstwhile supporters, to trying to form and maintain a government intact. As a result, he had much less time and energy available to govern the country. On numerous occasions the central government for all practical purposes came to a standstill as Siles exhausted himself juggling personalities and factions.

At the end of January a new cabinet was finally installed. In the place of the MIR, Siles recruited five new ministers, three from the MNRI and two independents. In the new scheme the PCB kept the Ministry of Labor and the Ministry of Mining. Over the next few months the PCB emerged as a leading force in the government, articulating prolabor positions and raising questions of more radical structural reform. For political dynamics, this was an important turn.

The COB Vs. the CEPB

The private sector had kept a relatively low profile until then and had acted mainly to push its own programs for economic stabilization and economic reorganization before the public. However, as the power of the COB to press the government grew, the private sector became worried about the drift of the government. With the increasing role of the PCB, worry turned to alarm. In early February the CEPB took up the cudgels and assailed the government for adopting "subtle plans to little by little liquidate the private sector."[5] It was a notable political turning point. Since the late 1970s, the postrevolutionary national bourgeoisie, liberated from the paternalistic tutelage of the Banzer neopatrimonial state, had been consolidating itself as a relatively coherent and politically self-conscious class. The CEPB, in turn, had been emerging as an important speaker for that class, for which it was putting forward a neoliberal economic model. The perceived threat from the COB-pushed Siles government served to consolidate the national bourgeoisie into a self-conscious political class; concurrently, the CEPB under its new president, Fernando Illanes, assumed the role of main voice of the private sector and major defender of its interests.

For all intents and purposes the CEPB became to the private sector and the bourgeoisie what the COB was to the working class. Like the COB, the CEPB took an autonomous critical position toward the government, and like the COB, it sought openly and directly to put pressure on the executive (which in this case was the government). In its new, more aggressive role, the CEPB aimed a good deal of its fire at the COB, especially on matters of economic policy, labor policy, and issues of authority in enterprises. In so doing, the CEPB assumed the role of being the interlocuter with the COB. The two associations were acting out what was in effect a class struggle independent of political parties and the legislature. From that point on the Siles government was like a Ping-Pong ball being bounced back and forth by paddles held by the COB and the CEPB. The result was that the government vacillated even more as it succumbed now to the pressure of one and then to the counterpressure of the other.

The tensions between the two associations built up throughout 1983. The CEPB reacted to several attempts by workers to take over private businesses, and the COB accused the private sector of evading taxes and paying unjust wages. By early 1984 their set-tos had turned into full-scale confrontations that put the government squarely in the middle. For example, in January 1984 the COB launched a series of strikes and demonstrations against the government's economic policy and low salaries. The protests concerned what was to become one of the COB's central demands: a minimum salary indexed to inflation. It was demand that was resisted by the government's economic policymakers because of the fear that to accede to it would only further fuel inflation.

The CEPB immediately charged that the government sought to strangle the private sector by denying its enterprises the vital foreign exchange needed to import inputs. It argued that private enterprises had inputs sufficient to function for only approximately twenty days. To pressure the government, it warned that if within thirty days the policies had not changed, it would seek broad based civic mobilization against the government. To make the point of its power, the CEPB declared a forty-eight-hour private sector strike beginning February 6.

The government reacted in what had become a characteristic manner. In response to the pressure of the COB, it announced a series of wage increases. At the same time it recognized the legitimacy of the private sector's complaints and declared its intentions to work the problems out in consultation with the CEPB. This provoked the COB to question the legality of any private sector strike and to accuse the private sector of planning a coup d'état. The government, in turn, pleaded for time to get its programs into place. Siles, in announcing the wage increases, complained to the COB that proliferating strikes and work stoppages were undermining the democratic process. At the same time the minister of finance publicly pleaded that it was impossible for the government to formulate a rational economic plan when it was constantly subjected to such intense direct and contradictory pressures.

Throughout 1983 and 1984, the government's pleas notwithstanding, pressures mounted on all sides. Aside from the COB and the CEPB, pressures came from the opposition-controlled Congress, which was looking for ways to assert its prerogatives in policymaking, and from regional civic committees and development corporations looking to cut deals for their localities. For its part, the government limped forward as the cabinet declared without letup that it was studying and analyzing the country's myriad problems and searching for solutions.

The spring of 1983 (fall in Bolivia) saw the beginning of one of the more important struggles of the Siles period. In response to a strike by technical and administrative personnel of a state mine, the federation of mine workers (FSTMB), backed by the COB, on April 29 took control of the COMIBOL central offices in La Paz. Once in control of the offices, the COB demanded co-management of all state enterprises and ultimately of all enterprises in the private sector as well. The government split on how to respond. Siles and the MNRI declared a willingness to discuss some type of representation in management but denounced the occupation of the offices as well as the COB demand for majority control. The PCB, in turn, backed the occupation. For its part, the congressional opposition condemned the action. The CEPB was particularly incensed by the possibility of worker co-management in the private sector; it opposed the COB's demand and assailed the government's wage increases as capitulation to labor pressure.

The battle over co-management (co-gestión administrativa) continued into the month of July. Throughout the COB underscored the weakness of the government as Lechín openly dared Siles to try to dislodge the FSTMB from the COMIBOL offices. The government did not try. In the first week of July an agreement was signed whereby the government granted the FSTMB "parity management" in COMIBOL. Ostensibly a compromise with labor's demand for majority control, the agreement ended with the FSTMB and the COB gaining de facto majority control. Siles agreed to appoint one of the state's management representatives from a list drawn up by the FSTMB. The upshot was that the FSTMB had four representatives and the state two on the six-man board.

Co-management in COMIBOL was a great victory for the COB. It signaled an accumulation of institutional power that the COB had not had since the early days of the revolution. Moreover, the irony was not lost that the COB was rebuilding its power at the expense of the very man, Siles, who had engineered the beginning of the COB's slide in the late 1950s.

At the height of the struggle Siles had again sought to gain some control over the COB by offering it co-government with the attendant theoretical responsibilities. Lechín again refused. The refusal was a result of Siles's own refusal to a COB proposal for 51 percent control over the cabinet. The UDP rejected this demand in part because of the need to distribute power quotas to all its members. The COB also demanded control over the most important cabinet posts including labor, mining, planning, and finance.

The COB continued on the course it had taken over the years of building its power as an autonomous corporate entity with semisovereign authority. Its power was built on the government's recognition of the COB's monopoly position as labor's singular national representative and by the steady appropriation by the COB of power and authority that ostensibly inhered in the state. Be that as it may, by mid-1983 the COB was at the zenith of its power; a power that was clearly too much for the debilitated Siles government to handle.

A Weakening Government

The confrontation with the COB and the generalized pressure on the government provoked another cabinet crisis. On July 14 two independent ministers who had been crucial in economic policy, Flavio Machicado (finance) and Arturo Nuñez del Prado (planning), resigned. Over the next few weeks Siles maneuvered to induce either the MIR or the COB to enter the government. Both refused and the crisis continued until a new cabinet was finally constituted on August 25. Once again Bolivia went some six weeks without an effective government in place.

By July and August 1983 the economic situation had become even more grave. Production had continued to decline, deficits had mounted, and inflation had begun to move into the range of 300 + percent annually. One measure of the inflation was the fact that in July the official exchange rate was $b.200 to the dollar while the parallel rate passed the $b.800 mark.

If the deplorable state of the economy was not enough, nature also dealt Bolivia and the Siles government a series of bad blows. Shifts in the currents off the west coast of Latin America (El Niño) set off climatic changes that caused severe droughts in some parts of Bolivia while others were inundated by record floods. The combined effects of the natural disasters were a sharp drop in the production of basic food staples, raising the spectre of starvation in some areas, particularly the southern Sierra. During July and August hundreds of starving peasants descended on La Paz to beg in the streets and seek other means of survival.

Throughout late July and August the government negotiated openly with the COB over possible terms of its entry into the government. The talks revealed much about the divisions of the Left in Bolivia and the double bind that the Siles government had fallen into. Basically, the COB enunciated demands for entry that called for a break with the Western financial system, symbolized by the IMF, and a move toward state control of the private sector as well as bread-and-butter commitments to labor. Although the COB insisted that its terms were not socialist but nationalist, their acceptance would have meant that the government would have forestalled all options to the right and therefore definitely embarked on a course toward some mode of state socialism. Neither Siles nor the MNRI could accept the terms, in part because ideologically the man and the party were more populists than socialists and in large part because those charged with economic policy perceived that in the short term they had no choice but to seek some accommodation with the IMF and the Western capitalist financial system.

These differences in ideology and perception crystallized the split on the Left in Bolivia between populists and socialists that was all but unresolvable, especially with regard to the government and the COB. The fact was that Lechín and the COB were implacably opposed to any accommodation with the IMF and the system it represented. That hostility was partly ideological and partly rooted in the history of postrevolutionary Bolivia. Neither Lechín nor the COB had forgotten the heavy political and economic costs imposed on their constituency by the same Siles in the name of an IMF stabilization program in the late 1950s.

Likewise, the COB noted that the bulk of the debt had been contracted under military-based regimes (especially Banzer's and García Meza's) that favored the private sector even as they forcibly imposed costs on labor. From the COB point of view the debt was not a debt of the mass of Bolivian workers and peasants but of the private sector and the military; hence, the COB in the name of the workers and peasants simply refused to recognize the debt's validity. Its position at base was that the middle and upper classes had caused the debt and the crisis and they should pay for it. To some extent the Siles government's economic advisers agreed with the COB analysis but argued that whatever the roots of the debt and crisis, the government had no realistic alternative except to come to terms with Bolivia's creditors and to spread the costs of a solution across the population.

Throughout the cabinet crisis of July and August the CEPB kept up its own pressure on Siles. On at least two occasions it declared itself in a state of emergency. It also held conferences to discuss the economic crisis and analyze government policy or, from its point of view, the lack thereof. Most interesting, the president of the CEPB traveled extensively to Santa Cruz to launch his attacks and to rally the eastern private sector behind the national effort of the CEPB.

The Siles government kept trying to walk between the two antagonistic organizations of the COB and the CEPB; it ended by satisfying neither. The new cabinet installed on August 28 was a patchwork stitched together almost in desperation by Siles. The cabinet included eight ministers from the MNRI, two from the PCB, two from the Christian Democrats (PDC), two independents, one from an MIR offshoot faction, and one military officer. In forming this new government Siles explicitly defined its major mission as coping with the deteriorating economic situation.

The new team soon made clear its view that the economic crisis demanded that Bolivia come to terms with Western financial circles. On September 13 the Bolivians began negotiations with the IMF toward achieving a "flexible accord." For its part, the IMF indicated that Bolivia would have to adopt drastic austerity measures if an accord was to be reached. The COB immediately castigated the discussions and warned that any IMF-inspired program would put Bolivia's fledgling democracy in jeopardy. The pressures and counterpressures on the government were severe. The economic situation continued to deteriorate, and the government now found itself unable to meet its debt service payments. The pressure from the IMF and the CEPB was strong to bite the bullet and buy into an IMF package. The counterpressure from the COB was if anything stronger.

Throughout September and October strikes and stoppages mounted to avalanche proportions. The COB pressed against any accommodation with the IMF, as well as for its own emerging program and for immediate wage increases. The government tried to buy time by decreeing substantial wage and bonus increases even as it continued its efforts to define an economic package that would surely run counter to the COB's positions. Negotiations with the IMF continued.

November began in an air of great tension. All of the key groups knew that it was only a matter of time before talks with the IMF would produce another paquete económico. Knowing full well that the paquete would carry with it substantial social costs, numerous groups and parties led by the COB began a series of anticipatory attacks on government economic policy. The government took a conciliatory turn, especially to the COB, and on November 10 gave further wage concessions. At the same time the government entered into open talks aimed at concertación (harmonious agreement) with both the COB and the CEPB. Once again the government was going to attempt to put together an economic package by way of negotiation with two key societal sectors with deeply differing views regarding the immediate economic crisis, not to mention the long-term economic future. Both groups, furthermore, had consistently voiced dissatisfaction with the government's style and performance to that date.

On November 17 the much-anticipated package came forth. It was not particularly radical but rather yet another watered-down stabilization plan based to some degree on monetarist logic. The peso was devalued from $b.200 to 500 (on the parallel market it was running at 2,000), prices on commodities like gasoline were raised, subsidies on many food items lifted, and some tax adjustments were attempted. The paquete was immediately denounced from all sides, particularly the COB, the CEPB, and the opposition parties in Congress. As usual, the government had responded to multiple pressures and ended by pleasing no one.

As the customary battle with the key interest groups was being waged by strikes, stoppages, public pronouncements, and the like, a full-scale constitutional crisis erupted between Siles and Congress. Led by the Senate, Congress assailed not only the content of the paquete but what it charged was Siles's unconstitutional and dictatorial mode of formulating and promulgating policy. Again talk of various schemes to effect a constitutional coup *(golpe constitucional)* were rife. In most scenarios the justification for the action was the numerous alleged infractions of constitutional law by Siles, and most scenarios projected the substitution of Vice-president Paz Zamora for Siles. The schemes being hatched in Congress, however, were attacked by most of the key external groups, particularly the COB and the CEPB, both of whom called for an uninterrupted continuation of the "democratic" system.

It also became evident that the CEPB was acting independently of any political parties that ostensibly spoke for the private sector. In the wake of the paquete of November 17, for example, the Paz MNR made an obvious attempt at buying popular support by introducing a bill that provided a 100 percent wage increase over and above the paquete. The CEPB denounced the bill as inflationary and demagogic, but it nonetheless passed in the Senate with the aid of ADN votes. Clearly, the schemes of the parties to gain short-term political advantage ran counter to the perceived long-term interests of the CEPB. This reinforced the inclination of the CEPB, like that of the COB to follow an autonomous policy line and to aim its major efforts directly at the executive.

Although it backed off on the coup plan, the opposition-controlled Congress was determined to assert its institutional will against the executive. Through intense interpellations of ministers Congress was obviously moving toward a generalized censure of the entire cabinet. Sensing the strategy, the cabinet preempted Congress by resigning en masse on December 14, 1983, an action the members said was designed to forestall a constitutional coup. This latest round of the struggle between the executive and the legislature over constitutional prerogatives provoked another cabinet crisis that was to last for thirty-six days.

As 1983 drew to a close, the economic balance sheet did not carry encouraging news. The inflation rate was at 300 percent and climbing. The GDP had fallen by 7.3 percent; the per capita product, by some 8.7 percent. Unemployment was up, real income down. The deficit was expanding rapidly. And, Bolivia was falling further and further behind in its debt payments.

The United States was an important influence during the Siles period, although it by no means had the capacity to determine specific political outcomes. Under Ambassador Edwin Corr, the U.S. embassy maintained a high profile. The United States was openly supportive of the democratization process. It was mildly supportive of the Siles government but remained cautiously suspicious of Siles populist roots and the role the Left, particularly the PCB, played in his government. Although the United States did try to pressure Siles to break with the PCB, general assistance levels were increased somewhat over previous years as a gesture of support. Total economic and military aid jumped from $12.8 million and $19.7 million in 1981 and 1982, respectively, to $63 million in 1983 and $78.1 million in 1984.

There is little question that the United States backed the democratization process during the Siles years, but given its previous backing of authoritarian, antipopulist regimes, the U.S. like most of the key political actors in Bolivia—backed some mode of liberal democracy more as a second-best option in that specific context. Moreover, like the bulk of the center Right opposition, the United States saw a trend to the right that would come to fruition in the next elections. Also, the embassy opened its doors to the emergent private sector in Bolivia and encouraged its new political role as well as its program to roll back the state and stimulate more market-centered development. By 1984 the U.S. embassy, like many others, was oriented mainly toward riding out the Siles government until the expected turnabout in the next elections.

Yet, the United States did bring great pressure to bear on the Siles government, which in some senses created strains in the democratization process. Aside from the issue of the PCB, the United States urged Siles to come to terms with the IMF and Bolivia's major international creditors. Hence, it backed monetarist-based austerity programs that would put Siles into a confrontation mode with the labor Left. As in the case of many other Latin American countries at this time, the United States was walking a thin line between backing a shift to more open democratic regimes while pursuing economic policy goals that clashed with the maintenance of popular support for democracy.

The major U.S. pressure regarded controlling the flow of cocaine into the United States. Bolivia, along with Peru, is a principal source of the coca leaf from which cocaine is extracted; hence, the push by the United States was for the Siles government to break existing drug rings and push for a long-term program of crop substitution among the Bolivia peasantry. For a host of reasons beyond the scope of this work, both goals were extremely difficult for any Bolivian government, to pursue realistically—let alone one as weak as the Siles-UDP government. Nonetheless, the United States made control of coca production the main policy issue with Siles. The appointment of Ambassador Corr, an expert in the matter, symbolized the significance the United States attributed to the issue. A good chunk of the increased U.S. assistance to Bolivia went into drug enforcement. Despite the public commitment of the United States to the drug control program initiated by Corr, between 1983 and 1986 only $14.7 million was authorized by Washington to finance the program. By June 1986 only $7.2 million had been released; the remainder was cut off by the Reagan administration due to the Bolivian government's inability to eradicate 10,000 hectares of coca production.

The Beginning of the End

On April 12, 1984, the Siles government announced a new austerity package that represented the culmination of a nearly two-year attempt to reconstitute the UDP. After intense negotiations the MIR had returned to the cabinet, but upon announcement of the paquete Walter Delgadillo of the MIR's *fabril* (factory worker) sector resigned as minister of housing and broke with the MIR altogether.

For the next two months the nation was rocked by a concerted reaction from the COB. The Central Bank's employees' union refused to implement the measures decreed by Siles, and the COB declared a general strike to protest the economic policy of the regime. By the end of May the confrontation between Siles, the UDP, and the COB required a drastic solution. Siles gave in to the COB's pressures: he accepted the resignation of Flavio Machicado as minister of finance; conceded another series of wage and salary increases, and an unprecedented move also acceded to the COB insistence in stopping payment on Bolivia's foreign debt to private international banks.

June, July, and August were difficult months for Siles and for Bolivia. The deteriorating economy, constant strikes, demonstrations, battles with Congress, enervating cabinet crises, and so on all combined to sap the Siles-UDP government of its last vestiges of authority. In a bizarre incident in late June Siles was actually kidnapped for a brief period by the officers involved with a special police unit set up with U.S. backing to combat drug trafficking. As a result, coup rumors began to circulate, as did rumors of a possible dramatic resignation by Siles. By August the government was in complete disarray.[6] The political weakness of the government was made clear at the beginning of the month when, with the help of MNRI dissidents, the combined opposition led by the MNRH and the ADN gained control of all the leadership positions of both houses of Congress. From that point on the rump factions of the UDP were completely powerless in Congress, and the government was isolated and cut off from any support in the legislature. It also became clear then that for the opposition-controlled Congress, a way had to be found to oust Siles while maintaining intact the concept of a civilian transfer of power. Once again, talk of constitutional coups and other schemes abounded.

In late August the opposition was given the card it needed to fill out its hand against Siles. Under intense U.S. pressure, August was declared a key month in the battle against *narcotráfico*. With great fanfare troops were moved into one of the main coca-producing areas and the issue of drug control took center stage. Almost immediately the government was attacked for publicizing its moves prior to their execution. Critics charged that the publicity served only to warn the drug chiefs, and that this fact revealed that the Siles government had been penetrated by the drug organizations. So, on top of all his other problems Siles now had to contend with a growing public image that he was presiding over a corrupt government, that was in cahoots with drug traffickers—as the government of García Meza had been.

Then an incident occurred that seemed to confirm all of the worst rumors and suspicions. It was revealed that Rafael Otazo, head of the National Council on the Control of Narcotráfico and a close personal friend of Siles, had established contact with the alleged kingpin of the Bolivian drug trade, Roberto Suárez. Otazo publicly claimed that acting with the direct authorization of President Siles he met twice with Suárez and discussed, among other things, a scheme whereby Suarez would provide the government with $2 billion to help with the nation's economic problems, especially the foreign debt. Siles repudiated the Otazo story. Otazo fought back by giving credence to charges of governmental connections to the drug trade; in particular, he pointed to Minister of Interior Mario Roncal, whose name had long been bandied about in popular rumors. In spite of Siles's denials, political damage had been done. The opposition in Congress moved quickly to exploit what had become known as the Otazo affair. A joint committee was set up to investigate the matter. As September wore on, Congress was moving toward an attempt to impeach Siles for his government's alleged involvement with Suárez and other drug organizations.

Even as the Otazo affair was heating up, the public struggle between the CEPB and the COB escalated, as did the COB's ongoing conflict with the government. On August 29 Gonzalo Iturralde, the owner of the Collana cheese farms was murdered by one of his farm foremen. The CEPB and its supporters in Congress charged that its was a political murder mounted by COB-backed peasant unions aimed at seizing private farms. In fact, prominent figures on the Left did publicly defend the act and cast it in the political terms of a justifiable strike by the oppressed against an oppressor. A publicity battle between the CEPB and the Left raged for days in the newspapers and in the halls of Congress. For its part, the Siles government tried to ignore the whole matter in the obvious hope that it would go away, but the passions mobilized by the incident did not fade and complete polarization between the CEPB and the COB was set in place. The question was, could Bolivia's fragile democratic institutions contain and survive the intense conflict between these two politically significant class organizations?

Early September also proved to be a turning point in the relationship between the COB and the Siles government. In spite of its actions the COB to that point had been officially following a policy of supporting the Siles government in principle while it sought to pressure it to move Bolivia in a more populist and left direction. At its convention in September the COB basically broke completely with the Siles government and declared its revolutionary intention to move Bolivia toward a socialist society based on "popular democracy." The final resolutions passed by the convention condemned the Siles government as a "bourgeois government" dedicated to imposing an IMF economic program on Bolivia that was aimed at consolidating a bourgeois society that would continue to oppress workers and peasants. The resolutions went on to charge that the Siles government had broken with the masses by resisting co-management, refusing the emergency plan of the COB, and leaning toward imperialism. As a result, there was now an irreversible rupture between the government of Siles and the movement of workers and popular forces.

The COB resolutions returned to the concepts of popular power versus bourgeois state power that had been pushed in 1970 during the Asamblea Popular. They argued that the popular forces had to seize political power and use it to expel the native agents of imperialism and the dominant classes. The task was more urgent than ever because of the political crises provoked by the exhaustion of the UDP formula. The COB had to convert itself into an alternative source of power for the nation.

The problem that the COB confronted, however, was the same one that it had come up against over and over during the previous three decades. It simply did not have the power to impose its will on Bolivia. The best it could achieve on its own was to pressure ostensibly Left populist regimes to accept its demands. But even here the COB had more success defending populist bread-and-butter demands than in pushing for a definitive movement toward socialism and popular democracy. However, in pressuring populist governments the COB generally had undercut their ability to govern and in the past had often provoked a response from the Right that had set off antipopulist reaction and repression.

In September of 1984 the COB was in a familiar dilemma. There was no longer any real possibility that the existing government would or could act as an instrument to reach the COB's stated revolutionary goals. Moreover, given the existing political game, the prognosis for the COB was not good. Having won many battles in the sense of blocking unwanted policy initiatives, the COB now found itself in a position where it was in danger of losing the war, for within the confines of a liberal democratic or bourgeois system the drift of power was clearly away from the COB.

The COB officially had never been comfortable with liberal pluralist or bourgeois democracy. At best the formal democratic formula was seen as a way out of right-wing military governance and as a first step on the way to socialism and popular democracy. In short it was a formula to be used and transcended. Now that the COB confronted the reality of its inability to use the system to achieve its long-term goals, it was forced to look for other formulas.

In the immediate context the COB declared its intention to defend the existing "democratic process" from any disruptions from the Right, be they based on what COB leaders called traditional "fascist coup formulas" or one of the newer notions of a "parliamentary coup." But, at the same time it called upon "patriotic forces" in the military to contemplate what was necessary to achieve a truly democratic society. Hence, as it had done in the past, the COB sought to draw factions of the military to its side. It also kept up pressure on the Siles government through yet more strikes and demonstrations.

By October the position of the Siles government had become completely untenable. The opposition parties in Congress had seized upon the Otazo affair to batter the government unceasingly. The plans for impeachment marched forward as almost daily some new scheme to remove Siles was floated through the halls of Congress and the newspapers. The COB at that point aimed its ire at Congress, using demonstrations and threats to employ the popular forces to shut Congress down. The COB concurrently called on Siles to carry out a coup himself *(auto golpe)* by which he would shut down Congress and decree the COB's socialist *emergencia.* The best Siles could do was yet again to shuffle his cabinet, this time including the two top army commanders in key positions. The manuever at best brought buy time.

Beset on all sides, Siles on October 25 declared himself to be on a hunger strike to defend democracy. His action was in response to a resolution passed in Congress the previous day condemning the government's supposed negotiation with Roberto Suárez. The hunger strike, Siles averred, was aimed at creating a climate of "peace and reflection" in the country. It turned out to be a failure, but did provoke the National Conference of Bishops to call a meeting of all political forces to seek some kind of "social, political and economic pact to save the nation." The conference was attended mainly by center Right opposition parties from Congress, and the main thrust of the discussions was of schemes to oust Siles while maintaining the liberal democratic electoral framework intact. The COB condemned the conference and called its own conclave of Left parties and "patriotic" military men.

Throughout the conflict with Congress and the parties, the COB continued to assail the Siles regime. It had refused to support Siles's hunger strike, and on November 10 called for a general strike to protest the government's refusal to give in to its demands for implementation of the Plan de Emergencia.

In the midst of all this, on November 23, the government tried again to launch an economic package. Again the COB used its power in the streets to eviscerate the plan. The government did manage to devalue the peso to 9,000 to the dollar. However, the potential effects of that were offset by wage adjustments in which the minimum wage was raised from $b.128,000 to $b.204,000. Meanwhile the black market rate was at $b.18,000 to the dollar and still climbing.

In the same month, November, Siles symbolically threw in the towel and looked to the bishops conference to find a salida whereby he could leave his office in dignity and with the democratic system intact. The action shifted to the bishops conference, where the opposition parties continued to press rival schemes to bring Siles down. After intense maneuvering the parties agreed to a scheme pushed by Banzer's ADN to have early elections. Once the parties were more or less in line, Siles also formally accepted the salida.

The COB leadership was infuriated by the settlement, which it denounced as yet another ploy at the expense of the working class by the Siles government and the right-wing parties. A good deal of the anger came out in demonstrations against the economic measures of November 23 and subsequent attempts to grapple with the economic crisis. Although the COB could still undo economic policy it was powerless to block the emerging political formula. In early December Congress convened to put the salida into legal effect: elections were to be held on June 16, 1985, with the transfer of power to occur on the traditional date, August 6. The ratification of the political formula arrived at by the opposition parties in November immediately created a lame duck government and changed the nature of the political context. Most of the parties shifted their emphases to prepare for the June balloting. The UDP came to an end as the MIR and the PCB abandoned the government to join in the general jockeying; both not unexpectedly sought to distance themselves from administrative policies. On December 14, Vice-president Paz Zamora resigned and declared his candidacy for the presidency, although this was technically prohibited by the Constitution. The move by Paz Zamora led to a serious split in the MIR, with Antonio Aranibar, who had his own presidential ambitions, gathering his followers to form a new "MIR-free Boliva." It took Siles twenty eight days, until January 10, 1985, to put together a new government, formed almost exclusively from the MNRI.

The Struggle For Position

From the point of view of political power and ideology, the new electoral round was to be extremely important. The great weakness of the Siles government over and above its policy failures was that it was unable to resolve any underlying power issues and point the nation in any particular substantive direction. That weakness was built into the Siles government because from the first it was the product of a salida, or compromise, engineered among the main parties, interest groups, and the military. It did not have its own mandate to rule either through elections or the commitment of an institution with muscle, such as the military, to back its policies and programs.

Moreover, the salida that produced the Siles administration entailed an arrangement that for all intents and purposes guaranteed a standoff between the ideologically opposed executive and legislative powers. Indeed, it is clear that the center Right parties, the private sector, the civic committees, and parts of the military backed the salida of October 1982 precisely because it assured that they could block Siles, the UDP, and the COB from leading the nation into some definitively left populist or socialist direction.

The structural weakness that hampered the Siles government from the outset was compounded by the deep ideological and policy differences between the populists and socialists within the UDP coalition. A fact that was compounded further by the position of qualifiedly antagonistic support taken by the COB toward the UDP government. In spite of its earlier electoral performances, the Siles-UDP government inaugurated in October 1982 in fact had no stable base of institutional or popular support and was never able to achieve such a base.

The fundamental ideological and policy differences over alternative models of political economy, the meaning of democracy, the relationship between the central government and the regions, and so on that had plagued Bolivia for years were still wide present; salidas may buy time but they do not resolve key power and ideological issues. Indeed, during the Siles period the many differences were brought into even sharper relief. The June elections would not be simply a matter of choosing a government within a functioning system but yet another attempt to constitute a power bloc to back a government capable of defining and implementing a coherent system of governance and an economic model. So, aside from campaign strategies, a critical question for all political groups was, what position should we take toward the elections and, by extension, toward electoral democracy in a Western liberal democratic mode? This was no mean question, for, as we have seen, pluralistic elections as a means of distributing power were hardly an entrenched value in any of the key power groups.

The center Right political parties, like the MNR and the ADN, and the private sector backed the electoral process itself. Again, their support for the process sprang not out of deeply held values but from the perception that they would do well in the elections, that the socialist Left would do poorly, and that the traditional nondemocratic alternatives were much less unappealing. The main-line MIR of Paz Zamora, which was forging a social democratic line, saw an opportunity to become the major "legitimate Left" opposition in a new scheme set in motion by the center Right. Elections were to these groups a pragmatic means to address power issues and assure them the ability to stay in the political game and pursue their long-term interests.

The situation confronting the COB and the more Marxist socialist Left groups was considerably more difficult. The COB and its backers had failed to push the Siles regime to implement the state socialist system embodied in the COB's Plan de Emergencia. Moreover, they were now perceived to be the main culprits in the failure of the Siles administration, especially in economic policy as well as for the general air of political and economic chaos. The leadership of the COB and the parties that backed the COB knew that they would do poorly in the elections. They also knew that the chances were good that the elections would produce a center Right regime that would push a model of political economy that they perceived to be anathema to both their short-term bread-and-butter interests and their long-term ideological interests.

There was little to gain and much to lose. It is not surprising that the COB/Left condemned the elections as a bourgeois fraud. Reflecting the infinite capacity of Bolivia's political elites to create pungent political expressions, the COB/Left characterized the elections as a *golpe electoral* (an electoral coup d'état) by which the private sector and the Right would illegitimately seize power. The immediate strategy of the COB/Left became to block or at the least postpone the elections, and if possible to induce a left-oriented coup to set up a regime that would establish a socialist system that, according to the COB/Left, would itself constitute democracy.

Owing to the complex and tenuous political situation, the political salience of the military was increased markedly. Civil factions from right to left sought to draw factions of like-minded officers to their side in a wide array of schemes that ran from outright coups to more complicated notions of military backing for constitutional coups and the like. The pressures within and around the military manifested themselves in late December when in an attempt to increase his control over the military, Siles ousted the army commander, General José Ólvis Arias. With the backing of the armed forces commander, General Simón Sejas Tordoya, Siles appointed the prominent generational officer General Raúl López Leytón to the army command post. Ólvis Arias resisted the action and a number of garrisons in the interior threatened to rebel in a gesture of support for him. Although the matter was debated in terms of military discipline and traditions, there were ideological overtones to the struggle, which many perceived as a move by Siles to undercut right-wing groups in the military.

In the end the matter was resolved within the military itself. Ólvis Arias was forced to step down and accept an undesirable border post, and Lopez Leytón assumed command. Whatever the ideological overtones, the relatively smooth resolution of the matter probably demonstrated a growing sense of institutional survival in the military rather than partisan politics. As the affair came to a close, General Sejas, long rumored to be a supporter of the COB/Left, strongly declared that he and the armed forces as a whole were committed to back fully the present democratic process and the electoral formula produced by the civilian politicians.

Although Siles was now a rather impotent lame duck president, he did regain some political clout around the question of organizing and backing the elections. The matter was involved, but it can be said that by and large the political forces from Paz Zamora's MIR on the left to the ADN on the right were to a great extent committed to an electoral outcome. Their immediate tactic, therefore, was to continue to induce Siles to support elections. In this they were backed by the U.S. ambassador, who continually sought to convince Siles that he could yet gain a respectable place in history as a president who helped put Bolivia onto a democratic path. The COB/Left on the other hand, because it saw the proposed elections as a completely losing proposition, it pressured Siles either to postpone the elections and institute left structural changes or to participate in a dramatic auto golpe aimed at bringing the COB/Left definitively to power.

As the process developed, Siles seemed to vacillate between one position and the other. In retrospect, however, his behavior shows a strategy aimed at holding onto formal power long enough to hand it over with dignity to an elected successor. To achieve this he had to, in effect, do battle with the COB again on the terrain of economic policy. His modus operandi here was to hold back the Left on matters of structural change while trying to buy short-term support from labor by giving in across the board on immediate bread-and-butter issues. The strategy worked in the sense that a formal, democratic electoral outcome was saved, but it came that at the price of plunging Bolivia even more deeply into its economic morass.

The first salvo in this new struggle was fired by Siles on February 8, 1985, when in a dramatic midnight move he announced yet a new paquete. Like many of the previous paquetes, it contained contradictory elements (devaluation offset by wage increases) that satisfied neither the private sector nor the COB. In reality, the package was too little and too late. The formal devaluation of the exchange rate to $b.45,000 to the dollar was simply drowned by the black market rate that pushed beyond $b.100,000 to the dollar.

In the face of the relentless inflation, merchants abandoned the official exchange rate and began to peg their prices to black market rates. The black market became so pervasive that it overwhelmed attempts to control it through the police. In La Paz the center-city thoroughfare, Avenida Camacho, was thronged daily with people freely exchanging dollars and pesos; most were middle-class public employees seeking to protect their salaries. But, again short-term logic was defeated by longer-term economic realities. As payday for public employees arrived, the crowds of buyers and sellers increased and of course the rate deteriorated accordingly. For most Bolivians, survival was a daily struggle. It was estimated that by February 1985 the average Bolivian worked for an effective take-home pay of ten dollars per month. Clearly, alternative survival strategies had to be brought into play.

The COB reacted to the new paquete with what amounted to a last-ditch struggle to bend Siles to its will and/or block the elections. It declared a state of emergency and publicly geared up for a mass mobilization against Siles and the paquete. On March 4 the COB brought some 10,000 miners to La Paz to take part in a "march against hunger." They were backed by other unions, including civil servants. Accompanied by the band of the La Paz municipality, they trudged past the presidential palace, tossing sticks of dynamite and calling for Siles's resignation and the transfer of power to the workers. The march turned into a twenty-day siege of the capital that became known as the *jornadas de marzo*. Coincidental with a general strike, the miners' harassment of the government was a daily occurrence. By mid-month Siles, who had tried to ignore the marchers, sought to buy peace with large wage concessions and guarantees that the subsidized stores in the mines would remain stocked. The COB refused, and upped the pressure by means of street blockades and other actions. Siles then offered the COB parity co-government. The COB again refused, citing its unwillingness to participate in a soon-to-be-ended government. It was now generally agreed that the COB was trying to precipitate a political crisis and force the government to declare a state of siege and postpone elections.

The situation in La Paz was becoming difficult as people ran out of cash and market stalls grew bare. Siles moved against striking civil servants, threatening dismissal and refusing pay for days on strike. The COB responded by ordering the strikers "to bring their case to people" by blocking the major arteries of the capital. The fact is, however, that although the COB had tied up La Paz almost completely, the rest of the country was returning to normal. The COB was clearly losing its hold on the situation and the elongation of the strike was undermining its power.

Perhaps in recognition of the COB's weakening position, Siles decided to mobilize force against the occupying miners and their supporters. On March 20 troops took up positions in the capital while planes of the air force overflew the city. The looming confrontation was sad testimony to the deterioration of the political situation in Bolivia. Here stood Siles, a father of a "populist" revolution and the man who had led the working class to apparent electoral victory in 1980, arrayed against Lechín, another father of the revolution and leader of a working class that felt betrayed by the revolution in general and Siles in particular. A bloody and tragic clash seemed inevitable. Then as it had done in the past, the conference of bishops stepped between the contenders. After two days of intense negotiations a deal was struck in which the COB lifted the strike in return for further wage concessions, a bonus, and guarantees that the stores in the mining camps would be kept stocked. On March 23, after a final gathering in the center city, the miners dispersed. The *jornadas de marzo* were over.

Politically, the *jornadas de marzo* were a defeat for the COB. The rupture with Siles was definite, and the possibility of the COB's blocking the upcoming elections was receding quickly. The COB/Left, which had seemed so politically all-powerful in the early days of the Siles regime was now politically weaker than at any time since the Banzer dictatorship of the 1970s. The COB could now do little beyond maintain a defensive posture on wages and salaries while searching frantically for some way to blunt or stop what would surely be defeat of major proportions at the polls.

If the COB lost, it is by no means clear that Siles won in any but the most formal sense. His government survived, but it had lost all semblance of popular backing from his "natural constituency." Bereft of support from the Left, Siles now had no real choice but to push the electoral salida and cling to the formal symbols of office until the elections. At that point most other considerations were let slip as everyone came to focus on June 16.

It is interesting that Congress and most of the main-line political parties stood back from the jornadas de marzo. Basically, the parties sought to avoid being tied to either side as they maneuvered in preparation for the elections and let Siles and the COB exhaust themselves in the crisis. What the parties like the MNR and ADN most wanted now was for Siles to hold on long enough to bring off the elections.

In late March Congress ratified the call for elections and stipulated the rules to be followed. A most significant feature was that voters were to choose municipal officials and national officials at the same time. This marked the first time since 1948 that local officials were to be elected; between 1948 and 1985 local officials had simply been appointed by whatever government sat in the national palace. The absence of elections all those years probably contributed to the emergence of local civic committees as the truly effective centers of power in the capitals of the more important departments.

Needless to say, local civic committees took a keen interest in the upcoming local elections. Many of them were distressed by the electoral law that ratified the preexisting single-ballot list system in which each voter cast one ballot for one party that was counted for all open offices, i.e., the presidency, congressional seats, municipal positions, and so on. The list system theoretically gave tremendous power to national party officials to control their lists from the center; however it also tended to reinforce the disconnection of the main parties from key groups in civil society, especially the regional civic committees. It threatened as well to reinforce further the disconnection of key governmental institutions from civil society, rendering them to some degree epiphenomenal to the problems of governance.

For whatever reason, the civic committee was the real center of power and governance in places like Santa Cruz. Hence, although the parties held the reins in regard to the single complete lists, they also wanted to maintain good relations with the local committees. Top people of the MNR and the ADN, led by their presidential candidates Paz and Banzer, traveled widely seeking the support of the civic committees by, among other things, giving them a say in designating party candidates for municipal offices. To gain the support of regional elites party leaders had to cede at least some of their control over party lists.

In the first elections lineup some 79 parties and electoral fronts signed on, and twenty-nine presidential candidates presented themselves. After scrutiny, the electoral court eliminated a number of parties and recognized eighteen presidential contenders. Significantly, Juan Lechín's PRIN was among the disallowed parties because it had failed to get a minimum percentage in the previous elections and then had failed to pay the legally mandated fine for such a low vote. That ratified the reality that Lechín's power was rooted exclusively in his personal standing in the FSTMB and the COB, and could not be converted into a national electoral base. Indeed, one might argue that especially in recent years his visibility as the COB's main protagonist with the government diminished his national-level electoral salience. Put another way, Lechín had to confront the fact that in a liberal democratic system his power would be restricted to that of a sectorial leader with little or no chance of achieving the presidency. This reality reinforced the COB and Lechín's lack of enthusiasm for the upcoming elections.

The Elections of 1985

The ideological nomenclature by which the electoral fronts behind the presidential candidates sought to describe themselves is interesting. With the exception of Banzer's ADN, all parties asserted that they represented what they referred to as the "national Left" *(izquierda nacional)*. The ADN did not claim the coloration of right or conservative but, rather, declared itself to be of the "national democratic" center. This concern with nationalist identity reflected the fact that most of the main parties wanted to associate themselves with the ideological strains manifested in the revolution of 1952; the "national revolution" itself had become a kind of symbol around which most groups rallied, regardless of their interpretations of the meaning of the revolution. Even the ADN was careful to depict itself not as counterrevolutionary but as oriented toward shifting the balance within the revolution away from the state and back to the market.

As in previous elections, party fragmentation forced the formation of fronts and the often rather opportunistic cohabitation of ostensibly hostile ideological groupings. This time out, however, it was the more minor parties, especially on the left, that formed coalitions; this was owed to the collapse of the UDP and the fact that there was no Left candidate comparable to Siles around which a broad Left coalition could be formed. In addition, the three major parties ran mostly on their own hook. The major exception was the continuance of an improbable electoral alliance between Paz's MNR and the small leftist group of Oscar "Motete" Zamora known as the Marxist Leninist Communist Party (PCML).

There were really only three major parties contending for the big prize. Politically, the outstanding story was the great success Paz Estenssoro had in reconstituting the MNR coalition. Most of the disparate strains of the party, including a large slice of the MNRI, returned to the broad canopy of the original MNR, beneath which they rallied for yet another run by the old warhorse Paz. The Paz MNR was offset by two relatively new groupings. By far the most important was Banzer's ADN, which in just a few years had risen to where it was challenging the MNR for the position of majority party. The third major contender was the Paz Zamora MIR. Still young by Bolivian standards, the MIR had split into three groupings: two had moved in a more Marxist left direction and the main branch staked out a social democratic position.

In the 1985 contest there was no real serious contender to the left of the MIR. In the short term at least the COB/labor Left and its party manifestations were completely exhausted and outmaneuvered in electoral terms. The elections spelled little more for the Left than possibly ruinous defeat.

The principal figures by far were Paz Estenssoro and Hugo Banzer. It was clear that ideology and program were to some extent relevant, but the personal pull of a potential presidential *caudillo* (leader) was still the chief element in any electoral contest. The clear strategy of the fragments of the political class was to form around a *presidenciable* (presidential contender) whose coattails they hoped to ride into the power and perks of office.

At its core Bolivia's was still a personalistic and patrimonial kind of political system in which institutional and programmatic considerations of all kinds were secondary to the dynamics of patron-client networks. This was true not only of the MNR, whose electoral unity was patently the product of the agglutinating force of Paz Estenssoro. Such was the reality in the ADN as well. The ADN was, in fact, split into two broad groupings. One, a group of prominent individuals (drawn in large part from the private sector) who had developed their careers as personal retainers of Banzer during his dictatorship. These Banzeristas were loyal to Banzer the man and became members of the ADN primarily to use it on Banzer's behalf. The other grouping was made up of ADN organizational men who, realizing the continuing role of dominant personalities, had sought out Banzer as their candidate. Both wings had disparate goals and ambitions and it was only Banzer who held them together. The main-line MIR, in turn was obviously the creature of Paz Zamora; in fact, it was personal as well as ideological issues that had led its other two factions to split off behind their own personalistic leaders.

Actually, in terms of ideology and program there was little separating the three chief candidates; all had come out of the cardinal definitions of the revolution of 1952. During the 1970s both Paz and Banzer were clearly identified with the state capitalist trend in the revolution and the central emphasis of that line on capital accumulation by controlling popular consumption. The main evolution in their respective positions was a clear tilt away from the state toward the market and the private sector. The MIR of Paz Zamora, on the other hand presented itself as a younger, politically cleaner generation ready to pick up the banners of the MNR revolution. In programmatic terms the MIR gave itself a bit more of a populist cast, through which it tried to stake out the territory to the left of the Paz MNR and Banzer's ADN.

The three parties all blasted away at the failure of Siles and what they painted as the "extreme Left." Among themselves the issue was not ideology or program but the concept of which leader followed by which party could most effectively pick up the pieces and impose some kind of solution on Bolivia. Further, the other contenders condemned Banzer individually for the harsh repression and authoritarian ways of his regime during the 1970s. The MIR in particular excoriated him, and it also tried to tar Paz with the same brush because of his cooperation with Banzer early in that decade.

In addition to the weakened parties of the traditional Left, the fledgling peasant movement entered the campaign. In the early 1980s the main group known as the Revolutionary Movement of Tupac Katari (MRTK) had backed the UDP; now it joined forces with one of the wings of the long-standing Trotskyist Partido Obrero Revolutionario (POR). The group's electoral prospects were not good. The peasantry remained an inchoate political force divided along such various lines as ethnicity, regionalism, type of activity, class, and so on. Moreover, most peasant votes were still perceived to belong to the major national parties, especially Paz and the MNR.

The campaign turned out to be a glitzy media-dominated struggle somewhat out of sinc with the dismal economic and social situation. The ADN in particular ran a media-centered campaign the likes of which had never been seen in Bolivia before. But, Paz and the others also sought to use the media, especially television, to project images independent of programmatic substance.

The three ranking parties patterned their campaigns around images of their presidential aspirants. Both the MNR and ADN focused on the maturity and experience of their candidates. Banzer was advanced as a stable figure associated with a period now described as one of order and progress; if he did it once he could do it again was the message. Paz was presented as a sagacious and battle-tested statesman associated with the great revolution of 1952. The MNR stressed above all his ability to maneuver through difficult political terrain. The MIR, in turn, played up the theme of new and fresh ideas, which it linked in the media to Paz Zamora's youthful good looks. Paz Zamora's campaign took more than a few pages on image creation from the successful presidential campaign that Alan García had just run in Peru.

As we have seen, Bolivian politics has a way of making dramatic shifts; politicians long thought politically dead have a way of suddenly rising phoenix-like from the ashes. Such was the case with Banzer. From the beginning of the campaign he was considered the front runner, a belief that became firmer as an increasingly self-confident ADN ran its extremely slick campaign. Banzer's enhancing image strengthened his hand in the party and helped him to overcome the tension between the Banzeristas and the ADN organizational people. He consolidated his hold over the party apparatus when he forwent the temptation to impose a Banzerista as the party's vice-presidential candidate and allowed a convention to choose one of the party founders, Eudoro Galindo.[7]

The development of the ADN is in many ways one of the more interesting and important recent developments in Bolivian political life. In a short period of time it went from zero to the second major party, wholly displacing the now-moribund FSB. Although it has a personalistic element, the ADN has established itself as a modern political organization in its own right. During the campaign it forged links with the Republican party in the United States; it was able to turn that and its ties to the local private sector into a campaign war chest that dwarfed those of all other parties. It brought in U.S. campaign professionals, media consultants, and pollsters—all of whom were used to launch an impressive, highly visible campaign.

Banzer's perceived lead was such that Paz all but conceded him a popular vote plurality. The campaign of the MNR and Paz was predicated on holding down Banzer's total vote and shifting the election to the new Congress. Basically, the MNR aimed at winning more seats in Congress as a base to form an anti-Banzer congressional coalition that would put Paz in the presidency. Paz Zamora and the MIR focused mainly on posting a respectable popular showing that they could convert into a congressional bloc, with which they could establish themselves as the major legitimate "Left" opposition group.

As the campaign wound on, the practical political and economic situation continued to deteriorate apace. The Siles government had for all intents and purposes given up on governing and simply sought to hold on until the elections. Sensing that a new government would take a firmer hand with the economic situation, all of the various sectors of civil society sought to wrench whatever concessions they could from the debilitated Siles government; strikes, roadblocks, regional civic actions and the like mounted in frequency and intensity. The Siles government retained office by giving in to whatever current demand was pressed upon it.

The government's inability to resist group demands led to bread-and-butter concessions far beyond the capacity of Bolivia's enfeebled economic base to finance. The result was such a flood of unbacked expenditures that bank notes printed in neighboring Brazil became Bolivia's second-largest import. With these developments, inflation raged. Previous devaluations paled into insignificance in the face of an inflation that became truly catastrophic. The rate so accelerated that it was impossible to calculate accurately; estimates put the 1985 figure anywhere from 14,000 percent to 20,000 percent. The value of the peso plummeted: by July it was over $b.600,000 to the dollar and a scant few months later close to 2 million to the dollar. Some international economists have adjudged it to have been the seventh-highest in recorded human history. To say the economy was in a state of collapse is an understatement.

The main political parties, of course, played up "economic chaos" in their campaigns. Paz and Banzer directed their pitches to the urban sectors most hurt by it. Paz and the MNR in addition made great efforts to carry the message to the countryside. Both candidates also made appeals to workers based on the argument that the Left leadership had led them into an economic blind alley.

Given the fact that the COB had in essence rejected the electoral process, the key class-interest group from an electoral point of view was the CEPB. If the COB was electorally in a no-win situation, the CEPB was in a no-lose situation politically. Both Paz and Banzer directly sought private sector support, and the MIR as well developed a leadership wing of young private sector entrepreneurs. Because of the association of many prominent entrepreneurs with the Banzer dictatorship, the CEPB was considered by many to be the preserve of Banzer and the ADN. This was not the case. First and foremost, as we saw, the CEPB had gone through an important political metamorphosis and became a true national class organization over the previous seven years. Hence, whatever the personal ties of some members to Banzer, they could not deliver the organization as such.

At one level the CEPB continued to back an electoral salida mainly because it was to its class advantage to do so. In terms of specific candidates, the most prominent of its leaders were split between Banzer and Paz. The split had its roots in the Banzer era, and especially among some in the medium mining sector who assailed Banzer's tax policy toward the sector as well as his general "statist" orientation. In the current electoral battle the split widened. Those who had figured personally in the Banzer period continued to back him on the grounds that his seven-year rule proved he was good for business. Others swung behind Paz because of a previous rejection of Banzer and because, they argued, Paz was the one national leader with the political skills to bring Bolivia out of its current predicament. Be that as it may, prominent figures from the top strata of the CEPB played visibly partisan roles in the campaigns of both Banzer and Paz. When all was said and done, the sector expected favorable policies from whichever man won. The issue was which could more effectively lead Bolivia in the preferred direction.

Throughout the first half of 1985 tensions mounted and numerous groups continued in their attempts to derail the elections. As a result of serious complications in the registration process, the elections were postponed from June 16 to July 14. The registration problems were primarily in the countryside, and most observers agreed that the problems worked mainly against Paz's candidacy. Nonetheless, Paz and the MNR continued campaigning.

The electoral results did not themselves resolve the central issue of the transfer of power. As expected, Banzer won a plurality with 493,735 votes, but at 28.57 percent, it was far from a convincing victory. Moreover, Bolivia's complex proportional vote system worked against the ADN in the congressional races, a factor that was reinforced when the MNR-dominated electoral court threw out a large number of ADN votes on technical grounds. In the end, the ADN's congressional delegation was forty-one deputies and ten senators, far fewer than necessary to elect a president in Congress.

The MNR electoral game plan turned out to have been well designed. Paz polled 456,704 votes, 26.42 percent of the total. More important, the MNR won more congressional seats than the ADN, forty-three deputies and sixteen senators. The MNR moved quickly to mobilize an electoral coalition in Congress to bloc Banzer and seat Paz. The MNR maneuvered to build a coalition to the left, taking advantage of the deep personal antipathy toward Banzer among the parties that had felt the brunt of his repressive regime. The key to MNR strategy was to win over the MIR, which had come in third: 8.85 percent of the popular vote, and fifteen deputies and one senator. The MIR was quickly joined by three other parties, including the rump MNRI, which was enough to put Paz over the top. After a ceremonial first-round tally, the coalition went into place and Paz was elected president of Bolivia for the fourth time. He was two months short of his seventy-eighth birthday.

Banzer and the ADN were not happy with the outcome, of course. In the immediate wake of the election they had cried fraud and threatened to reject the results. As tempers cooled, they began to shift ground. A turning point came when Banzer and the ADN decided to ratify the electoral process as such and accept Paz's ascension to the presidency. Whatever motives one ascribes to them, the fact remains that this was a historic decision from the point of view of implementing a liberal democratic system based on elections. As an ADN spokesman put it, they accepted the legality of Paz's election if not its legitimacy. To accept defeat and remain in the political fray according to the existing rules is one of the more crucial ethics of a democratic system.

Paz and the New Economic Policy

There was little question in anyone's mind that the first order of business of the new Paz government, inaugurated on August 6, 1985, would be the economic crisis. Nor was there any doubt that a strong austerity package would be the first line of attack. The question was, when would the paquete come and how severe would it be?

Over the next three weeks Paz shrewdly kept his plans close to his chest. Some hints came in his inaugural address when he launched bitter accusations against the Left, particularly regarding its opposition to foreign investment, and announced his intention to decentralize the state mining (COMIBOL) and petroleum (YPFB) corporations. There was little doubt that he would look to a revitalization of the private sector to lead an economic recovery.

Many were somewhat dismayed by Paz's lackluster cabinet appointments; they seemed to herald a return to the old-style patronage politics of the MNR in its early days. However, behind the scenes Paz had formed a select group to formulate an economic plan. It was made up mostly of newer MNR figures from the private sector, and a few independents from the private sector who also had reputations as economic technocrats. The group was led by Gonzalo Sanchez de Lozada, a prominent medium mine company owner and MNR senator (elected president of the Senate), and Guillermo Bedregal, a longtime and enigmatic MNR figure who was minister of planning in the new cabinet.

To some extent the select group was a formalization of informal groups that had been meeting to discuss economic policy in the years prior to the elections. The informal pro-MNR groups paralleled similar groups in the ADN; some independent figures, like economist Juan Cariaga, were included in both informal groups. Given the fact that others in both groups had long-standing patterns of contact and interaction, there was a great deal of cross-fertilization going on between the two parties' economic teams.

In the months prior to the elections, the ADN working group had traveled to Harvard University, where it sought advice and counsel in developing an ADN economic plan. Members returned with an austerity program based on free market logic and a prominent role for the private sector. Most of the members of the MNR working group were familiar with the ADN-Harvard plan as well as its rationale and the values behind it.

It is important to note that the plan that ultimately came forth was formed in camera between Paz and his select group exclusively. The cabinet and the MNR congressional delegation were not involved. It is clear that for the wily Paz, timing and secrecy were essential to the successful launching of his economic program. On August 29, 1985, without warning or prior consultation with anyone other than the select group, Paz implemented by simple presidential decree (no. 21060) a drastic and far-reaching program of stabilization and economic recovery. The manner in which the decree was formulated and announced indicated that although democratic elections determined governmental succession crucial economic policy was going to flow in a quasi-authoritarian manner from a revitalized presidential office that, in the short term at least, had experienced a great reconcentration of decision making power.

Decree 21060 was significantly more than another austerity paquete. In many respects it is a program that if completely implemented will profoundly redirect the entire thrust of the political economy. It signals an end to the logic of the political economy introduced by the revolution of 1952 and followed throughout the twists and turns of subsequent decades. It was as if President Paz was closing the book on the revolution he helped to launch in the 1950s and opening a book on a whole new process.

It would be a mistake however, to view the decree as a rejection of the national revolution by a Paz who had evolved from revolutionary to counterrevolutionary. It would be more accurate to see it as a radical adaptation to a difficult set of circumstances in which there is a reorganization of the central values and logic of the original revolution, especially as pertains to the relationship between the state and the economy. Still, the decree does flow directly out of the original approach of Paz and the core MNR elite.

The original MNR concept of revolution was one of using the state to wrench Bolivia out of its semifeudal past and promote development and modernization. The MNR originally used the language of anti-imperialism, but the core leadership always stressed its intention to remain within the western capitalist sphere. Hence, the goal was a system of state-directed capitalism. The belief was that state capitalist development could be achieved simultaneously with populist redistribution.

In light of the terms of the revolution of 1952, decree 21060 denoted four important shifts in emphasis. First, because it embodied severe austerity policies, it definitively broke with the notion of any short-term compatibility between populist redistribution and capitalist development. It stressed stabilization and capital accumulation at the expense of popular consumption. The emphasis reflected the press of immediate circumstance but also was a ratification of the priorities to which Paz and other MNR leaders had shifted in the late 1960s and early 1970s.

Second, and more important from a long-term structural point of view, is the revised conception of the role of the state in directing development and modernization. The policies in the decree aimed at reducing the size of the state, increasing its efficiency, and above all providing the mechanisms for the executive to control the state apparatus, especially the resources it extracts from civil society. Behind the policies was the accurate perception that when it comes to the state, size does not necessarily mean strength. Indeed, as we noted earlier, the state in Bolivia has grown consistently since 1952 but its capacity to direct society has diminished. One of the major reasons is that the substantial resources that the state has extracted have been dissipated into the clientelistic networks that permeate the labyrinthine public sector; they have not provided a basis for governmental administrative action. The purpose of decree 21060 is a leaner, stronger state executive apparatus under the control of specific governments.

Following from the first two shifts is a shift from the long-standing primacy of the state in promoting development to a lead role for the market and the private sector. And, the fourth shift embodied in the decree is the promotion of an opening of the economy to the international system. Hence, at both the domestic and international levels market forces should become preponderant.[8]

To a large extent decree 21060 represented a triumph for the private sector. It surely signaled a change in political fortunes for the COB and CEPB, the Left and the Right in that sense. Throughout the early 1980s, the CEPB had been pushing three major ends in economic policy: economic stabilization by way of a strict austerity program; emphasis on capital accumulation over consumption; and a rollback of the state's role in the economy in favor of the private sector. In sum, it was oriented toward a neoliberal economic model.[9] Yet, it would be too facile to see decree 21060 as a measure revealing the capacity of the private sector or bourgeoisie to dictate government policy in some manifestation of class dominance. The fact is that owing to the farrago of factors—both national and international—Bolivia's options, like those of many other Latin American countries, are severely limited. The policy embodied in the decree reflected a convergence of positions that had been developed by Paz and the main-line MNR over the years with the relatively recently formulated positions of the private sector; the context of crisis and limited options played a large part in melding the positions.

Once the full implications of 21060 were manifest, many components of the private sector, especially in manufacturing, were far from happy. The decree opens the economy to what from the point of view of local companies is potentially ruinous competition. Many local Bolivian companies are simply unable to compete in an open economy and will surely go under. The rationale of the decree is that the cleansing effects of the market are necessary to introduce efficiency into the economy.

Decree 21060 was therefore received most cautiously by the CEPB, whose leadership was already receiving disquieting messages from local manufacturers. The pressure was such that its president, Fernando Romero, resigned when he was attacked by membership groups for his enthusiastic support of the decree. His successor has been much more circumspect in discussing the decree and has publicly criticized many of its provisions. Division within the CEPB over 21060 reflects a variety of factors. The private sector in Bolivia suffers from the same divergence between perceptions of long-term sectorial or class interests and short-term interests of specific persons and companies that besets other sectors in Bolivia and elsewhere. Furthermore, although many could subscribe to the abstract principles of neoliberal economics pushed by the CEPB since the late 1970s the fact is that a large portion of the private sector had developed under the protective wing of the state. It was going to be difficult and painful for many components of the sector to be weaned from dependence on the state. The point is that a view of decree 21060 as a policy orchestrated by a monolithic bourgeoisie rooted in the private sector is far too simplistic to be useful.

The COB/Left was not confused regarding the decree and immediately attacked it, but its capacity to affect national economic policy had declined drastically. Paz, as expected, proved an effective and shrewd maneuverer against the COB/Left. The manner in which the decree was promulgated, the timing of its announcement, and its contents, all caught the COB/Left off guard. Then, before it could regroup, Paz moved to repress open opposition. On September 17 an attempt at a general strike was crushed when he declared a state of siege and rounded up major COB leaders like Lechín, who were sent into temporary exile. When the military held behind the government, the COB/Left yet again found itself helpless, temporarily at least, before a strong and determined executive.

The successful launching of decree 21060 in late August of 1985 reflected a reconcentration of decision-making power in the executive. However, unless a political base for the power was consolidated it could have proved a pyrrhic victory followed by yet another dissipation of governmental power. Unlike Siles in 1982, Paz was obviously taking full advantage of circumstances to increase his power: the severity of the crisis; the discrediting of the Left; and the general backing he had in Congress.

In the longer term a key component of Paz's ability to govern was the relative restructuring of the MNR into a broad-based organization with a plurality in Congress. The MNR, however, could have proved a fragile reed had it been all the president had to lean on. Paz was not through demonstrating the tremendous skills he had acquired in almost five decades of active political life.

Perhaps, no one was caught more off guard by 21060 than Banzer and the ADN, for Paz had in effect adopted their program and then some. The ADN was in the difficult situation where it could hardly challenge Paz for implementing an even tougher version of its own economic program. The upshot was that it had to support the decree and back the state of siege. Having maneuvered the ADN into de facto support of his economic initiatives, Paz opened talks with Banzer to contemplate Bolivia's political and economic future. The discussions produced an agreement that the MNR and the ADN would enter into a formal "pacto por la democracia." If it holds, it is a historic development that could well alter the structure of power for some time to come.

The pact, signed on October 17, 1985, is not a governing alliance but an agreement that the two parties will cooperate in Congress to push through full implementation of decree 21060, including follow-up legislation. In addition to providing for shared backing of a joint economic program, the pact provides for a step-by-step process whereby the ADN will share in control of key public sector corporations and the associated patronage. The latter will allow the ADN to consolidate its organizational base and position itself for the next round of elections.[10]

The pact not only furnishes a base of support for the Paz economic program but goes a long way toward overcoming the structural disjuncture between the executive and the legislature. It does not increase the role of Congress in the formulation of public policy but converts it into a base of support for policies formed by the executive. Unlike Siles and other recent democratic presidents, Paz can rely on the MNR-ADN majority to uphold and legitimate his policies. Thus, for the first time in recent memory, there is a mechanism by which the electoral system can generate a structural base of support for executive power.

Even more significant, perhaps, is that if the pact holds it will reinforce the concentration of decision power in the executive. Because Congress at the moment is mainly ratifying rather than making policy, the pact in effect creates an authoritarian decisional capacity in the executive within a framework of formal democracy. In any event, for the short term at least, Bolivia has a civil democratic regime in which the government can govern.

Throughout its first months the pact for democracy has held quite well. Attempts by the Left to censure the economic policy of the government have been fought back. More important, crucial pieces of legislation, especially a new tax code, have sailed through Congress. During its first year the Paz government has been able to retain the initiative and maintain a forward thrust. This is not to say that all is well. There are serious strains in the MNR-ADN alliance as well as within both parties. Old-line MNR cadres are particularly disturbed by having had to share a reduced patronage pie with the ADN, a pool of jobs that will be cut further as the policies in decree 21060 take hold. The ADN, in turn, has been experiencing internal turmoil over control of the party between the Banzeristas and the ADN organization men.

The main thing the pact has going for it is the continued agreement between Paz and Banzer, who are now the undisputed titans of Bolivian politics. Ironically, this residual strain of personalism might well serve to force the parties to move into a more modern style of politics. Banzer is using the ADN and the pact to build his image as a statesman and a democrat in preparation for the next election. Paz, for his part, is now playing a different game, his last hurrah. He wants his place in history, and not as a politician maneuvering with one eye on the next election.

The MNR in particular senses that Paz is more concerned with securing his place in history by leading Bolivia out of the current crisis than with the interests of the MNR and its job-hungry cadres. Many in the party were particularly upset in January 1986 when Paz, fearful that the party people were not following through with 21060, precipitated a major cabinet overhaul. Party men in key economic posts were either ousted or transferred; Bedregal for example, was shifted to the Ministry of Foreign Affairs. Paz then brought into the cabinet a number of the independent and private sector figures who had helped formulate decree 21060. Gonzalo Sanchez de Lozada was moved into the Ministry of Planning, from which post he took direction of what now amounted to a cabinet within the cabinet for economic policy and management. The major task of the group of ministers was to see to it that the provisions of 21060 and follow-up legislation were vigorously implemented. Although unhappy with this loss of power and jobs, the MNR cadres must face the hard reality that for them Paz is the only game in town for now.

Bolivia in a sense has come full circle. Victor Paz Estenssoro and the MNR have put a period to the chapter begun with the revolution of 1952. At the same time they have opened a new chapter in the unfolding drama of Bolivia. It is a chapter fraught with hazards and possibilities. We can now only wait to see what script they write.

Notes

1. General background on the economic crisis and the debt is contained in Michael D. Mortimore, "The State and Transnational Banks: Lessons from the

Bolivian Crisis of External Public Indebtedness," *CEPAL Review* (August 1981): 127-51; Nicholas Asheshov, "Financial Brinkmanship in Bolivia," *International Investor* (April 1981). For other general views, see Fernando Baptista Gumucio, *Estrategia nacional para la deuda externa* (La Paz: Los Amigos del Libro, 1984); José Luis Roca, *Derrotemos el hambre* (La Paz: 1985).

2. Two general accounts of cocaine and politics in Bolivia are Gregorio Selser, *Bolivia: El cuartelazo de los cocadolares* (México City: Editorial Mex-Sur, 1982); and Amado Canelas Orellana and Juan Carlos Canelas, *Bolivia: Coca, cocaina* (La Paz: Los Amigos del Libro, 1983).

3. The role of the IMF in Bolivia's economic policy is discussed in "Power and the IMF: The Example of Bolivia," *Euromoney* (January 1982): pp. 104-13.

4. The relationship between Siles and Congress is treated at length in Eduardo A. Gamarra, "Political Stability, Democratization and the Bolivian National Congress," (Ph.D. dissertation, University of Pittsburgh, 1987), ch. 5.

5. The CEPB came into its own as a political force in this period. Over the next three years it carried out a very public assault on the COB and government policy, which is chronicled in the documents contained in Confederación de Empresario Privados de Bolivia, *Pensamiento y acción de la empresa privada, 1982-1985* (La Paz, 1985).

6. For a general perspective on the Siles period, see the essays in Roberto Laserna, ed., *Crisis, democracia y conflicto social* (Cochabamba: Ceres, 1985).

7. Eudoro Galindo has strong ideological views, which he spelled out in *Bolivia: Otro camino* (La Paz: Los Amigos del Libro, 1985).

8. The plan is evaluated at length in "La nueva política económica," *Foro Económico* nos. 5, 6 (La Paz: Foro Económico, 1985). A critical view of the plan is presented in James Dunkerley and Rolando Morales, "The Bolivian Crisis," *New Left Review* 155 (January/February 1986): 86-106.

9. These views are spelled out at length in the two previously cited volumes published by the CEPB: *Pensamiento de la empresa privada Boliviana* (1981) and *Pensamiento y acción de la empresa privada, 1982-1985* (1985).

10. The pact and its signing is laid out in a pamphlet published by the ADN as *Pacto por la democracia* (La Paz: Acción Democrática Nacionalista, 1985).

6

Conclusion: Policy Cycles and Regime Transition—Bolivia in Comparative Perspective

Bolivia today is in a state of acute crisis, perhaps the worst crisis in the nation's history. The crisis has two dimensions economic and political, and each has its own challenges for key decision makers. The central tasks in the economic sphere are foremost to stabilize the economy and then to promote economic development. The critical challenge in the political sphere is to establish and maintain a system of open representative democracy after more than thirty years of authoritarian and quasi-authoritarian rule. At the moment there is severe tension between the two spheres. Accordingly, efforts to solve one side of the problem (economic) often create problems on the other side (political) that then feed back negatively to the first. As we saw in the last Siles administration, for example, attempts to decree austerity programs put great strains on Bolivia's fledgling democratic institutions, which later undercut the government's ability to mount economic policy. A climate of extreme economic crisis is not a propitious one in which to establish a democratic regime.

Bolivia is not a unique case in the above respect. Most of the countries of South America are going through similar dual economic and political crises characterized by a need to stabilize economies while simultaneously trying to shift from authoritarian to democratic modes of governance, and hence their established political systems are under stress. The general crisis is in no small part due to factors internal to each country, but it is also evident that it is due to other factors arising in the international political economy, which itself is in crisis and going through a process of restructuring. The fact is that the countries of Latin America must adapt to what is an emerging new stage in the global capitalist system, an ever-present need that demonstrates clearly the dependent position of Latin America in general and Bolivia in particular within the global system.

Dependence has had a number of effects on these countries, two of which stand out. First, it has acted to limit the options available to national decision makers, especially in moments of crisis. Second, it has increased the salience in national decision making of external decision-making centers, be they other governments like that of the United States or international agencies like the International Monetary Fund (IMF). These effects are particularly relevant in understanding Bolivia, one of the most extreme cases of economic dependence in the entire region. Its extreme dependence has conditioned the internal processes of its political economy for most of this century, and particularly since the revolution of 1952. Again, it has been an extreme variation on a Latin American theme.

Indeed, the view that Bolivia is essentially a variation on a regional theme has shaped the fundamental orientation of this book. Because of its contextual position, Bolivia becomes more comprehensible if we view it from the perspective of tendencies and processes common to the region. We can understand the particular case by means of generalizations drawn from the whole.

There are also good reasons to study the Bolivian case as a way to grasp the larger processes common to the region. A central assumption of this study is that because of its very extreme conditions, Bolivia constitutes an excellent case to elucidate some of the major dynamics of the region. This is not to say that Bolivia is an analogue of the region, or of countries that operate on a much larger and more complex plane than Bolivia. Bolivia is a relatively small country in regard to population (5 million), with limited significance in international affairs. Yet, the very extremeness of the Bolivian case and its smaller scale allow us to highlight much more clearly certain processes that also operate within larger and more complex nations and societies. To restate a point made in the introduction, Bolivia is worth studying both as a case in itself and for its significance in the development of the literature on the comparative political economy of Latin America.

The Region in Perspective

In this concluding chapter, then, we will first look briefly at some of the major analytically defined processes that in our view have been shaping the political economy in Latin America since at least the 1930s. Then we will give a general analytical summary of the main lines of the political economy in Bolivia, especially since 1964, in light of our view of it as a case in a regional context. The focal point of this analytical retrospective is the current dual problem of economic crisis and the transition from authoritarian to democratic regimes.

The basic time frame to be taken into account in putting today's crisis into historical context is the 1930s to the present. The Great Depression was a watershed in modern Latin America. Much as today, it was a period of economic collapse brought on by a generalized crisis in the global capitalist system. Specifically, the economic crisis reflected the exhaustion of the primary-product export model of growth that had linked the region into the world economy to that point. As a result of the changes in the global capitalist system the nations of the region were forced to accommodate their economies to a new evolutionary stage in the global system.

Beginning at least with the depression the countries of Latin America have been faced with three fundamental, recurring needs. The first has been the need to define and implement political models of economic development and specific growth strategies, and here it has been imperative to create structures of adaptation to the global system. The second need has been to bring about institutional structures capable of incorporating into existing systems newly mobilized social sectors, most particularly organized labor. The third need has been the ongoing need to assemble coalitions of power capable of sustaining regimes that are able to fill the two other needs. The interrelationships of the three needs have been crucial in shaping the unfolding process of the political economy in the region.

From an analytical point of view the development of the political economy in Latin America during this period did not proceed linearly. Rather, it has tended to be characterized by a pattern in which linear developmental sequences have occurred within cycles. We will look at two fundamental cyclical alternations: one at the level of the political regime; the other involving broad policy strategies to deal with models of development and the incorporation of politically relevant social sectors. In the first there has occurred a shift from authoritarian to democratic regimes and vice versa; in the second, from populism to antipopulism.

There has been no clear cultural or developmental bent in Latin America toward any particular regime type. In most countries we see a clear cyclical alternation from de facto authoritarian regimes backed by the military to regimes modeled more on Western concepts of open pluralist democracy. Some linear evolution has taken place, especially in the context of authoritarian regimes, which over the years have in most countries shifted from personalistic dictatorships to more sophisticated regimes based on the armed forces as an institution. Be that as it may, the fact is that neither type of regime has been very successful for long periods at solving, or creating a framework for the resolution of, the three basic questions of models of development, political incorporation, and coalition building. Indeed, the cycles have moved mainly as a result of the failure of one regime type (democratic) giving rise to the other (authoritarian), the failure of which in turn gives rise to the first again, and so on. This basic circularity of regime types indicates perhaps that the real recurring need in Latin America has been to create effective decision-making centers at the core of these societies independent of outward regime form.

Behind this central dilemma is a contradiction of political economy that besets all modern capitalist societies, whether in the advanced industrial center or the less developed periphery: the tension between the economic imperative to accumulate capital for investment and the political imperative to build legitimacy for specific regimes as well as generate support for them. Although the contradiction is common to all capitalist societies (and socialist, too), it is particularly difficult among the less developed countries of regions like Latin America.

In the less developed context the contradiction is translated into one between what we can call economic and political logics. Owing to the lack of capital in the less developed countries, economic logic demands that capital be accumulated mainly by curtailing consumption relative to production; success in curtailment allows for capital accumulation. Political logic, on the other hand, demands regime legitimation and the mobilization of support for governments mainly by meeting the demands of broad sectors of society, which usually translates into politically mediated increases in consumption levels. Hence, the contradiction and dilemma.

The problem has been particularly severe in dependent developing countries, where along with capital, political options available to decision makers are also limited. Moreover, as we saw, external actors like the IMF have considerable influence in shaping the options available to policymakers. From these issues there arises the inescapable fact that regardless of the model or strategy of development followed, some groups in society will have to bear some of the considerable costs associated with capital accumulation and investment.

Because few if any groups will for any length of time voluntarily assume the cost burden, the fundamental political question becomes, who is going to pay the costs of development and how? A derived question is, what type of government operating in what kind of regime form will have the power and capacity to define and enforce a resolution to the cost question? Both of these questions have been posed over and over in Latin America since at least the 1930s. They have been posed with new urgency today. The present domestic and international crisis is disturbingly akin to the crisis of the 1930s in most countries. In Bolivia the present crisis is in fact worse than that of the Great Depression. The contemporary language of debt renegotiation, IMF stabilization programs, and economic packages (paquetes económicos) is in fact addressing an old congeries of issues that is emerging with particular urgency today both because of the internationally induced regional crisis, and because over the years neither authoritarian nor democratic regimes in the region have been able to solve the underlying contradictions and questions of political economy.

Over the same period another dramatic cyclical process has been played out at the level of policy and strategy: populism and antipopulism. Populist political movements arose in Latin America during and after the 1930s. Some, like APRA in Peru and the MNR in Bolivia, took the form of organized parties aimed at seizing power; others, like that of Vargas in Brazil and Perón in Argentina, were more leader centered and organized from positions of power. Whatever the form, populism and populist ideologies became the almost characteristic regional response to the Great Depression. In almost all countries they outpaced parties of the Marxist Left and came to dominate the political stage.

Populism in all its guises projected a multiclass alliance between entrepreneurs, the middle classes, workers, and peasants to use state power in the name of nationalistic development strategies. Particularly, the alliances were oriented toward use of the power of the state to promote a development model that essentially was state capitalism. Moreover, they all held out the hope that they could sustain regimes capable of promoting stable capitalist development simultaneously with broad processes of income distribution.

Populism as a movement and a development strategy carried within it the basic contradictions between political and economic logic. The concurrence of the imperative to accumulate and the political predisposition to distribute occasioned tensions within populism over costs of development. Over the years the tensions produced ruptures between those more oriented to accumulation, such as entrepreneurs and the technocratic middle class, and those more oriented to distribution, such as organized labor and the popular sectors.

Populist movements did not come directly to power everywhere, but the record shows that populist reformist ideology did penetrate and become predominant throughout the region. Given populism's pervasiveness, the tensions and contradictions produced by populism in our view became the driving force behind the cycle of authoritarian and democratic regimes.

One can see the connection between the two cycles—authoritarian-democratic, and populist-antipopulist—and the driving force of the latter in the recent dynamics of the political economies of a number of countries. It is clear in the case of Peru, for example. In 1963 the populist Belaunde Terry was elected president, but owing to legislative immobilism created in part by the intransigent opposition of the older populist APRA party, he was ousted by the military in 1968. In its first years the military regime tried to implement a species of military populism. By the mid 1970s the contradictions in the approach were evident, and a second phase was begun in 1975 whereby the military pursued antipopulist politics aimed at capital accumulation. After a controlled process of redemocratization sponsored by the military, Belaunde was elected again in 1980 and proceeded to implement a decidedly antipopulist economic program based on an opening of the Peruvian economy. Most recently APRA, headed by its new leader Alan García, was voted into power and at the moment is attempting to pursue economic activation and some populist distribution. It remains to be seen how successful García and APRA will be in pursuing their economic strategy and maintaining an open democratic system.

Most analysts would agree that the recent cycle of authoritarianism, initiated in the 1960s, and then redemocratization, in the late 1970s and 1980s, was connected to previous reformist strategies oriented to promoting development and incorporating key social sectors like organized labor. To simplify an extremely complex reality, the emergence of authoritarianism was connected to the exhaustion of the import-substituting growth strategy pursued in many countries during the 1940s and 1950s. Again, it was a matter of a need generated extraregionally for the major Latin American political economies to adapt to structural changes in the global capitalist system. Import-substituting industrialization had allowed some countries to defuse revolutionary pressures by pursuing populist distributional programs to benefit labor and other popular sectors in the form of wage policies and state-delivered services such as social security programs.

Bolivia was an important variation on the process. A one-product exporter with a small population, it did not have the capacity to buy political time through distributing surplus earned by import substitution. Hence, the old regime collapsed under the internal pressures that set off the revolution of 1952. The populists of the MNR found themselves astride a revolutionary process that threatened to escape their control. A good deal of political energy was expended by the MNR in trying to pull the process back into an essentially populist trajectory. This was accomplished by the mid-1950s, but then the MNR came up against the basic dilemmas and contradictions embedded in the populist developmental model.

In other countries the contradictions of populism and democracy brought to the fore with the exhaustion of the import-substitution process created an environment that pulled the military center stage. A new kind of developmentalist military regime based on the armed forces as an institution with a sense of mission acting in concert with civilian technocratic elites appeared. This new type of regime, which was probably epitomized by the government of the armed forces in Brazil, was termed by the Argentine sociologist Guillermo O'Donnell a bureaucratic-authoritarian regime type, or B/A regime.[1]

O'Donnell's concept has become the analytical standard, and we have used it in connection with Bolivia in the 1970s. Aside from the B/A regime's institutional characteristics, which mark an evolutionary organizational advance within the basic cycle of regime types, the B/A regime also has a policy thrust linked to the populism cycle. Basically, such regimes emphasize the economic imperative and therefore pursue antipopulist policies aimed at curbing broad-based popular consumption. Hence, in the context of the B/A regime costs are imposed none too gently on organized labor and other popular sectors. Politically, these sectors, which previously have been incorporated into the political game, are forcefully excluded and subjected to stern state control.

In spite of some periods of apparent economic success the new B/A regimes in Latin America were in the long run failures both politically and economically. Indeed, in many cases the military handed power back to civilians in the midst of worse economic crises than those obtaining when they seized power. And, after they had saddled the economies with massive foreign debts, which aside from being immense burdens served to increase the role of external decision-making centers in national affairs. Ironically, many of the same populist groups that had been ousted or suppressed by the military in the 1960s found themselves coming back to formal power in circumstances that mandated that they themselves implement antipopulist stabilization programs.

The new authoritarian regimes were unable to win anything other than transitory popularity. They were not able to establish any real legitimacy for authoritarianism as a regime type or for the military as the foremost power broker in society. Indeed, the great political weakness of these regimes was their inability to build any ongoing institutional links between the state and civil society. As a result, there was a growing alienation between the state and civil society as well as the military and civil society. There was, moreover a general political atrophy of key national institutions, including the military.

One of the main reasons that the military began to look for ways to leave power was the growing decomposition of the military as an institutional force. Within the new authoritarian model the military had sought to repress politics in civil society; however, the price paid for short-term success in doing so was the importation of those dynamics into the military itself. The longer it was in power, the more it experienced the ideological, personal, and factional divisions characteristic of civil society. That fact threatened the very self-concept of the military as well as put the institution onto a more direct collision course with the primary groups of civil society. Collision with labor was foreordained because of the model of development imposed by the military, but it is clear that repression is at best a short-term measure that in no way addresses the deep need to incorporate labor and other social sectors into the system in a stable way. These regimes demonstrate again the old truth that repression postpones problems but it does not solve them.

One of the more fundamental and unexpected contradictions fostered by the authoritarian regimes was with the private sector. They came to power as favorable to the private sector because they protected the sector from leftist threats, imposed order and accumulated capital to spur development. For these reasons, they began with private sector support. Over time it became evident that the military had its own perceived interests and that the state side of the state capitalist equation had its own logic. At a minimum the regimes had to maintain the state apparatus and therefore at a certain point the state, although guaranteeing the capitalist system, began to enter into conflict with the private sector over appropriation of the surplus produced by the system. Thus, in a number of cases, like Brazil, the private sector turned on the regimes and led the fight for a rollback of the state and a return to formal democratic procedures.

Thus, Latin America is again experiencing redemocratization. Again the engine driving the cycle is the generalized failure of the B/A regimes and the development models they pursued. In the end they were unable to institutionalize a system of ongoing governance capable of managing the economy and mobilizing support from civil society. Likewise, many of the groups pushing democracy are not doing so out of a commitment to democracy itself but because experience with the alternatives has them convinced that it is the only viable option. Thus, as many have noted, democracy is coming around once more mainly because it is perceived as a second-best option. Let us now return to the Bolivian case to see how the above analysis helps to clarify it, and to see how it can contribute to further elaboration or clarification of broader analytical schemes designed to make sense out of the regime as a whole. The case of Bolivia puts the above dimensions into dramatic relief as well as highlighting other dimensions of its own, especially since the revolution of 1952.

Bolivia's MNR was a classic populist party that somewhat reluctantly headed up a mass-based revolution instead of the preferred strategy of reform imposed from above. From the outset the MNR coalition was rife with the contradictions discussed earlier. The first difference of opinion was ideological and involved those oriented toward a more populist state capitalist model and those oriented toward a more Marxist state socialist model. By the mid 1950s the former had pretty much bested the latter but by no means had eliminated them from the scene.

Bolivia

No sooner was the state capitalist model dominant than the MNR was face to face with the basic contradictions between economic and political logics and the question of who within the MNR's original coalition was going to bear the lion's share of the costs of development. The issue drove a wedge between those oriented toward emphasizing accumulation and those pushing distribution; this meant a split between the new private sector and the middle class on one hand and organized labor on the other. For a variety of complex reasons the peasantry at that point lined up more with the former group, which was coming to form a center Right faction in the MNR.

The drama was played out in the late 1950s and early 1960s in a context with striking similarities to the present scene. It was a period of serious economic crisis characterized by, among other things, a demand-driven hyperinflation produced by policies that sharply increased general levels of consumption. To receive needed external assistance, the government had to accept externally defined programs: first an IMF stabilization program, and later a United States-designed program to rehabilitate the tin industry. The first program was implemented by Hernán Siles in the late 1950s; the second was implemented by Paz Estenssoro in the early 1960s. Both programs carried within them cost allocations that fell most directly on organized labor. Not surprisingly, that drove a wedge between the MNR elite and labor elites. Most fatefully, the MNR government of Siles negotiated a resumption of U.S. military aid that was used to rebuild the armed forces as a counterweight to worker militias. Whatever else it did, the move put a renewed Bolivian military into a pivotal political position. The tensions and conflicts generated by the underlying contradictions began to pull the MNR apart and undercut its ability to act as a mediator between the revolutionized state and civil society. This was to prove rather important.

Like many populist movements, the MNR did not carry within it a primary commitment to democracy in the classic Western sense of competitive pluralism. Rather, the MNR took as its model the PRI of Mexico and aimed at creating a de facto single-party system operating behind a democratic facade. However, unlike the PRI, the MNR was not successful in incorporating key social sectors such as organized labor into the organizational structure of the party. This turned out to be a fateful organizational weakness.

The MNR's problems with labor did not derive solely from the dispute over social costs but also from earlier organizational decisions. Basically, the MNR elite ratified the independent organizational strength of labor by granting labor in the first years of the revolution legally autonomous or *fuero* status, as well as formal co-government. Organizationally, this defined labor more than an independent ally of the MNR rather than as a constituent organization. Hence, when the dispute over allocation of costs arose, labor simply shifted its position from one of alliance to one of antagonism.

The MNR failed to incorporate the COB but granted it semisovereign status within the state. When the break came, then, the COB perceived the MNR as well as the state as alien entities either to be captured or defended against. Moreover, the break oriented the COB as an entity toward bringing direct unmediated pressure to bear on the executive in a species of quasi-interstate relations. The structural and institutional consequences of these early decisions were many, profound, and long-lasting.

First, the decisions obviously left open the question of incorporating labor into a general new regime type in which, as in Mexico, cost allocations could be made and enforced within a single corporatist party structure. Thenceforth any attempt at a state capitalist model in Bolivia would immediately mean unmediated confrontation between the executive and the autonomous COB. Practically speaking, although this pattern strengthened the COB as an entity, it remained far from strong enough to impose its own model on the MNR or the country. Accordingly, over the years the COB became more of a defensively oriented organization aimed mainly toward attempts at vetoing the executive-based actions of other political organizations and coalitions.

More significant, the COB's patterns of interaction with the government and the state became a model or precedent for other class, sector, and regional organizations. Thus, there developed a pattern in which all the major group organizations of civil society sought direct unmediated interaction with the executive and the state apparatus. In short, the pattern undercut the articulation of an intermediary structure capable of institutionalizing relationships between the government and civil society. Conflicts between the government and groups, and among groups themselves were quite direct, and Bolivia began to move toward the kind of unbuffered context of conflict that Samuel Huntington defined as a praetorian situation.[2]

A derived consequence of this pattern was a transformation in the role and function of the MNR and other political parties as well. Unlike the PRI, the MNR did not become the vertebra linking the key groups of civil society to the state or a structure for mobilizing support for governments. Nor was the party able to assume the classic functions of interest articulation and interest aggregation. In short, the party declined dramatically in performing intermediary roles between civil society and the state, and thereby was part of the process of weakening Bolivia's intermediary institutional structure.

For reasons we will go into shortly, the MNR was converted mainly into a patronage machine, which set off intense factionalization as the party divided into groups of petty leaders and their backers. The assault upon state coffers was an important driving force in the steady expansion of the state apparatus. It also weakened the ability of the MNR to act as a support base for governments because once a particular MNR government had distributed the patronage, the party members who had been denied jobs began to turn against it. The internal coherence of the MNR finally fell apart, and the party became a collectivity of personalistic nonideological factions that collapsed in total disarray in November 1964.

In retrospect, then, it is clear that although the economic situation, the logic of development models, and the behavior of external actors were factors crucial to the situation, they did not determine its evolution but served to create climates of constraint and limited options. Critical political, administrative, and organizational decisions were still there to be made. The decisions made by the MNR elites in interaction with sectorial elites like labor put in place another set of logics whose structural consequences ultimately led to the political demise of the MNR as a ruling party and contributed to a general decomposition of intermediate political institutions. Not coincidentally, the resulting praetorian situation combined with the intense conflict over development models and costs basically forestalled the possible persistence of any civil regime operating even in a facade democracy. Military intervention and de facto authoritarianism were the all-but-guaranteed outcomes.

Institutional Disintegration

The military intervention of 1964 and the subsequent twenty years of military-backed authoritarian regimes were not the product of some perverse motivations internal to the military, nor of a specific social class's use of the military to assert its will and interests. They were, rather, the product of a complex structural milieu created by the interaction between scarcity and dependence, the logics and contradictions inherent in populism and state capitalism, and the decisions made and not made by key political elites, especially those of the MNR and organized labor.

In any event, 1964 marked the initiation of the cycle of populism and antipopulism: a period of antipopulist state capitalism until 1969, followed by two attempts at military populism, terminated by a definitive return to antipopulist state capitalism between 1971 and 1978. Throughout these years and into the 1980s the military was the de facto preeminent political force in Bolivia. As we noted earlier, the process of fragmentation in civil society continued apace, as did the disintegration of political institutions. Moreover, the elites of all principal groups, factions, classes, and regions demonstrated over and over that they were not averse to fomenting and backing authoritarian regimes that they perceived to be in their interests. No elite demonstrated a firm and ongoing commitment to establishing formal democracy until the 1980s.

The period 1964-69 was characterized above all by imposition of a state capitalist development model within an essentially authoritarian framework. The costs of the model fell mainly on organized labor, which was forcefully repressed and excluded from the political game. The costs also fell indirectly on the traditional agricultural sector. However, the leader then, Barrientos, was able to exploit a charismatic image and traditional clientelistic links to peasant leaders to generate a degree of support in the countryside. Peasant support was theoretically given institutional form in the so-called military-peasant pact *(pacto militar-campesino)*. That the support was shallow was made clear when the Barrientos regime provoked widespread peasant opposition with a proposed new tax.

Barrientos sought to build a coalition based on the peasantry, the urban middle class, and the emergent private sector, and from a position of power he tried to legitimize the coalition in an outwardly democratic system crystallized in the constitution of 1967. Whenever the legislature challenged him, he simply exercised de facto authoritarian rule. More fundamentally, Barrientos was unable to give any real institutional form to his regime, and most particularly he was unable to build any party structures to link support in civil society to the formal structures of government.

To remain in power, Barrientos had to resort to personalist manipulation of clientelistic factions that began to penetrate even further all of the nation's key institutions. Clientelistic factionalism carried with it a tendency to personalistic favoritism or corruption, which began to erode even further the coherence of the institutions. This in turn undermined the perception of the state as an objective expression of society and fed the negative perception of it as an alien entity to be captured and used for the particularistic benefit of individuals, factions, groups, and regions. These dynamics had already permeated civil institutions, such as political parties, and under Barrientos the process was reinforced there and most fatefully introduced into the military as well.

In spite of Barrientos's popularity in some quarters, his government ended as one disconnected to civil society. Moreover, under Barrientos the state and particularly one of its major institutions, the military, were set off in antagonistic relationships with key groups like organized labor. Indeed, to hold on to power, Barrientos and the military slipped into an almost permanent state of war with labor.

Although the regime was able to repress labor and impose costs on workers, it was unable to eliminate labor as a central actor or to incorporate labor in a controlled fashion. This became more than clear during the interludes of military populism led first by General Ovando and then General Torres. Both of these governments demonstrated the growing weakness of the central state and specific governments to take charge of the flow of popular mobilization through means other than coercion.

Although the governments of Ovando and Torres took the lid off labor, they were powerless to structure labor's relationship to the national political process. Fatefully, labor adopted an autonomous position toward both populist governments, for which any degree of its support was predicated on immediate response to labor demands. Labor thereby pushed both in a more radical direction, which provoked opposition from the middle class and the private sector without providing the governments with a stable base of offsetting support. Indeed, the Ovando and Torres governments were even more disconnected to society at large. And, even though the labor elite was able to batter these weak populist regimes, they were not able to form a power base capable of imposing a labor-backed model of either populism or state socialism. The Asamblea Popular served mainly to polarize civil society along class and ideological lines even as it contributed to the enervation of the state and the nation's formal public institutions.

Although they were ostensibly based on the military, the Ovando and Torres governments were extremely weak and incapable of governing in any but the most formal sense. Moreover, the military was showing severe strain as personal, factional, and ideological differences began to pull it apart. Indeed, it was only the threat to the institution per se by the popular assembly that in 1971 brought enough unity within the military to put it at the head of a military-civil alliance to end the interlude of military populism and again forcefully impose a state capitalist model that emphasized capital accumulation and enforced social order. From the point of view of both the Left and Right, authoritarian solutions were the only viable route; enlistment of aid from the military factions therefore became a strategic goal of all the principal civil players.

It is important to remember that what brought Banzer to power for seven years was not a simple coup d'état but a quasi civil war based on a broad civil-military coalition that reflected the advanced extent of fragmentation and ideological polarization that had permeated civil society. It was not unlike the kind of ideologically charged civil-military movement that brought a new kind of authoritarian regime to power in Brazil in 1964.

Indeed, in many ways the Banzer regime was a Bolivian variant on the wave of new authoritarian regimes that swept across the region after 1964.

Patrimonialism

At one level the Banzer government was an attempt to institute a Bolivian version of the B/A regime type. There was a concerted attempt to present the military as an institutional force driven by a coherent vision of Bolivia's future. This image was enhanced by the revitalization of the Altos Estudios Militares (School of High Military Studies) modeled on similar schools in other countries. Such schools mixed civil and military elites in their classes. From this there began to emerge in Bolivia as well as elsewhere linkages between military elites and civil elites from the private entrepreneurial sector and the technocratic middle class. In Bolivia this became the basis for a Bolivian version of the so-called military-civil technocratic alliance that is a defining structural characteristic of B/A-type regimes.

As we saw, Banzer also attempted to gain institutional coherence by integrating the MNR and the FSB into a formal pact to support the government. This was further elaborated in a corporatist-type arrangement in which the military, the political parties, and the private sector were formally designated as the government's support pillars and links with civil society.

Even as he sought to build an institutionalized authoritarian regime, Banzer moved with alacrity to push a return to the antipopulist state capitalist model. In the early and mid-1970s the model seemed to be succeeding as Bolivia, like other countries in the region, posted very healthy growth rates. Thus, the Banzer period can be said to have marked the full realization of authoritarian state capitalism in Bolivia. To many observers, it was a regime that brought apparent prosperity and political order; Banzer was credited with a kind of miracle of economic and political development.

It is now more than apparent that development at both levels was either superficial or nonexistent. Although economic growth took place, it was not reflective of any real development in the sense of creating structures for future self-sustained growth. Moreover, the growth that occurred was not the result of any policy or management skill of the government.

The government spurred growth mainly because it guaranteed the capitalist system by force and imposed the costs of capital accumulation on labor and the popular sectors. In a sense it created a climate that was, in the short term at least, propitious to capitalist growth. Once that climate was in place, however, the major source of growth was demand generated by the international economy. The profits from such growth were not recycled to the productive sectors, and as a consequence they did not develop during this period. Hence, when the international economy slumped in the late 1970s, Bolivia went into an economic tailspin, demonstrating thereby that the country was as dependent as ever within the international political economy.

The superficial growth of the 1970s was bought at a very high social price paid by the mass of workers and peasants. Bolivia was to demonstrate what had become clear in other cases as well: repression in the long run is inefficient and ineffective. The Banzer government did not in any sense, solve the central political issue of structuring a productive relationship with organized labor, particularly the miners. To the contrary—throughout his tenure the mine camps were like conquered territories under permanent occupation by army troops. The legacy of organized labor's hatred and suspicion of the military intensified greatly during this period.

Aside from the disjuncture with labor the Banzer government also had serious trouble with the peasantry, which put an end to the idea of a special pact between the military and peasants. In the 1970s peasant groups began to realize that the state capitalist strategy pursued since the 1950s by the MNR and subsequent military regimes was systematically working against the interests of the traditional agricultural sector. Protest brought bloody repression in the Cochabamba Valley in 1974, which led not only to a rupture between the peasants and the military but to the proliferation of new racially and regionally focused peasant organizations. Like labor, these organizations fostered a hostile view of the central state and its primary arm of repression, the military. The Banzer regime, then, created a growing gap between the military and the state, and two of the most numerous and significant social groups in Bolivia, the working class and the traditional peasantry.

The Banzer period also saw the definitive rise of regionalism in Bolivia led by Santa Cruz. Effective power in the regions did not inhere in formal government institutions empowered by the central state but in regional civic committees. Committees like that of Santa Cruz, although beneficiaries of the state capitalist policies of the Banzer regime, came increasingly to play a zero-sum game in which they perceived the central state as an alien highland *(kolla)* entity to defend themselves against and/or to be assaulted for particularistic privileges. The support of the regional committees was therefore more and more contingent on the Banzer government's response to their every demand.

The Banzer government's relations with the private sector were also complex and problematic. At base were the underlying contradictions between the private sector and the state manifested in state capitalist development models, contradictions that were exacerbated by the peculiarly important role the state had come to play in Bolivia—a role that led to a hypergrowth of the state in size and function. To understand the political economy of Bolivia, it is necessary to understand the role of the state. Again, we are dealing with an extreme version of a pattern common throughout the region.

The role of the state in Bolivia was determined historically in large part by the country's underlying social structure, which in turn was a product of Bolivia's extremely dependent monoproduct economy. In brief, the economy has been characterized by the fact that sources of hard wealth have been few, and because of ownership patterns, have not tended to circulate readily. Hence, there has always been a dual problem of social mobility and the maintenance of social status linked to the circulation of wealth.

One result of the relative immobility in the stratification system has been a tendency to use political office as a substitute medium to circulate wealth and to achieve and/or maintain status. Thus, because political office was one of the few things that circulated readily, it was converted into a commodity; one of the principal dynamics of politics has been that of job circulation or what the Bolivians call *empleomanía* (obsession with political jobs). This dynamic in turn stimulated fragmentation among the elite and subelite segments of society into personalistic factions formed around strongmen apt to ascend to positions that controlled patronage.

Historically, this dynamic has been most relevant to the middle class and some segments of the upper class. The urban middle class has throughout this century been an extremely dependent grouping in that it does not control hard sources of wealth but has needed wages, salaries, and fees to achieve and maintain status. Given the scarcity and low circulation of sources of hard wealth, one of the few sources of jobs has been the state. The middle class has always experienced concrete existential motivation to enter politics as a medium of job circulation. In this way the middle class had fed the tendencies toward factionalism and clientelism that have pervaded and in a sense subverted Bolivia's political institutions for most of this century.[3]

These dynamics were heightened by the revolution of 1952 and the subsequent policies followed by the MNR. Indeed, one of the main reasons the urban middle class supported the statist-oriented MNR was the implicit promise of the expansion of the public sector and thereby middle-class employment. In any event, since 1952 the state apparatus has become the primary mechanism of incorporating the urban middle class into the system. This structurally rooted fact has been one of the main engines driving the steady expansion of the role and size of the state in Bolivia since 1952.

Moreover, these dynamics have fed into and exacerbated the tendencies toward personalistic clientelism, which have had at least two important consequences for political system. First, personalistic clientelism has pervaded the entire state apparatus and undermined the formal outward rationality of state organizations. Second, as we have seen it has distorted political parties, converting them from mechanisms to underpin governments and institutionalize links between key groups in civil society and the state into vehicles to mediate the distribution of jobs.

All of these forces asserted themselves most powerfully during the Banzer period. Although Banzer sought to create a modern institutionalized regime, the underlying predisposition toward personalistic clientelism and factionalism simply overwhelmed his efforts. As we saw, when these dynamics began to operate, through the political parties, for example, Banzer turned more and more to direct manipulation of personalistic factions, which further undermined the formal rationality of the state and national political institutions. He ended up by creating what was in effect a traditional patrimonial mode of authoritarian rule that gave the lie to any pretense of a bureaucratic-authoritarian regime. Patrimonial dynamics were so strong under Banzer that in spite of his procapitalist rhetoric the state apparatus grew larger and faster under him than during any previous regime. By the time he was done, the state was by far the dominant dimension in the state capitalist model.

The great growth in the size and role of the state had numerous consequences. First, it exacerbated tensions between the state and the private sector. Under Banzer the state expanded the economic space it penetrated as well as increased its appetite for resources to maintain its expanding apparatus. Thus, the inherent tensions in the state capitalist model between the state and the private sector came to a head. By the mid 1970s important voices in the private sector began to question the wisdom of supporting Banzer and his system of patrimonial prebendal capitalism.

The relationship between the Bolivian state and the private sector has always been a complex one. The contemporary private sector in many respects was brought into being by the revolution of 1952 and the model of development defined by the revolution. Over the years it grew under the wing of the state and had come to rely on it. It had become dependent on coalitions' use of power of the state to safeguard it from threats from the Left, and to sponsor the accumulation of capital and selective allocation of costs. In addition, the sector looked to the state for economic protection, subsidies, and lucrative contracts.

The private sector was particularly enmeshed in the state under Banzer. Still, as we saw, it did not relate to the state and public policymaking as a sector or class with its own clear sense of collective interests but as an aggregate of elite individuals and firms that were linked to the state by personal ties to the patrimonial ruler. As the state's appetite for resources grew, its policies—such as the mode of taxing the medium mining sector—exposed situations in which individual entrepreneurs tied into the prebendal system were acting in ways contradictory to the objective interests of the private sector or class. This led to the appearance of a wing of the private sector that began to question the preeminent role of the state and the sector's dependence on it.

By extension, components of the private sector started to doubt the long-term viability of any military-based authoritarian system. They pointed out that whatever its anticommunist credentials, the military had developed a stake in an expanding and activistic state; they realized, in short, that there was a contradiction between a military-based authoritarian state pushing a state capitalist model and a private sector seeking autonomous growth and development. These same components of the private sector not only had serious reservations regarding Banzer and his supporters in the sector but also raised necessity for establishing some mode of democracy as being crucial to the sector's own health and that of the economy. A major source of this emerging position was the association of medium miners.

Aside from these issues, the hyper-growth of the state raised particularly sharp issues of coordination and administrative capacity because the consolidation of a patrimonial system subverted the formal rationality of the state. The state was being disaggregated into petty fiefdoms headed by personalistic civil and military factions. This reality diminished the institutional coherence of the state and undermined its capacity to govern and/or manage society. The upshot was that by the mid-1970s the state was large, consumed a great deal of resources, but in practical terms was weak in the sense of possessing an ongoing capacity to direct society.

The general weakness of the state translated into the practical weakness of specific governments. This was also evident under Banzer. Although his government started off capable of enforcing its will, over the years that capacity diminished markedly. Actually, after a relatively brief period Banzer had to spend most of his time and energy manipulating the Byzantine web of civil and military factions simply to remain in formal power. As we saw, he was constantly trying to reorganize the state in vain attempts to restore some ruling capacity at the center. He held formal power for seven years, but by the mid-1970s he could scarcely rule, in the sense of defining and implementing policy.

In Bolivia, then, as elsewhere authoritarian systems proved no more capable than democratic systems of long-term governance and social management. Power to rule based on the willingness and capacity to use concentrated force is a short-term situation that in no way fulfills the requirements of governance in the modern world, especially for a dependent and vulnerable country like Bolivia.

The ultimate weakness of the Banzer government was reflective of two structural problems that had developed in Bolivia and that were to be crucial in structuring the political process in the post-Banzer era: the way that a government relates to the state, and the way it relates to civil society.

By the late 1970s the state apparatus had become such a large and dense web of clientelistic feudalities that governmental authority over the state apparatus was cast into doubt. For all practical purposes governments could not use it as a mechanism to execute and administer policy; the components had developed logics of maintenance and survival that ran counter to central notions of rational administration. This was seen in the growing problems of corruption, inefficiency, and failure to act in concert with governmental policy. Another important dimension of the decline of governmental authority over the state apparatus was that a considerable portion of the resources extracted from society by the state were dissipated within the apparatus and never emerged as a resource available to governments to back policy.[4]

The other side of diminished governmental authority was a lack of institutional mechanisms to coordinate the flow of demands and support from civil society to the government. Indeed, Banzer ended with no stable sectorial bases of support but mainly a reality in which all key sectors were either actively hostile or at best only formally supportive in return for government favors. Dependent on its ability to manipulate a panoply of patron-client arrangements that generated an intense dynamic of "ins" and "outs" that transcended ideological or class lines, the Banzer government was confronting a civil society that generated substantial demands but offered little by way of coherent and institutionalized support. What support was there was contingent on immediate demand satisfaction. The upshot was that the government was for all practical purposes structurally doomed to be weak and obsessed with survival.

The irony of the Banzer period is that although it was a period of superficial economic growth, it was also a period of political retrogression. The concept of modern political development implies, at the least, the elaboration of a set of abstract institutional structures that link the state and civil society and channel the flow of political energies produced within society. In theory at least, such a set of structures can be articulated into a variety of regime types from totalitarian, to authoritarian, to some mode of democracy. This is one of the reasons that the B/A regime type was considered "modern" and an advance over earlier personalistic dictatorships.

In Bolivia under Banzer there was a retreat from institutionalized rule of any type into a more traditional system of personalistic patrimonialism.

The process of decay and decomposition of the nation's institutional infrastructure continued apace. All of the major institutions had weakened and become increasingly epiphenomenal to the real process of governing. Institutional retrogression was also evident in the armed forces, which by the late 1970s were as fragmented and ridden with clientelistic factionalism as were civil institutional structures. The military's condition rendered it less able to generate support for the government, and in fact reinforced the tendency of the patrimonial ruler to dissipate his energies in trying to create and maintain coalitions of backers in the military.

Thus, as in other cases, authoritarian antipopulist rule in Bolivia was a dismal failure from the point of view of creating a viable political system capable of structuring economic development. The Banzer regime left a legacy of a large, debilitated, and out-of-control state apparatus that was divorced almost totally from civil society. The central government was extremely weak and incapable of governing in any meaningful sense because the atrophy of the institutional structure left it without buffers between it and civil society and without authoritative capacity to control the state apparatus. Particularly pronounced was the decay of the institutional coherence of the armed forces, which were also alienated from most of civil society. These realities were manifest in the complete inability of Banzer to manage events during his last years in office. Thus, when the conclusion of his term came at the hands of a coup from the divided military, the onetime strongman ended with an ignominious whimper rather than a bang.

Regime Transition

Since the fall of Banzer and the collapse of his patrimonial system in 1978 the main political problem has been to constitute a central decision-making authority within a democratic framework. The problem has been complicated by an economic crisis that began in the late 1970s and by 1985 was catastrophic. The extreme weakness of most of the governments during this period precluded their articulating and implementing programs to deal with the economic circumstances. There have been of course many factors behind this impasse. One is the all but permanent contradiction between political and economic logic and the derived question of social costs, which has intensified in the current international and domestic crisis. At present the most pressing aspect of the cost question is who is going to pay for the needed stabilization program.

The reality of Bolivia's internal condition and its dependence in the world system have created a situation in which all proposals for stabilization that have been designed by domestic and international elites have been based on austerity programs that fall most heavily on organized labor and other popular sectors. Thus, the irony of a country seeking to establish a mass-based democracy while it is forced by domestic and international circumstance to impose substantial burdens on the mass of the population, and the inability of governments to have launched earlier austerity programs not only aggravated the economic crisis but meant that higher future costs of doing so would add to the difficulty of pushing such a program through—a classic vicious circle.

It is important to remember that because of the collapse of the country's institutional structure, governments per se, regardless of form, were weak during this period. Military-based authoritarian governments were as weak and vacillating as civil democratic governments; even the brutal García Meza government was incapable of defining policy, and was able only to cling to office and loot the country during its year at the helm. One crucial reason for the weakness was the dispersal of practical power from the state to the various class, sectorial, and regional entities of a civil society that was increasingly fragmented along multiple lines. An important development was the rise in political salience of the regional civic committees, especially those of the eastern departments and above all Santa Cruz.

The central structural problem was the decay of institutional infrastructure to mediate between the dispersed power of civil society and the large but extremely debilitated central state apparatus; governments in effect were caught in the metaphorical middle. The enervation of the state, however, did not mean a reciprocal increase in the strength of civil society in a positive sense. Owing to a propensity to pursue particularistic interests, none of the components of civil society either alone or in concert was able to define and implement a solution for the rest of society. They were strong only relative to the fragile governments, on whom they could press their demands and/or against whom they could exercise de facto vetoes over all or portions of the various economic packages floated. In a deep sense it was an enfeebled state and a fragmented civil society feeding on each other in a manner that diminished the capacity of the society as a whole to address its problems.

Aside from the structural weakness of the state, there were also some structural factors inhibiting the constitution of effective governments within the context of formal, competitive democracy. The main trouble in this regard has been the way that political parties and the electoral system relate to the process of forming a government. As we saw, parties in Bolivia are now driven mainly by the logic of penetrating and distributing state patronage among their members. This helps account for the fact that one of the few things Bolivia produced in quantity in the 1980s was political parties. The proliferation, which cannot be accounted for in terms of ideological or programmatic differences, was stimulated further by the modified proportional representation system whereby the legislature was elected, a system that allowed minor parties to win seats.

The dynamics of the party system has had a number of serious consequences. Because of the proliferation of parties, it has been extremely difficult to form a majority in the bicameral legislature. Moreover, as we learned earlier, the party system of multiple tiny parties has increasingly been separated from the associational structure of civil society and therefore does not link the sectors of civil society into the system by way of the legislature. These two factors have led to a serious structural disjuncture between the executive and legislative powers and between the electoral system and the process of governing.

From 1978 to 1985 no government had anything resembling a majority in the legislature, even with coalitions. Party fragmentation has precluded the legislature from acting as either a source of major programs and policy or as a base of political support for executives and their policies and programs. Indeed, legislatures have been set off against executives in an antagonistic dynamic. Legislatures not only blocked executive action but were a consistent source of conspiracies to bring down executives that they themselves had empowered. Congress over and over showed a willingness to contrive all manner and means to subvert the outcomes of the democratic electoral system.

In Bolivia the government has meant a freestanding executive branch that has not been politically connected to the legislative branch. This fact is evident when key interest groups like the CEPB, the COB, and the civic committees bypass the parties and Congress and bring pressure to bear directly on the executive. The executive branch during this period has had to contend with two separate political dynamics: an antagonistic and obstructionist Congress; and pressure groups seeking to veto, blunt, or modify policy formulated by teams of experts. The former has not provided the political support for the executive to deal with the latter, and in fact has diminished its ability to do so.

To function at all, the executive has had to resort to a de facto species of authoritarian rule by decree, a reality that simply fed the propensity of parties in the legislature to attack the executive for violation of the democratic rules of the game, and provided the parties with rhetorical cover for various schemes to oust presidents by equally undemocratic means. The executive as a result has tended to ignore Congress and negotiate with the interest associations, tantamount to de facto legislative fora outside the formal democratic structures. This was particularly true of the COB and CEPB, which often held meetings to discuss and pass on government programs, especially economic packages.

One can see that the formal democratic electoral system has in a real sense been divorced from the actual process of governance. As a result, elections have not created political bases of support for governments (executives), nor have they linked society at large or parts thereof to the executive or to the democratic system as such. In sum, in Bolivia, as in a number of other countries like Peru and Ecuador, there developed a marked disjuncture between electoral-parliamentary politics and the executive-based process of governance. Elections have not tended to produce unitary governments with executive and legislative faces but rather dualized governments in which there has been a tendency toward standoffs between the legislature and the executive. To avoid immobilism, presidents are often tempted or inclined to govern around or over legislatures, sometimes bending or ignoring the democratic rules of the game as they do.

There have been other factors at work in Bolivia's shaky transition from authoritarianism to formal competitive democracy. Ironically, one was the internal collapse of the military and the fact that, especially after García Meza, it had to beat a hasty retreat from power. The experiences of Peru, Ecuador, and Brazil all show that the transition has been smoother when the military, acting as an institution, decided for its own reasons to absent itself from power and was able to control the transition at least to the point that it played a large role in defining the rules of transition. In that type of situation civil groups were forced to unite behind the push for democracy and were able to focus on negotiations with the military rather than on direct confrontations with one another before the new system was in operation. In Bolivia the sudden departure of the military threw civil groups into a situation where they had to gerrymander rules of procedure among themselves in an atmosphere of tension and ongoing crisis. Rather than focusing on a set of democratic rules per se, all groups sought short-term solutions that served their immediate power and patronage aspirations. As we saw, groups of every ideological persuasion often were willing to seek nondemocratic shortcuts to power at the expense of their rivals.

In Bolivia, as in many other countries in the region, the elites of civil society have backed into democracy as a regime form. An orientation toward democracy among most of them turned into perceiving it as a second-best option arrived at after bitter experiences with the alternatives. Most important in this was experiencing of the García Meza government, which led many to lose all confidence in playing the military card. By the early 1980s most key elite groups had concluded that in the short term at least formal democracy would at a minimum allow them to stay in the political game whereas military-backed authoritarian regimes could lead to exclusion.

Democracy in a sense, then, has emerged in Bolivia as a result of a negative consensus. This is not necessarily bad in that it does create some short-term concrete interests in maintaining a democratic system. The principal question will be whether civil elite groups, especially the political parties, can find enough tolerance and trust to come up with new ways of organizing a democratic process.

In the transition to democracy the experience of the Bolivian private sector has been interesting. Until the late 1970s the elites of the private sector had been clearly inclined to seek the protection of military-based authoritarian regimes. Moreover, they tended to relate to authoritarian regimes more as individuals than as a sector or social class. In the latter Banzer years, they began to grasp the latent contradiction between the sector and a statist-oriented authoritarian regime. Then after the Banzerato, operating in a competitive environment forced the sector to adopt a class-based orientation, which was manifested with the emergence of the CEPB as its key interest group. Finally, the García Meza tenure had a complex effect on them: it challenged their trust in the military even as it provoked fear that the military institution could be ruined and hence not available as an ultimate protection from a leftist revolutionary threat.

After these experiences the private sector became a strong proponent of democracy, mainly because it disliked the alernatives and simultaneously felt more confident of its ability to play a democratic game. However, the sector has showed that it now is capable of acting as a class and is committed to defending its interests. So, although it is committed to a democratic solution to the problem of organizing governmental power, it is clear that it would not hesitate to seek alternatives should it feel its fundamental interests threatened by the Marxist Left.

A set of attitudes and strategies similar to that of the private sector can be attributed to other crucial players, such as the COB and the civic committees. The way to gain civil elite support for a democratic system is the perception on all sides that there is more to be lost outside a democratic system than within it.

All of the structural problems and contradictions came to the fore during the Siles presidency of 1982-85. The disjuncture of legislative and executive power and the collapse of his party coalition enfeebled his government. At the same time he was unable to assert authority over the huge and sprawling state apparatus, which itself was incoherent and weak vis-à-vis civil society. The weakness of the government in dealing with the state apparatus was clear in the emergence of public employee unions, especially the employees of the central bank, as a key power group not subject to government control.

When Siles confronted the power groups of civil society, he did so from a position of extreme political frailty. This was particularly true in his relations with the COB and labor, who theoretically should have been his major support group. Siles found it progressively difficult to govern, especially in terms of stabilizing the economy. Simply to retain formal power he had to respond to the myriad unmediated demands pressed on his government by the power groups of civil society like the COB, the CEPB, and the civic committees. Capitulation to the demands raised consumption levels such that hyperinflation was fueled, thereby contributing to the general deterioration of the economy.

The experience of Bolivia since the late 1970s demonstrates that its biggest political problem remains to create and sustain an effective center of decision-making for over these years both authoritarian and democratic regime forms have proved incapable of doing so. In our view the key for Bolivia to weather its present political and economic crisis is the creation of a strong central government capable of defining and implementing practical solutions to concrete policy issues. Settling the forms and structures of governmental power is prerequisite to the dealing with the economic crisis.

The trick for Bolivia will be to come up with a formally democratic system that can produce strong governments. The recent history of the country and of the rest of the region demonstrates that only formally democratic regimes stand any real chance of establishing long-term legitimacy. Authoritarian regimes will always be perceived as governments of exception and therefore temporary in nature. Such regimes ultimately produce widespread societal resistance, and have proved that over the long haul they are no more effective than democratic regimes at coping with the central issues of the political economy.

There are no blueprints to indicate how these political problems can be solved. The experience of Bolivia indicates that just as all of the chief elite groups of society have, in a manner of speaking, backed into democracy, they have also showed both a need and a capacity to improvise their way into a viable democratic system. The rules of the democratic game have been emerging as a result of negotiated ways out *(salidas)* of specific dilemmas. The salidas have not always proved worthwhile, but the process itself has forced disparate elites to sit down together. And, the process itself could help build a necessary set of informal norms of tolerance and compromise that are a crucial part of the infrastructure of any ongoing democratic system. Effective democracy, if it emerges in Bolivia, will not conform to externally derived models or to onetime global solutions to all of Bolivia's contradictions and conflicts. In Bolivia, as elsewhere, democracy will of necessity be built over time, not decreed into existence. If it comes, it will be produced by serendipitous salidas reflecting the pragmatic creativity of political elites and not grand solutions reflecting intellectual imports or architectural schemes.

The recent developments under the Paz Estenssoro government inaugurated in August 1985 illustrate the process and give some ground for cautious optimism. In the first place, the ADN and Banzer demonstrated a clear will to let a democratic system work when they accepted the way Paz and the MNR took the presidency through shrewd manipulation of the electoral court and the new legislative assembly. It showed a willingness to abide by outcomes of the system and a willingness to begin to play the critical role of loyal opposition. It was an important if small step toward legitimating a competitive electoral system by the party elites.

Just as important, President Paz used the crisis situation to concentrate substantial decision power, in the short term at least, in the executive office. To do that he had to design a stabilization program quickly with a small group of decision makers and decree it with no public discussion of its terms. He thereby caught all of the potential opponents off guard, and when they did try to react negatively, he swiftly used state coercion to neutralize their opposition. In short, a government produced by a democratic electoral formula acted decisively by assuming to itself an essentially authoritarian style of decision making.

The crucial question was and remains whether that de facto authoritative capacity to act by the executive could be encased in and politically legitimated by a formal democratic framework. The key to that question was and is the relationship between the executive and the legislature as mediated by the political parties. The most dramatic move in that regard was the "pact for democracy" by the MNR and the ADN. The pact, as long as it holds, for the first time in years guarantees that the executive has majority political support in the legislature. In effect, the pact provides a way of giving political and democratic legitimacy to policies formulated by a few decision makers around the executive, for the pact makes the legislature a device to legitimate executive action rather than a lawmaking body in its own right. Should the pact hold and be further elaborated, it may point the way toward a hybrid regime type that fuses the executive with authoritative decision capacity with a democratically legitimated legislative assembly.

While it is still too early to tell, recent Bolivian experience along with that of countries like Venezuela and Colombia indicates that a way to solidify formal democratic regimes is to engineer pacts among the major political parties. The exact nature of the pacts can and must vary from case to case, but at least two provisions are crucial: losers in electoral contests must not be excluded from the game, and regardless of who wins there must be some sharing of state patronage. Both provisions are incorporated in the Bolivian pact.

Political pacts, however, speak to only one of the two sides to executive decision making. The executive must articulate viable public policies, but then they must be implemented and administered. The first side of that is political in the classic sense and needs a party majority or coalitional underwriting in the legislature. The other side is political and administrative, and demands that the executive have the capacity to assert authority over the state apparatus. If anything, the second aspect is actually much harder to deal with in Bolivia than the first. Thus far at least it has proved a stumbling block to the Paz administration, which in various statements has made clear that it grasps the importance of asserting authority over the state apparatus.

In the Bolivian context party pacts can help with the first aspect but in some senses are actually an inhibiting factor with the second. A central issue in asserting executive control over the state apparatus pivots on control of the size of the state and discipline over state employees. However, one of the keys to the success of party pacts is division of state patronage, which reinforces clientelism in the state apparatus, which in turn conflicts with the needs of the executive to control the size and behavior of the corps of public employees. It is by no means immediately clear whether and how the Paz government can overcome this problem. Still, if a long-range capacity to manage the economy is to be achieved, the state apparatus must be brought to heel and the authority of the executive over it must be established.

Another problem that must be addressed in Bolivia and elsewhere is the relationship between governments and the state with the organized expressions of civil society. As we saw, in Bolivia a situation developed whereby the relationship has been direct and unmediated, and although groups have made a wide array of demands, they have not given a proportionate amount of support. Indeed, as overall economic production has steadily declined in recent years, there have been major increases in the production of demands and of parties. In fact, a demand overload has threatened to overwhelm the fledgling democratic system, as manifested in hyperinflation.

Behind the situation is a sociopsychological reality in which the political economy is perceived as a zero-sum game in which the only rational course is for groups to pursue their short-term interests by seeking to bend governments and the state to their will. This is a standard behavioral mode that locks into play in a situation of scarcity, economic crisis and hyperinflation like that obtaining in Bolivia since the late 1970s. Although the short-term behavior of each group reflects situational logic, the aggregate results of those behaviors is irrational for the collectivity and in the long term for specific groups as well. The only way out of this situation is for strong governments to begin to establish the credibility of the state as the articulator of a general collective interest and rationality. Again there are no simple solutions or blueprints. The problem can be overcome in part only as governments have policy successes that over time begin to accumulate and accord the legitimacy that builds the public's confidence in government and the state.

An important step was taken by the Paz government when it used the pact for democracy to push through an income tax that supplants the previous indirect taxes. The tax system is important because aside from generating needed resources, it speaks to the issue of legitimating a democracy by establishing a reciprocal tie between the state and the citizenry. It is a crucial step because it is a concrete, ongoing way by which citizens manifest support for, and develop a stake in, the democratic system. In short it is an important component of a necessary attitudinal base in the nation's collective social psychology.

When all is said and done, however, no long-term serendipitous creativity can work unless governments can get a handle on the economic crisis and create some sense of light at the end of the tunnel. This reality brings us and Bolivia right back to those intractable contradictions between economic and political logics and the thorny issue of costs. Bolivia, like a number of other nations, has come full circle in that the original populists are seeking to find a way out of the crisis through antipopulist strategies that impose harsh costs on labor and other popular groups, that is, the very same groups that have been forced to pay the costs of previous strategies that failed to put Bolivia on a constructive developmental path.

The new economic policy instituted by the Paz government in August of 1985 is not so much an end to the revolution as a readjustment of the relationship between the state and the market in the state capitalist system that it clearly continues. Basically, the policy is predicated on an opening of the economy to initiatives from both the internal and external private sectors. Whether the domestic private sector can or will respond to this opportunity and challenge remains to be seen. One can say, though, that if it does not, the approach is in trouble and with it the fledgling democratic system.

Whatever the response of the private sector, the approach in the short term imposes some heavy costs on the popular sectors, especially organized labor. The reality is that one of the basics of any long-term stability is the incorporation of labor into the system. The experience of exclusionary authoritarian regimes in Bolivia and elsewhere has made manifest that a system based on the repression of labor and on disproportionate burdens cannot work for long. Hence, some means must be found to build labor's confidence in a central state relating to society through a formal democratic system. Again, answers are not readily obvious. But, the sina qua non for a rapproachment is an easing of costs imposed and a demonstration that the costs will pay off in benefits in the not too distant future. This means the creation of jobs and an adequate salary base, but because of the present domestic and international situation, no Bolivian government has resources adequate to cope with these necessities.

Thus we come full circle to Bolivia's overwhelming dependency within the world economy. Because of that inescapable fact, at every step of the way external actors will play a crucial role in expanding or contracting the options open to the Paz government. Bolivia's chances to come out of this crisis with some mode of democratic system will be shaped largely by what external actors like the United States do or do not do. Is the United States willing to put the resources behind its stated goal of fostering democracy and development in Latin America, including Bolivia?

Notes

1. This concept of bureaucratic authoritarianism was developed in the important works of Guillermo O'Donnell, like *Modernization and Bureaucratic-Authoritarianism: Studies in South American Politics* (Berkeley: University of California, Institute of International Studies, 1973) and "Corporatism and the Question of the State" in *Authoritarianism and Corporatism in Latin America*, ed. James M. Malloy (Pittsburgh: University of Pittsburgh Press, 1977), pp. 47-87.
2. Samuel Huntington, *Political Order in Changing Societies* (New Haven: Yale University Press, 1968).
3. For an extension of this analysis, see James M. Malloy, *Bolivia: the Uncompleted Revolution* (Pittsburgh: University of Pittsburgh Press, 1970).
4. The issue was singled out by the technocrats around President Paz in designing the new economic policy launched in 1985. See Foro Económico, *La nueva política económica.*

Appendix A

BOLIVIAN PRESIDENTS SINCE 1952

President	Period in Office
Victor Paz Estenssoro	April 1952-August 1956
Hernán Siles Zuazo	August 1956-August 1960
Victor Paz Estenssoro	August 1960-August 1964
Victor Paz Estenssoro (a)	August -November 1964
General René Barrientos Ortuño (b)	November 1964-July 1966
General Alfredo Ovando Candia (b)	
General René Barrientos Ortuño (c)	August 1966-April 1969
Luis Adolfo Siles Salinas (a)	April 1969-September 1969
General Alfredo Ovando Candia	September 1969-October 1970
General Efraín Guachalla (d)	October 6, 1970
General Fernando Sattori (d)	
Admiral Alberto Albarracín (d)	
General Juan José Torres Gonzalez	October 1970-August 1971
General Hugo Banzer Suárez	August 1971-July 1978
General Juan Pereda Asbún	July 1978-November 1978
General David Padilla Arancibia	November 1978-August 1979
Walter Guevara Arce (a)	August 1979-November 1979
Colonel Alberto Natusch Busch	November 1-16 1979
Lydia Gueiler Tejada (a)	November 1979-July 1980
General Luis García Meza	July 1980-August 1981
General Celso Torrelio	August 1981-July 1982
General Guido Vildoso Calderón	July 1982-October 1982
Hernán Siles Zuazo	October 1982-August 1985
Victor Paz Estenssoro	August 1985-present

(a) Overthrown by military coup d'état.
(b) Served as "co-presidents" after May 1965. Barrientos stepped down in January 1966 in order to run for office. Ovando ruled between January and August 1966.
(c) General Barrientos was elected to office in July 1966.
(d) Triumvirate ruled only for a few hours.

Appendix B

BOLIVIA: LEADING ECONOMIC INDICATORS
1964-1984

year	% change prices	GDP growth rate	GDP per capita
1964	10.1	4.81	
1965	2.9	6.9	
1966	6.9	7.01	
1967	11.2	6.32	
1968	5.5	7.18	
1969	2.2	4.76	
1970	3.8		
1971	3.1	4.94	
1972	6.5	5.91	
1973	31.5	6.91	
1974	62.8	6.1	3.4
1975	8.0	5.3	2.4
1976	4.5	6.8	4.1
1977	8.1	4.0	1.4
1978	10.4	3.3	.7
1979	19.7	2.0	.6
1980	47.2	.8	− 1.8
1981	31.1	− 1.1	− 3.7
1982	123.5	− 9.2	− 11.5
1983	249.0	− 7.3	− 8.7
1984		− 3.1	− 22.2
1985		− 2.1	
1986		− 4.0	

Source: *Latin American Statistical Abstract 1982-1984* IDB, *Economic and Social Progress in Latin America 1986* Instituto Nacional de Estadisticas, *Bolivia en Cifras, 1980 and 1985.* Confederacion de Empresarios de Bolivia, various reports.

Appendix C

U.S. ECONOMIC ASSISTANCE TO BOLIVIA
1964-1984

Year	Total Assistance (a)	Military Assistance	Narcotics
1964	57.6	3.6	
1965	19.2	2.0	
1966	17.8	2.5	
1967	22.3	3.0	
1968	30.6	3.7	
1969	17.3	1.7	
1970	29.7	1.2	
1971(b)	19.5	2.0	
1972(c)	66.2	6.2	
1973	32.4	5.1	
1974	54.9	7.9	
1975	33.2	7.4	
1976	38.6	3.4	
1977	73.4	3.1	
1978	53.2	0.8	2.4
1979	51.1	6.7	3.2
1980	30.1	0.3	0.2
1981	12.8	—	0.2
1982	19.7	—	0.2
1983	63.0	—	1.7
1984	78.0(d)	0.1	14.9

(a) Includes: technical cooperation and developmental grants, cash grants and other grants, foodstuffs under P.L. 480, and developmental loans.

(b) Data for 1964-1971 adopted from James W. Wilkie, "U.S. Foreign Policy and Economic Assistance in Bolivia: 1948-1976," in Jerry Ladman ed., *Modern Day Bolivia* (Tempe: Arizona State University, 1982); 85-86 Table VI-I.

(c) Data for 1971-1984 taken from Agency for International Development, *Overseas Loans and Grants* (Washington, D.C. 1972-1985).

(d) This figure includes aid granted during the drought in Western Bolivia caused by changes in the *El nino* current

Appendix D

BOLIVIA: FOREIGN DEBT
1971-1984
(Millions of $US)

Year	Total (a)	Private	Official (b)
1971	782.1	256.9	525.2
1972	966.3	321.6	644.7
1973	1,047.3	343.3	704.5
1974	1,209.8	435.9	773.9
1975	1,549.8	643.9	905.9
1976	1,978.7	803.4	1,175.3
1977	2,441.6	1,041.9	1,399.7
1978	3,101.8	1,420.3	1,681.5
1979	3,498.6	1,484.2	2,014.4
1980	3,641.9	1,411.7	2,230.2
1981	3,765.2	1,463.2	2,302.0
1982	3,785.7	1,221.3	2,564.4
1983	4,820.0	n.a.	n.a.
1984	4,947.6	1,368.1	3,504.5

(a) Includes undisbursed debt.
(b) Multilateral and bilateral loans.
Source: Instituto Nacional de Estadisticas, *Bolivia en Cifras, 1980 and 1985*. Organization of American States, *Short Term Economic Reports Vol IX Bolivia* (Washington, D.C. 1984): Table SA-30

Index